The Asyut Project

Edited by
Jochem Kahl, Ursula Verhoeven
and Mahmoud El-Khadragy

Volume 1

2007

Harrassowitz Verlag · Wiesbaden

Jochem Kahl

Ancient Asyut
The First Synthesis
after 300 Years of Research

2007

Harrassowitz Verlag · Wiesbaden

Photo on the cover: Fritz Barthel

Bibliografische Information der Deutschen Nationalbibliothek
Die Deutsche Nationalbibliothek verzeichnet diese Publikation in der Deutschen
Nationalbibliografie; detaillierte bibliografische Daten sind im Internet
über http://dnb.d-nb.de abrufbar.

Bibliographic information published by the Deutsche Nationalbibliothek
The Deutsche Nationalbibliothek lists this publication in the Deutsche
Nationalbibliografie; detailed bibliographic data are available in the internet
at http://dnb.d-nb.de.

For further information about our publishing program consult our
website http://www.harrassowitz-verlag.de
© Otto Harrassowitz GmbH & Co. KG, Wiesbaden 2007
This work, including all of its parts, is protected by copyright.
Any use beyond the limits of copyright law without the permission
of the publisher is forbidden and subject to penalty. This applies
particularly to reproductions, translations, microfilms and storage
and processing in electronic systems.
Printed on permanent/durable paper.
Printing and binding: Memminger MedienCentrum AG
Printed in Germany
ISSN 1865-6250
ISBN 978-3-447-05666-3

To the people of Asyut past and present

Contents

Preface IX

Introduction: Why write a book about ancient Asyut?... 1

Chapter One: Asyut: a wounded city.. 3

Chapter Two: History of research 21

Chapter Three: Asyut: its sacred landscape... 35

Chapter Four: The mountain at the desert edge: functions and changes 59

Chapter Five: Living and dying at Asyut 107

Chapter Six: Men of influence and power 129

Chapter Seven: Popular religion in Asyut (Meike Becker) 141

Chapter Eight: Ateliers, school, and knowledge 151

Map 1: Gebel Asyut al-gharbi 155

Chronology of Ancient Egypt 157

Bibliography 159

Indices 177

PREFACE

This book would not have been completed without the support of many a people. The commitment of Prof. Dr. Ursula Verhoeven (Johannes Gutenberg-Universität Mainz) and assoc. Prof. Dr. Mahmoud El-Khadragy (University of Sohag) was and still is invaluable. Together with the author, they have directed the Asyut Project and have contributed considerably to the revival of the extensive fieldwork done in Asyut after more than eighty years of interruption. Furthermore, thanks are due to Prof. Dr. Wolfgang Schenkel and Dr. Mahmoud el-Hamrawi. I owe it to them and their good offices that the German-Egyptian cooperation was able to work out as well as it did.

I am also very much indebted to the Supreme Council of Antiquities, particularly to Dr. Zahi Hawass, Dr. Sabri Abd el-Aziz, and Mr. Magdy el-Ghandour; the General Director of Middle Egypt, Mr. Samir Anis Salib; the Inspector General at Asyut, Mr. Ahmed el-Khatib and his predecessors, Mr. Hani Sadek Metri and the late Mr. Mohamed Abd el-Aziz; the inspector of the magazine at Shutb, Mrs. Nadia Naguib, the accompanying inspectors Emad Bostan Ata, Rageh Darwish Khalaf, Magdy Shaker, and Mohamed Mustafa Al-Shafey; as well as the restorers Ahmed Abd el-Dayem Mohamed, Khalid Gomaa Sayed, Gamal Abd el-Malik Abd el-Moneam, Naglaa Abd el-Motty Fathy, Helal Qeli Attalaa, Mahmoud Hasan Mohamed Sallam.

I am equally indebted to Johannes Gutenberg-Universität Mainz (2004), the *Fachbereich 9 Philologie* of the Westfälische Wilhelms-Universität Münster (2004) and the German Research Foundation (2005 up to the present). Fieldwork to this extent would not have been possible without their financial backing.

Fieldwork would have never succeeded so well without the genuine support of the local *ghafirs*, especially the *Urgestein* Quraim (Mohamed Saad Moursi), as well as the police, the military, and *reis* Ahmed Atitou and *reis* Zekry supervising the numerous workmen—not to mention the driving skills of Sobhi, who all participants in many ways owe their safety and well-being to.

I cannot thank all of them enough.

In the same fashion, the following colleagues and assistants in the field also deserve to be mentioned. For the last four years, through their own indefatigable efforts, they have contributed to expanding our knowledge of ancient Asyut and the surrounding area. Participants of the previous four seasons were (in chronological order):

Mahmoud El-Khadragy, Egyptologist (2003-2006)
Eva-Maria Engel, archaeologist (2003-2005)
Ursula Verhoeven, Egyptologist (2004-2006)
Ulrike Fauerbach, surveyor (2004-2006)
Monika Zöller, Egyptologist (2004-2006)

Yasser Mahmoud Hussein, Egyptologist (2004-2006)
Omar Nour el-Din, Egyptologist (2004)
Sameh Shafik, epigrapher (2005-2006)
Meike Becker, Egyptologist (2005-2006)
Dietrich Klemm, geologist (2005)
Rosemarie Klemm, Egyptologist (2005)
Christiane Dorstewitz, Egyptology student (2005)
Diana Kleiber, Egyptology student (2005)
John Moussa Iskander, Egyptologist (2005)
Ilona Regulski, epigrapher (2006)
Ammar Abu Bakr, draftsman (2006)
Fritz Barthel, photographer (2006)
Hazim Saleh Abdallah, Egyptologist (2006)
Eva Gervers, anthropology student (2006)
Andrea Kilian, Egyptology student (2006)
Mohamed Naguib Reda, Egyptologist (2006)
Laura Sanhueza-Pino, Egyptology student (2006)

For permission to reproduce photographs I am grateful to Bodo von Dewitz (Museum Ludwig, Köln), James Ede (London), Regina Hölzl (Kunsthistorisches Museum Wien), Christian Leitz (Eberhard Karls-Universität Tübingen), Gertrud Platz (Antikensammlung Staatliche Museen zu Berlin), Christiane Ziegler (Musée du Louvre, Paris), and the Museum of Fine Arts Boston.

This book owes its final form to the invaluable support of my wife, Eva-Maria Engel. Christoph Engel produced the layout, the English correction was in good hands with James Goff, Terence DuQuesne, Troy Sagrillo, John Daly, and the Flying Fish Theatre. I feel much obliged to all of them. Finally I am indebted to the Verlag Otto Harrassowitz for publishing this manuscript.

Vienna, May 2007   Jochem Kahl

INTRODUCTION

WHY WRITE A BOOK ABOUT ANCIENT ASYUT?

In pharaonic times Asyut never played a central role in the ancient state. It was never the capital of the splendid empire of those kings who made history for nearly three thousand years from 3200-332 BC.

Asyut was often an important support for the royal court, but sometimes even the opposite. It seems always to have had its own and original creative power. Sometimes in accordance with the canon of the royal court, but more often by seeking and developing its own concepts of art, architecture, and religious beliefs, ancient Asyut as far as modern researches concern is today well known for its own school, a school of craftsmanship and theology, which produced many unique pieces of art and texts, which were highly valued in ancient times and that also have today a permanent place in the scientific discipline of Egyptology.

Not only did Asyut have a relatively distant position with respect to the high culture of the court, but it also provided important impulses to the court and other towns. Often it is mentioned in religious texts as being one of the most important towns in Middle and Upper Egypt. This special role of Asyut, i.e. its position between residential influence and regional traditions, deserves to be examined as an example for high culture outside the royal court.

Due to a poor history of research and the deprival of many of its monuments, Asyut had been forgotten for a long time. Only some of its most beautiful objects, today found in museums and collections all over the world, receive any attention at all. The ancient site, its town, its temples, and its necropolis had not been the focus of any interest since the 1920s. In the 1980s and the beginning 1990s some attempts to start scientific work in Asyut failed due to the danger of terrorism. Only in 2003 a new field-project began: The Asyut Project. A joint mission of the Westfälische Wilhelms-Universität Münster (Germany) and of the Universitiy of Sohag (Egypt) surveyed the ancient necropolis, and in 2004 members of these Universities, as well as members of the Johannes Gutenberg-Universität Mainz (Germany), conducted the first archaeological fieldwork there in more than eighty years. According to modern understanding of archaeology, the goals of this fieldwork are not the discovery of single objects, but the reconstruction of the history of the ancient necropolis, and thereby of the ancient town and its different fortunes as a city of culture, as a border town, and as a wounded city, as well as the determination of various phases and functions concerning the use of the western mountain at Asyut. Goals are also safeguarding and restoring ancient monuments in the necropolis, which have suffered much through stone quarrying, tomb robberies, and climatic influences.

This book is intended to contribute to establishing ancient Asyut's place in the memory of modern mankind. It will provide an overview on our present knowledge about the history, the art, and the people of ancient Asyut—an overview, which will hopefully be enlarged by further studies and ongoing fieldwork activities in the near future.

CHAPTER ONE

ASYUT: A WOUNDED CITY

Wounded cities, like all cities, are dynamic entities, replete with the potential to recuperate loss and reconstruct anew for the future.
(SUSSER/SCHNEIDER 2003: 1)

Present-day Asyut in Middle Egypt (Fig. 1) has a population of more than 400,000 and is one of the eight largest cities in Egypt. In antiquity Asyut almost certainly consisted, as did other cities, not only of temples, mansions, and palaces, but also of the humble dwellings of functionaries and peasants, as well as their workshops, granaries, storage magazines, shops, and local markets. The urban population of ancient provincial capitals was most likely fairly small by today's standards, and the town had a population of perhaps 2,000 or 3,000 people during the dynastic period (HASSAN 2001: 271).

The only site currently accessible for exploration is the necropolis situated in the western mountains. The ancient city and its temples have been almost completely buried and lost under the strata of the alluvial plain and especially the rapidly growing modern city (Pl. 1a; Figs. 2-3). Neither the city nor the temple have ever been examined. Furthermore, the ancient necropolis is also covered today by parts of the modern Islamic cemetery (Fig. 4), which cannot be disturbed.

Finds that provide information about the ancient city as it existed are rare and discovered only occasionally, the results of purely arbitrary measures. In the 1930s for example, an Asyuti houseowner came across fragments of a Ramesside temple by chance while he was digging for gold underneath the foundations of his house (Fig. 22).

Written sources from outside the town itself, and inscriptional and archaeological evidence, which are preserved in the nearby necropolis (Fig. 5), are thus our only sources of knowledge of ancient Asyut.

These sources reveal that Asyut was home to the temples of the gods Wepwawet, Anubis, Osiris, Hathor, and Thoth (cf. Chapter Three), as well as a sanctuary called "House of the Eight Trees" with relics of Osiris, namely his fingers. This sanctuary existed during the Roman Period and is most probably earlier. In addition, an obelisk and a magazine for a group statue made of gold and iron ore once existed. They represented the contending gods Horus and Seth (OSING 1998b: 143-150).

The ancient necropolis is situated in the mountains, on the west bank of the Nile (Map 1). The mountain peak rises to over two hundred meters above sea level (Fig. 6; Pl. 1b). The necropolis extends over several kilometers along the cultivated land.

Several hundred tombs at the very least—scholars believe actually there were more than a thousand—were hewn into the mountain, which makes it look strikingly similar to a honeycomb (Fig. 7). Stone quarrying, tomb robbery, graffiti, excreta of bats and pigeons, unprofessionally performed excavations—sometimes using dynamite—

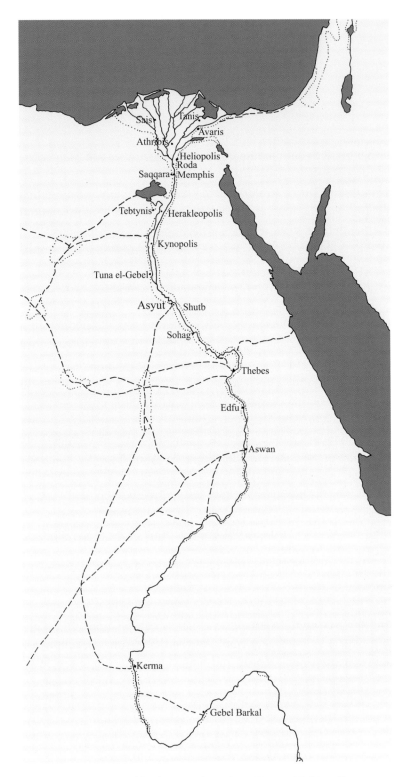

Fig. 1: Geographical map of Ancient Egypt (© Engel).

and the forces of nature in the form of rainfall and earthquakes, have all led to the tombs being all but destroyed.

Initially, I shall tread a new path, so as to demonstrate why it is rewarding to study this ancient town. From the few set pieces handed down to us, I will for the first time try to illustrate Asyut's importance, its continuity over the course of at least five thousand years, and of its special fate and its character.

The internationally renowned architect, former mayor of Belgrade, and contemporary unyielding dissident, Bogdan Bogdanović, wrote in 1981 the following statement concerning cities:

How many times have I told myself, that a city is only a real city, when it has its own personality, its psychological profile, its character, its appearance, its way of dealing with itself and the outside world, as well as with guests, with the environment, with nature and with other cities. For several often repeated reasons cities should be as readable and wise as books.
(BOGDANOVIĆ 1993: 49-50; translated from German)

In the following pages, I shall try to read the "book" called Asyut. But will we be able to open it at all? Are we able to read and understand the city of Asyut, to reconstruct its profile, its character, and its appearance, even though nothing of it has been excavated? Or will Asyut remain a book written inside and outside, and sealed with seven seals? And indeed, many mysteries will still remain.

Let us however open a first chapter, entitled "Asyut: A Wounded City."

I have chosen this title, which refers to a series of workshop papers edited by Jane Schneider and Ida Susser from the City University of New York (SCHNEIDER/SUSSER 2003), for a special reason. In these papers several scholars explore how urban populations are affected by "wounds" that have been inflicted through violence, civil wars, overbuilding, as well as natural disasters such as earthquakes.

And indeed the chapter which I have chosen to open this study will confront us with the saddest story in the history of every town, namely that of its destruction. But it will also provide us with an understanding of the most valuable possibilities a city has to offer, namely its culture.

If, like BOGDANOVIĆ 1993, we imagine the city as the place of crystallization of Myth and Logos, Ethnos and Demos, as well as of the development of a civilized society, then the destruction of the city turns out to be the destruction of the memory of culture, as well as of the remembrance of the people and of the civil customs and values of social life (cf. also BOGDANOVIĆ 1994: 17-50).

A characteristic feature of Asyut's history is its repeated destruction, or that of certain areas of the city. Another element is that the town has always been able to recover over and over again and that it has had a strong will to survive, as can be recognized from the First Intermediate Period (about 2060 BC) until the present day.

Fig. 2: View from the rock necropolis on to the Nile near Asyut during the height of the inundation (BORCHARDT/RICKE 1929: 119).

Let us now examine the destruction previously mentioned of the town or of a single area of it, for instance the necropolis and the hinterland. All these examples of destruction included death, pain, and a loss of culture. These events were rarely recorded in the sources, because negative events such as murder, epidemics, and defeats did not conform with Maat, the principle of cosmic balance, and were therefore not to be recorded, according to the ancient Egyptian concept of history (VON BECKERATH 1977: 566).

We can discover the earliest attestation of destruction at the end of the First Intermediate Period. After the Eighth Dynasty, centralized government definitely lost its power and the country broke up into several regions governed by local rulers. Step by step, two nuclei of power emerged (cf. SEIDLMAYER 2000). In the north, Herakleopolis (SEIDLMAYER 1997: 81-90) continued the Old Kingdom tradition, and in the south Thebes aggressively expanded to the north and south, thus becoming a threat to the northern Herakleopolitan kingdom (QUACK 1992: 98-113). This rivalry culminated in a war, which lasted for at least sixty years.

Asyut obviously was the last bastion of the Herakleopolitan kingdom and the final theatre of war, since the Asyuti magnates were the closest allies of Herakleopolis. These events must have happened between 2063 and 2045 BC.

Iti-ibi, a local magnate of Asyut, lived around 2060 BC, and in a long autobiographical inscription in his tomb he reports on a counterattack by the Herakleopolitan

Fig. 3: Modern Asyut (© Kahl).

troops against the Theban forces. Before the text was fully inscribed, it was covered with plaster and a politically neutral inscription was painted on it. Today, parts of both inscriptions have remained visible (Pl. 3b). This change in decoration is taken as evidence for Iti-ibi's defeat.

In fact, the inscriptions in the tomb of his son Khety II confirm this interpretation. Even if some details of the translation are uncertain, the essential points are clear: Khety II seems to have been driven out of Asyut, but with the support of the Herakleopolitan King Merikara he managed to repel the Theban aggressors and gain possession of his territory once again.

We read in his autobiographical inscription:

You [i.e. King Merikara of Herakleopolis] did convey him [i.e. Khety II from Asyut] upriver, the heaven was cleared for him, the whole land was with him, the counts of Middle Egypt, and the great ones of Herakleopolis. The district of the Queen of the Land came to repel the evil-doer [i.e. the Theban ruler]. The land trembled, Upper Egypt bailed water [i.e. its ships sank]. All people winced [i.e. all people were in terror], the villages in panic, fear entered into their limbs … The land burned in its [i.e. Herakleopolis'] flame … The head of the fleet extended to Shutb [this town is situated six kilometres to the south of Asyut], its end to Uu-Heri [an unknown place to the north of Shutb]. Heaven was blowing the north wind. Papyrus fell on the water. Herakleopolis was landing. "Welcome," the town [i.e. Asyut] cried jubilantly to its ruler, the son of a ruler, women together with men. The ruler's son [i.e Khety II] reached his town, he entered his father's [i.e. Iti-ibi's] territory. He brought back the refugees into their homes. He buried his old people.
(Siut IV, 10-18)

But some time later the Theban party seized Asyut.

After this second defeat of Asyut, the Theban aggressors reached Herakleopolis quickly, conquered it and won the war. The Theban dynasty then ruled over all of Egypt and the consensus is that Asyut did not recover from its destruction for over seventy years and slipped back into provincialism. However, the exact opposite was the case, as recent archaeological work has revealed.

The discovery of two hitherto unknown tombs of local magnates, the so called nomarchs, as well as two other already known tombs of nomarchs, bear witness to the high quality of art and architecture in Asyut which was maintained even during the Eleventh Dynasty and the beginning of the Twelfth Dynasty.

In particular, the Northern Soldiers-Tomb (H11.1; Figs. 64-65) from the end of the Eleventh Dynasty deserves to be mentioned. The northern wall of its inner hall has been demolished and a roof weighing several tons has collapsed, burying the rest of the tomb. Only a part of the southern wall has survived. Its decoration shows among others wrestlers and marching soldiers (EL-KHADRAGY 2006a; cf. KAHL/EL-KHADRAGY/ VERHOEVEN 2005: 164, Pl. 14.1).

A reinvestigation of the sequence of the Asyuti nomarchs reveals a continuity from the First Intermediate Period to the Twelfth Dynasty (Fig. 8). The owners of Tombs III, IV, and V acted as nomarchs at the end of the First Intermediate Period, probably in the order Khety I, Iti-ibi, and Khety II. In addition Iti-ibi(-iqer), the owner of the recently discovered Tomb N13.1, might have held the position of nomarch at the very end of the First Intermediate Period (a study of Tomb N13.1 by Mahmoud El-Khadragy will throw more light on its chronological position). We can also reconstruct the following sequence of nomarchs between King Mentuhotep II, who reunified Egypt, and the early Twelfth Dynasty. Mesehti, the owner of the Northern Soldiers-Tomb, and Anu held the highest positions in Asyut. It is highly probable that Djefai-Hapi II and Djefai-Hapi I were their successors.

The nomarchs' soldiers repeatedly appear in their tombs, either as a wall decoration as in Tomb IV (Fig. 56), Tomb N13.1 (Fig. 60), and the Northern Soldiers-Tomb (Fig. 65); as wooden models as in the tomb of Mesehti (Fig. 63); and in inscriptions such as that of Djefai-Hapi I (Siut I, 230-231). Warfare and the disposal of their own troops was of highest importance for the Asyuti nomarchs not only during the civil war in the First Intermediate Period, but also for some time—even generations—after the reunification of Egypt.

Despite the meager inscriptional evidence which we possess about the nomarchs after Khety II, their once impressive tombs with paintings and fine funerary equipment certainly leave no doubt that Asyut was prosperous enough not only to provide the nomarchs with rich tombs but also to repair the temples which would have been damaged during the civil war in the First Intermediate Period, especially given that taking care of the local gods was a traditional duty of Egyptian nomarchs.

These considerations form the background for the interpretation of a passage in the autobiography of Djefai-Hapi I, who was Asyuti nomarch during the reign of King Senwosret I (Twelfth Dynasty). Djefai-Hapi I was the owner of the largest Middle Kingdom private tomb in the whole of Egypt (Pl. 6b). We read in his autobiographical inscription:

Djefai-Hapi, he says: I am a brave heir with enduring monuments, a protector, one who restores ancient things. I erected the walls which had been destroyed. I covered […] ancestors. I rebuilt the house of my father. I renewed all that was primeval in Asyut. I was one who was beloved of the king and one who was favored by his township, one who gave orders to the […]
(Siut I, 234-236)

Djefai-Hapi reports on the restoration of one of the ancient temples in Asyut, presumably the temple of Wepwawet, when he says that he rebuilt the house of his father. Egyptologists used to connect this restoration work with damages the temple apparently suffered during the First Intermediate Period. But in this case the long time span of nearly one hundred years from the demolition to the restoration is perplexing; during this time, the continuity of life and work in Asyut should have been paralyzed. This supposition, however, is disproved by the once impressive tombs of the nomarchs who lived during the Eleventh Dynasty and the beginning of the Twelfth Dynasty. It is very hard to believe that no restoration work on the temples had been done during this time. In addition, the nomarchs of the Eleventh Dynasty and the beginning of the Twelfth Dynasty known today were chief priests of Wepwawet (Mesehti and Anu) and Anubis (Mesehti), which is a clear sign that the cults of these two principal gods remained intact.

One key to the interpretation of the crucial passage in Djefai-Hapi's autobiography lies in the political history of the reign of King Amenemhat I, the predecessor of Senwosret I. We also have evidence that a civil war took place during the reign of Amenemhat I, who was an usurper and the founder of the Twelfth Dynasty (cf. WILLEMS 1983-1984; QUACK 1992: 122-123). Two literary works, *The Tale of Sinuhe* and *The Teaching of Amenemhat to his Son*, supply further evidence that Amenemhat I was assassinated. These political events under Amenemhat I most probably form the background to Djefai-Hapi's rebuilding of the Wepwawet-temple and lead to the logical conclusion that this temple was ransacked and demolished during the riots under Amenemhat's reign (BUCHBERGER 1993: 375).

A further collapse of the centralized state led to the Second Intermediate Period. This epoch is characterized by the first foreign domination of Egypt. The Egyptians called this foreign period the Fifteenth Dynasty, that of "rulers of the foreign countries" (Greek: Hyksos). These Hyksos were a Canaanite people, who had immigrated into the eastern Delta since the second half of the Twelfth Dynasty. During the Fifteenth Dynasty the nucleus of power was Avaris in the eastern Delta. The rest of Egypt became dependent on the Hyksos, presumably in the form of loose satellite states. As far as we know, the northern part of Egypt, including Hermopolis in the 15th Upper Egyptian nome, developed and sustained close ties with the Hyksos.

The southern part of Egypt enjoyed a high degree of independence from the Hyksos, even if we do not know all the details. It seems as if the Theban ruler Nubkheperra Antef VI united several local kingdoms in about 1580 BC and founded the Seventeenth Dynasty, which coexisted with the Hyksos. This united kingdom of Upper Egypt extended to Asyut in the north (BIETAK 1994: 27). Asyut and its surrounding area thus once again marked the border of a divided Egypt.

The Hyksos maintained trade and diplomatic relations with the kingdom of Kush in Nubia to the south of Egypt. In Kerma, in Upper Nubia on the Third Cataract, statues of Djefai-Hapi I and his wife Sennwy were found (Figs. 99-100); they stood in a building whose function is disputed. Another statue of Djefai-Hapi I was discovered in the temple of Gebel Barkal in Upper Nubia. Since these statues bear titles and epithets that clearly refer to Asyut and which do not show any relation to Nubia, they must have been brought from Asyut to Nubia. The most plausible explanation is that the Hyksos donated or sold these statues to their Nubian allies (SÄVE-SÖDERBERGH 1941: 103-116; HELCK 1976: 101-115; KENDALL 1997: 24-27). This would mean that the Hyksos plundered the Asyuti necropolis, and eventually even the city itself. But a Kushite invasion and sacking of Asyut should be regarded as possibilities (cf. DAVIES 2003a: 6; DAVIES 2003b: 52-54).

Fig. 4: View from the ancient necropolis to the modern cemetery (© Kahl).

Our recent discoveries have made possible a reconstruction of Djefai-Hapi's tomb (Pl. 6a). Different sources, such as architectural observations, inscriptional evidence, and reports of early European travellers, have provided a more complete picture of the tomb (ENGEL/KAHL forthcoming). Not only did this tomb consist of a part cut into the rock, which is monumental enough, but also of a court, a causeway, probably a pylon or an entrance hall, a garden with trees, a pond and a small chapel. It even seems possible to locate the statues of Djefai-Hapi I and his wife Sennwy at a particular site in this tomb, namely the court, where they may have been erected. The Hyksos could have easily removed the statues from there.

A statue of Ramesses II, which is probably of Asyuti origin, was found in Tanis (PETRIE 1888: Pl. 11.172; DARESSY 1917b: 171). It gives evidence that the rulers of the Twenty-first Dynasty (or earlier Ramesside kings) deprived Asyut of some of its statues for reuse as building materials for their new capital in the Delta.

During the Assyrian invasion of Egypt in the first half of the seventh century BC, the Assyrian rulers Assarhadon and Assurbanipal installed governors in Egypt who were directly responsible to them. *Prism A*, one of several historical accounts of these military campaigns, mentions a governor of Asyut who was first installed by Assarhaddon,

Fig. 5: Map of Asyut (© Fauerbach).

then driven away by dissident Kushites or Egyptians, then reinstalled by Assurbanipal and who finally himself revolted against his protector (ONASCH 1994: 36, 55, 118-121).

Egypt was ruled from 306 to 30 BC by Ptolemaic kings and queens. Trinity College Dublin is home to a Greek letter from this period (TCD Pap. Gr. 274) which mentions a bloody uprising in the district of Asyut (CLARYSSE 1979: 103; PESTMAN 1995: 103, 121-122; MCGING 1997: 299-310). This uprising led to the depopulation of a village, the land of which was no longer irrigated and thus no longer cultivated. The text is not dated but can be linked to the revolt of the Theban rival King Ankhwennefer, who reigned over the Theban area from 200-186 BC. This Ankhwennefer fought for Egypt's independence from the Ptolemaic sovereigns (VEÏSSE 2004: 11-26). From 196 to 195 BC Ankhwennefer seized Aswan in the south of Thebes and advanced to the region of Asyut in the north. Since we have no information that Ankhwennefer led his campaign further north, the letter in Dublin indicates that, once again in Egyptian history, Asyut was the critical point of separation in a civil war. Asyut indeed seems to have been the turning point in Ankhwennefer's fortunes of war: he suffered serious setbacks and eight years after the battle in the district of Asyut he was effectively repulsed to the Theban area, where he lost his last battle against the Ptolemies in 186 BC.

In Late Antiquity Asyut was sacked yet again. Shenute's writings inform us about the marauding Blemmyes, a people from Nubia who penetrated Egypt as far north as Kynopolis during the middle of the fifth century AD (LEIPOLDT 1902/03: 129; EMMEL 1998: 86-88). Again, Asyut was stricken. More than 20,000 people from different cities found refuge at Shenute's monastery, the White Monastery, near Sohag.

The *Copto-Arabic Synaxarion*, which is a formal compilation of the lives of the martyrs, saints, and religious heroes of the Coptic church, reports that Nubian invaders murdered forty nuns at a monastery in the mountains close to Asyut (TIMM 1984: 238).
    The Arabic writer al-Maqrizi mentions the destruction of eight churches in and near Asyut in AD 1321 (TIMM 1984: 245).

During the Coptic Period at least two monasteries were erected in the ancient necropolis: Deir el-Meitin and Deir el-Azzam (cf. Chapter Four). One of them, Deir el-Azzam, is situated on the mountain plateau. Today, all that is left of this monastery is a ruin. If it is to be identified as the "Monastery of Seven Mountains" mentioned by al-Maqrizi (WÜSTENFELD 1845: 102), then it was destroyed AD 1418 by a raid. Its remains suffered further destruction by heavy rainfall in the late 1960s.

Let us summarize the results of this excursion into history. Because of its location in the middle of Egypt, Asyut several times played the role of a border town, which led to its being wounded, sacked, and destroyed. During the division of the country in the First Intermediate Period, the city was the north's bastion against the Theban faction.

Fig. 6: The necropolis in 1850 (Du Camp; © Museum Ludwig, Köln).

Asyut again marked the border of the southern Theban party against the Hyksos in the north during the Second Intermediate Period. When the indigenous Egyptians rebelled against their Ptolemaic rulers, Asyut once more defined the border between north and south, with the city this time belonging to the territory under Ptolemaic influence.

Asyut's special role as a border town is also reflected in the double vizierate during the New Kingdom, as well as in Ptolemaic and Roman provincial administration.

The vizierate, the highest administrative institution in Egypt, was divided into north and south during the New Kingdom (HELCK 1958: 21-25). The southern viziers' area of competence reached from Elephantine in the south to Asyut in the north.

During the Ptolemaic Period Asyut, or Lycopolis, as the town then was called, belonged to the large administrative district of Thebes, the Thebais. According to Agatharchides of Knidos, who lived from about 200 to 120 BC, and to Pliny the Elder (AD 23-79; *Natural History* V, 61), the Lycopolitan area marked the beginning of the Thebais (cf. CALDERINI 1980: 211).

The key question which we as scholars should ask is what was so special about Asyut that it repeatedly found itself on the border between two rival factions or zones of administration.

There are indeed two geographical factors which explain Asyut's role as a border town. The first is the Gebel Abu el-Feda to the north of Asyut (Fig. 9). The eastern mountain here directly faces the Nile. In this particular area, passage of the Nile is dangerous due to the river's many curves and its current, which here is stronger than usual. We possess a number of descriptions from previous centuries stating that ships were wrecked on the cliffs of the Gebel Abu el-Feda. It is thus reasonable to assume that the same applied in the Pharaonic Period. Sailing downstream, one sees that Asyut is situated at the beginning of these narrows and on the way to the north one had to stop at Asyut, and, if the winds were adverse, wait there for better weather. Asyut's unique geographical location, as well as the fact that the desert mountains are also in close proximity, explain Asyut's etymology: *s3ww.ti* "The Guardian", Coptic ⲤⲒⲞⲞⲨⲦ (OSING 1976: 320, 866 note 1377).

Another geographical factor, namely the desert road Darb al-Arbain, added to this role as a guardian. The Darb al-Arbain ("the Forty Days Road") began at Kobbe, Darfur Province, Sudan. It then moved north out of Sudan to al-Shab, continued north to the Kharga Oasis, and then on to the Nile Valley (Fig. 1). The road covers a total distance of 1,767 kilometers (VIVIAN 2000: 346). The stretch from Kharga to Asyut in particular was one of the most difficult and dangerous portions of the entire route.

We have a considerable amount of information about this desert road, which was a major route of the slave trade between Sudan and Egypt from the seventeenth to the twentieth centuries AD. Early travellers reported on the condition of the people who arrived with caravans at Asyut. In 1817, for example, the French traveller Frédéric Cailliaud saw a Darfur caravan arrive in Asyut with 16,000 people, including 6,000 slaves. It is important to realize that Asyut at this time had only about 20,000 inhabitants. Cailliaud describes the arrival of the caravan:

They had been travelling for two months in the deserts, in the most intense heat of the year; meagre, exhausted, and the aspect of death on their countenances, the spectacle strongly excited compassion. (cf. VIVIAN 2000: 352)

One can only guess at the logistical problems Asyut had to overcome regarding water, food, medical attention, and shelter.

This desert road may also have been of great importance in earlier times. In the Kharga Oasis, massive fortresses, placed on strategic hills, attest to an ancient security system dating back at least to the Greeks and the Romans (VIVIAN 2000: 359). They give evidence that the Darb al-Arbain was used in ancient times. It is therefore likely that the road was used as early as the Old Kingdom. Elmar Edel suggested that the Old

Kingdom official Her-khuf travelled on the Darb al-Arbain during his third expedition to Nubia (EDEL 1955: 62).

We can therefore conclude that Asyut's geographical position not only supported its special place in Egypt's history but was also responsible for its fate. Asyut served as a crossroads along the Egyptian trade routes. People travelling to the northern Nile Valley and the Delta region, or to the southern Nile Valley, crossed Asyut as did people travelling to the western oases and to the interior of Africa. We can therefore assume that Asyut was already a centre of trade in ancient times. Asyut was vulnerable and open to incursions, because it offered a direct link to the South. Therefore it has been a site of great strategic importance for the last five millennia.

The reliefs, paintings, and models of soldiers (Figs. 56, 63, 65) in the tombs of the Asyuti nomarchs of the First Intermediate Period and the Middle Kingdom attest to Asyut's military significance. So too does the finding of a hoard of several hundred votive stelae dating from the New Kingdom (cf. Chapter Seven), which point up the military importance of Asyut in the second half of the second millennium BC; soldiers were second only to priests in dedicating the majority of the stelae to the chief deity, Wepwawet.

Papyri of the fourth and fifth centuries AD also give evidence of soldiers in Asyut (TIMM 1984: 241). The *Notitia Dignitatum* mentions that Mauretanian cavalrymen were stationed in Asyut (TIMM 1984: 240), and a Middle Persian papyrus (cf. RICHTER 2003: 228-229) provides evidence that Asyut was a Persian military base during the third Persian occupation of Egypt (AD 618/19-629).

Even today Asyut is home to an extensive military base. Unfortunately it has been built in the western mountains, in other words among the only surviving remains of ancient Asyut, its necropolis.

Having seen that Asyut's extraordinary geopolitical situation led to its sacking and demolition, let us turn the page in this first chapter of the book called Asyut and once again pose questions concerning Asyut's personality, its psychological profile, its character, its appearance, its modus vivendi and its attitude to the outside world.

The geopolitical situation did not result solely in suffering. It also led to advances in art, architecture, and literature, in short to an intellectual culture (cf. Chapter Eight). It always seems to have been important for rulers of Egypt that the city be a melting pot of local and royal craftsmen, of people from the north and the south, as well as from abroad.

There was a writing school in Asyut for some time during the Middle Kingdom, which can be discerned in the orthography of the Coffin Texts (SCHENKEL 1996). Furthermore, there was an art school during both the First Intermediate Period and the Middle Kingdom (SMITH 1957: 223). According to William C. Hayes, Asyut was "the home … of an accomplished atelier of sculptors" during the New Kingdom (HAYES 1959: 347). In addition to this, royal sculptors would occasionally work for the Asyuti aristocracy.

Fig. 7: Tomb II (Twelfth Dynasty; © Kahl).

Texts from Asyut were valued and regarded as significant all over Egypt for thousands of years. Asyut formed part of Egypt's *cultural memory*, that is to say, the stored knowledge and memories of the past which are specific to a given culture and through which a culture creates its identity in an ongoing process (cf. ASSMANN 1992).

Elements of the tomb of Djefai-Hapi I and of the other nomarchs' tombs had a profoundly enduring effect on Egyptian culture for the next two thousand years (KAHL 1999). Excerpts of these tomb inscriptions were still copied outside Asyut in the second century AD in the form of epithets, autobiographical formulae, liturgical texts, contracts, and lists of decans (OSING 1998a).

Techniques of textual criticism, which included the construction of stemmata, have revealed that later copyists used papyrus transfers for inscription patterns which were stored in an Asyuti library (KAHL 1999). These patterns were drafts for the inscriptions on the tomb walls and they seem to have been transferred to Thebes some time between the reign of King Senwosret I (about 1900 BC) and the reign of Queen Hatshepsut (about 1460 BC). These patterns seem to have been copied again and again, as scribal errors show. Some of these scribal errors occurred because of misspellings of the hieratic script and can be dated back to the end of the Second Intermediate Period or

Nomarch	Tomb	Date
Khety I	Tomb V (M11.1)	First Intermediate Period
Iti-ibi	Tomb III (N12.1)	First Intermediate Period
Khety II	Tomb IV (N12.2)	Merikara (First Intermediate Period)
Iti-ibi(-iqer)	Tomb N13.1	End of First Intermediate Period
Mesehti	Hogarth Tomb III	Eleventh Dynasty
Unknown	Northern Soldiers-Tomb (H11.1)	Eleventh Dynasty
Anu	Location unknown	Beginning of Twelfth Dynasty
Djefai-Hapi II	Tomb II (O13.1)	Beginning of Twelfth Dynasty
Djefai-Hapi I	Tomb I (P10.1)	Senwosret I (Twelfth Dynasty)
Djefai-Hapi III	Tomb VII (Salakhana Tomb)	Amenemhat II (Twelfth Dynasty)

Fig. 8: Sequence of the nomarchs of Asyut from the end of the First Intermediate Period to the Twelfth Dynasty.

to the beginning of the New Kingdom, but there are no surviving monuments from the period during which these texts were copied. The first piece of evidence which shows that these patterns were used on monuments after the Twelfth Dynasty dates from the reign of Hatshepsut in Thebes.

In this connection we can observe that from the Eighteenth Dynasty to the Twenty-fifth Dynasty the transmitted Asyuti material was restricted to the elite of Thebes; for example to such famous men as Senenmut, Ipuemra, Rekhmira, Menkheperraseneb, Harwa, Ankhefenkhons, or Petamenophis (KAHL 1999: 321-325). This restriction to Thebes seems to have been deliberate; restricted knowledge was used as a demarcation of the highest elite against people from lower social strata.

The first use of the Asyuti material outside Thebes is attested for the tomb of Khonsardais at Naga el-Hasaya near Edfu at the beginning of the Twenty-sixth Dynasty. This means that the Asyuti material was used exclusively in Thebes for at least eight hundred years, from the time of Queen Hatshepsut (about 1460 BC) to the reign of King Psametik I (about 660 BC). And we can also offer an explanation as to why the material was transferred outside Thebes. Khonsardais was mayor of Thebes and mayor of Edfu. This distribution of offices gives us the clue for understanding how the Asyuti material was transferred to Edfu. It was not transferred from Asyut to Edfu, but from Thebes to Edfu. Some other circumstantial evidence also points to a transfer of the originally Asyuti material via Thebes to the rest of Egypt. Starting from the Twenty-sixth Dynasty, the dissemination of the material can be observed in Memphis/Saqqara, Heliopolis, Sais, Roda, Athribis, Kom Abu Yasin, Tuna el-Gebel, and the 12th Upper Egyptian nome (KAHL 1999: 325-329). The people who used the material at these sites were also high officials, but the material was now in circulation and seems to have been more easily accessible.

As far as we know at present, a library in Tebtynis in the Fayum desert was the final destination of the transmission of Asyuti material (OSING 1998a). Copies of the patterns for the Asyuti tombs of Djefai-Hapi I, three nomarchs of the First Intermediate Period (Khety I, Iti-ibi, Khety II) and other notables were discovered there. From their paleography these copies can be dated to the second century AD. The most interesting point is that these copies sometimes show more accurate readings than the tombs at Asyut, which means that they also are not copies of the inscriptions on the tomb walls, but rather copies of papyri which were once part of an archive in an Asyuti library.

The copies in the library of Tebtynis also transmit the names of the owners of the Asyuti tombs and epithets of the Asyuti gods. There can be little doubt therefore that the librarians from Tebtynis were aware of the provenance and at least of the approximate age of the originals, which were composed more than two thousand years earlier at Asyut.

But why were Asyuti productions, especially texts, held in such high esteem?

The answer to this question is threefold. The first reason is the literary and artistic quality of the Asyuti production. The second reason was the self-presentation of the Asyuti nomarchs, which the high officials of the New Kingdom and the Late Period took as an example. And last, but not least, the third reason was the importance of Asyut in respect to theology and the history of religion.

To augment the first reason, the quality of the language used in the inscriptions in Djefai-Hapi's tomb seems to have been regarded in ancient times as classical. Even now the language of these texts is referred to in universities as classical. For instance, in Alan Henderson Gardiner's standard work of reference on Egyptian grammar (GARDINER 1957) we find 282 quotations referring to the inscriptions from the tomb of Djefai-Hapi I. This means that Gardiner included more examples from this tomb in his grammar than, for example, from such famous literary works as the *Shipwrecked Sailor* (272 quotations) or the *Dialogue of a Man with his Soul* (157 quotations).

With respect to the second reason, the self-presentation of the Asyuti nomarchs was doubly attractive to later officials. Self-confidence and direct responsibility on the one hand and confidence in the gods and loyalty to the king on the other were the topic of the original Asyuti texts. Thus their cultural identification was a combination of loyalism in the Middle Kingdom and the principle of the responsible magnate of the First Intermediate Period who kept his territory alive and well in times of hardship and crisis.

Thirdly, Asyut was of particular importance as a sacred place, as is attested by religious and historical texts. Asyut played a prominent role in theology and religious history in Middle and Upper Egypt, after the religious centers of Thebes, Heliopolis,

Fig. 9: Gebel Abu el-Feda (EBERS 1880: 199).

Memphis, and Hermopolis. For example, the Pyramid Texts mention Asyut as the place where Isis and Nephthys watched over the dead Osiris:

Isis and Nephthys have watched over you in Asyut, over their lord, who you are in your name of "Lord of Asyut," and over their god, who you are in your name "God."
(PT 366; Pyr § 630 a-c)

We can imagine how much more injury Asyut had to suffer during its history than other Egyptian towns. Not only were its libraries, archives, schools, and temples demolished, cemeteries looted, churches and monasteries pillaged, but its individualistic ways of expressing its personality were also destroyed. Many times Asyut was unable to escape physical destruction, but it certainly escaped metaphysical destruction. Integral parts of Asyut's culture, memory, and self-confidence had already been transmitted outwards some time between the Twelfth and Eighteenth Dynasty: whether this was by force or peacefully remains unanswered. In any case Asyuti culture conquered much of Egypt during the following millennia and provided the city with an adamantine existence regardless of its physical fate.

Even if we do not know exactly how ferociously or how often Asyut was ravaged, we do know that it once escaped physical destruction.
There are texts (cf. Chapter Six) according to which Saint John of Lycopolis, who lived from about AD 310/320 to AD 394/395, saved his hometown of Asyut from anni-

hilation: After a sporting contest in Asyut, murders occurred between rival factions. Emperor Theodosius I threatened to extinguish the whole town. He said that this incident was similar to what had happened in Judah and Israel, where many young children were killed because of circus games, which were not in accord with Christian doctrine. Such things happening in Asyut would be the concern of pagans. Emperor Theodosius entrusted an officer to take soldiers to Asyut and ordered him to destroy Asyut by fire. The officer was further told that he should not let anyone escape. The emperor commanded this as warning to each town under his authority which might possibly dare to repeat the events there.

John of Lycopolis instructed the people of Asyut how to behave towards the imperial officer. He himself then received the envoy and sent the emperor an urgent request to spare his town. Asyut was thus saved and, in addition, John cured the officer's sick son.

It is exactly this escape which sheds a significant light on the history of cities past and present. Something exists which could be considered a ritual killing of towns and cities (BOGDANOVIĆ 1993: 33-39), namely the destruction of cities in the name of "conviction" and in the name of the highest, most stringent moral principles, in the name of religious, social, and racial doctrines which are apparently written in stone. We only have to call to mind the destruction of the proud city of Troy and the unfortunate recent examples of Grosny in Chechnya, Beirut in Lebanon, and the nameless villages in Darfur in Sudan, which were destroyed in civil wars, especially those motivated by religion and ethnicity.

We should remember that a city in general and every city in particular is a complex metaphorical system (cf. BOGDANOVIĆ 1993). Asyut is a unique home to memories which far exceed the memory of a single nation, race or language. Memories spanning the five thousand years of Asyut's history still exist, memories of a city harbouring pharaonic Egyptians, accomodating Copts, Arabs, Hyksos, Kushites, and Assyrians, Greeks and Romans, and Mauretanians and Armenians. It is our responsibility to retrieve what we can of these memories and to make the most effective use of them.

CHAPTER TWO

HISTORY OF RESEARCH

Asyut and the neighboring sites of Durunka and Rifeh have never received the comprehensive study that they richly deserve.
(SPANEL 2001: 155)

REPORTS AND TRAVELOGUES ABOUT ASYUT BEFORE 1799

Long before Asyut was of any interest for the scientific community, travellers described either the town or its peculiarities. At the end of the fourth century AD, a Jerusalem monk visited several monasteries and hermits in Egypt and gave a report on Egyptian monasticism in his Greek History of the Monks in Egypt, which was soon translated into Latin as the *Historia Monachorum in Aegypto* and spread beyond the borders of Egypt (FESTUGIÈRE 1971; RUSSELL 1981: 52-62; FRANK 1998: 483-505). This report contains valuable information pertaining to the saint and hermit John of Lycopolis, who lived in the fourth century AD (see Chapter Six).

Asyut maintained its role as a destination or way station for travellers even after the Arabic conquest of Egypt in AD 641. In the eleventh century AD the Persian traveller Naser-e Khosru for instance lauded the textiles and clothes woven out of sheep's wool in Asyut (NAJMABADI/WEBER 1993: 116). Two hundred years later, the Andalusian writer Ibn Said was so full of praise for the town that he exclaimed spending a day and night in Asyut made up for a whole life (EBERS 1880: 206).

However, the first time an interest in Asyut's monuments became tangible for us was at the end of the seventeenth century. In 1698, the French medical practitioner Charles Poncet beheld the remnants of an amphitheatre and Roman mausolea near Asyut (SAUNERON 1983: 91). The French antiquary and traveller Paul Lucas (1664-1737) visited Egypt in 1714 on behalf of King Louis XIV. The aim of his expedition was to further knowledge concerning Egypt's medicine and antiquities (LUCAS 1719: 338). He wrote a detailed report on the necropolis. Lucas states that he entered more than two hundred tombs, particularly the tomb called "Grotte de l'Estalle," which must be the tomb of Djefai-Hapi I (Tomb I; Siut I; P10.1). He reports seeing pillars, which had all but disappeared by the time the scholars of the French Expedition arrived in Asyut in 1799. Lucas estimated that more than one thousand other tombs had been situated in the mountain. He considered the large rock tombs to be among the most impressive structures he had ever seen during his journeys in the Mediterranean (LUCAS 1719: 343).

The Danish naval captain and traveller Frederik Ludwig Norden (1708-1742) ventured to Egypt in 1738 by order of the Danish king Christian VI. His purpose was to deliver a full and exact account of the country. Norden stayed in Egypt for a year and

Fig. 10: Asyut during the visit of Frederik Norden in 1738.

also visited Asyut. According to Norden, the necropolis situated in the western mountain was called "Tschebat ell Kofferi" (Fig. 10), which presumably can be traced back to Gebel el Kafirin ("Hill of the Unbelievers") (GRIFFITH 1889a: 245). A certain part of this mountain, in which seven openings in a row were visible, was called Sababinath after the seven virgins (seb'a benat) who apparently dwelt there (cf. GRIFFITH 1889a: 244). Norden only described one of the rock tombs in detail, in which he found a large chamber, four sexangular pillars, a painted ceiling and gold-plated decorations amongst other things (NORDEN 1784: 304-306).

Today these travelogues are of special value, even though they were written before academic scholarship discovered Ancient Egypt as a field of research; the first chair in Egyptian history and archaeology was created in 1831 at the Collège de France and hieroglyphs were first deciphered by Jean François Champollion in 1822 in his *Lettre à Monsieur Dacier*. What makes these travelogues special is that far more monuments were preserved at the time when they were written, in contrast to Bonaparte's French Expedition in 1799 and all following expeditions.

The mountain served as a quarry, which led to a continuous destruction of the tombs and diminished the mountain itself. The well-documented quarrying not only occurred in the nineteenth century (see below), but also in the eighteenth century, as is revealed by comparing Lucas' notes regarding Tomb I with those of the French Expedition (ENGEL/KAHL forthcoming). Furthermore, the Mamluks seem to have damaged the tombs by using them as shooting ranges for their target practice (JOLLOIS/DEVILLIERS 1821: 151; compare GRIFFITH 1889a: 177, who is more reluctant on this particular issue).

THE FRENCH EXPEDITION

The French Expedition marked the great turning point in regards to the academic preoccupation with the monuments of Ancient Egypt. Bonaparte not only sent soldiers to Egypt as part of his campaign, but also scientists, scholars, and artists, who were to take stock of the regional flora and fauna, the geography, and ethnography, as well as antiquities. The scientific achievements of the expedition marked a milestone in the history

Fig. 11: View of the harbour el-Hamrah in 1839 (drawing by Hector Horeau).

of Egyptology, even though the military campaign itself was an utter disaster in which the French fleet at Abukir had been sunk and the French army imprisoned. In 1802, Bonaparte arranged for the scientific results to be published, an arduous task which took twenty years to complete. The publication of the results was an invaluable contribution to furthering preoccupation with ancient and modern Egypt.

Asyut itself played a special role during the French Expedition, as its antiquities were the first to be seen by the expedition's members in Upper Egypt, thus offering a first glimpse into the art and writing of the ancient Egyptians (JOLLOIS/DEVILLIERS 1821: 125-126).

The French civil engineers René Édouard Devilliers du Terrage and Jean Baptiste Prosper Jollois were responsible for the chapter on Asyut. Both Devilliers du Terrage and Jollois mention the small village el-Hamrah (cf. Fig. 11) situated near the Nile, which was considered to be Asyut's port. El-Hamrah was connected to Asyut by way of an embankment, which was supposed to protect the wider area from annual flooding (JOLLOIS/DEVILLIERS 1821: 127). Jollois and Devilliers noticed granite and marble pillars at the town's entrance, most of which were fluted. In the town itself they mention a large bazar and nice houses made out of clay bricks with fragments of porphory, marble or granite pillars serving as thresholds (JOLLOIS/DEVILLIERS 1821: 128). Some of these pillar fragments were fluted as well.

Fig. 12: Asyut during the French Expedition (Panckoucke 1822: Pl. 43).

The main trade in Asyut in 1799 consisted of linen cloths, crockery, natron, and opium. The Darfur caravan ended slightly to the north of the town and brought thousands of slaves from Sudan to Asyut (Jollois/Devilliers 1821: 128; cf. Chapter One). In addition to this, the informants of the French Expedition spoke of ten oil factories in Asyut and cultivation in and around Asyut. Wheat was the main produce, followed by barley, flax, beans, and various other grains which were successfully cultivated there. Poppy seeds were harvested and used to make opium. Picturesque gardens and plantations with fig, apricot, pomegranate, orange, lemon, and palm trees could be found near Asyut, especially in the north. These gardens and plantations were very fruitful (Jollois/Devilliers 1821: 129).

The Mamluks lived in their houses between Asyut and the mountains, in direct proximity to the headquarters of the French Division Desaix (Fig. 12). The houses, showing embrasures, dominated the town and small cannons were placed on the highest points. This part of the citadel was on the left hand side of the path which led to the mountains. A wide plane was on the right hand side. This plane was covered by the Nile during the annual flooding. Jollois and Devilliers set up camp there along with their assistants in order to be closer to the antiquities they wanted to visit.

They report the following on the mountain and the Islamic cemetery (cf. Fig. 4):

When following the route from Asyut to the mountain, the traveller soon reaches the limit of the cultivated terrain—where a modern cemetery is located. These final resting places of the Moslems do not stir feelings of sadness; they present a more gay aspect than the interior of the towns. One arrives there by an avenue planted with acacias and sycamores. The principal tombs are of a light architectural construction, painted with different colours and surmounted by trees. Some enclosing walls are constructed in stepped form, superimposed one upon another, to form a type of pyramid. Amongst the painted ornaments, or, more properly, the daub on the walls, can be seen flowers, trees and objects which appear to have some association with the profession of the deceased … The enclosures of the tombs are crenellated. The tombs are square or pyramidal in form and are always painted white.
(RUSSELL 2001: 311)

Further on, they mention the antique tombs in detail:

More distant from the cemetery [i.e. the modern cemetery] is the foot of the Libyan Chain in which one sees a considerable number of tombs disposed at different levels up to the summit of the mountain. These excavations are of two or three types. The majority, and the most interesting, have been excavated by the ancient Egyptians to serve as sepulchres. We recognised these by the hieroglyphs with which they are decorated and by the artistry evident in their execution. Their walls are dressed perfectly and have a regular batter. Other rock-cut tombs have served as refuges for the first Christians of this country. On the walls of some of these are to be seen the figures of saints—drawn and painted in the worst taste. Some of the ancient tombs have also been inhabited by local people, who, as a consequence, have appropriated, removed and covered over—in effect have effaced—all traces of the ancient religion of the country. Sometimes, the form of the old hieroglyphs has been preserved and are only covered over by grotesque paintings. In addition to the two types of tombs, of which we have spoken, ancient quarries[1] can still be seen. At the foot of the mountain, a large canal passes by which served as a means of transporting stones. This canal connects with Bahr-Yousêf and is joined to the Nile by a small branch some two or three hundred paces below the town of Asyut.

The architecture and inscriptions of the larger tombs were studied by the expedition's scholars, the descriptions covering eighteen pages of text (JOLLOIS/DEVILLIERS 1821: 133-151). The tombs were measured and the plans published. The murals were copied and documented for posterity in copper-engravings and illustrations (PANCKOUCKE 1822: Pls. 43-49). The French copyists did a good job, even though the hieroglyphs had not yet been deciphered in 1799.

The descriptions of the French antiquary, artist and savant Dominique Vivant Denon (1747-1825) deserve special mention in addition to the article about Asyut in the *Description de l'Égypte*. Denon fulfilled his role of an "embedded correspondent" and described and drew the antiquities amidst periodic volleys of enemy bullets. Furthermore, his accounts and drawings of Asyut give a good impression of the town (VATIN 1989: I, 96-98; II, Pls. 30.2, 33.2).

THE SCIENTIFIC EXPLORATION OF ASYUT

The present-day exploration of Asyut has its roots in the achievements of the French Expedition. Travellers, Egyptologists, and archaeologists journeyed to Asyut after the

---
1 The translation of this excerpt differs from RUSSELL 2001.

results of the expedition had been published (cf. GRIFFITH 1889a: 244-251). The steadily growing interest in Ancient Egypt during the nineteenth century also played a major part in sparking curiosity and the desire to travel there.

The reports the French Expedition produced are just as valuable as the earlier travelogues. All of these texts provide an overview of how Asyut changed during the course of time. Shortly after the French Expedition had visited Asyut, the town and its surrounding landscape experienced a phase of change. In 1817, saltpetre factories were established in Asyut with French aid. In addition to this, large amounts of mulberry trees were planted and Druzes were employed to make silk (RIDLEY: 224). The mulberry trees, which grew to be thirty meters tall, served as food for silkworms. The silk industry had been introduced to Egypt five years earlier in 1812 so that independence from Syrian silk imports could be achieved. It is not difficult to imagine how the saltpetre factories and silk industry changed the landscape of Asyut the French Expedition had described.

The cultivation of corn, indigo, opium, and sugar is reported during the reign of Mohamed Ali (1823-1838; BOWRING 1998: 38, 46-47). At the end of the nineteenth century the British invested heavily in irrigation infrastructure to enhance agricultural productivity. Starting in 1899, the Asyut barrage was constructed until its completion in 1902. The barrage was part of a network of modern dams and canals stretching from the Aswan Dam at the First Cataract to the Delta (BOWMAN/ROGAN 1999: 3).

Not only was the town subject to change, but the ongoing process of modernization proved to be detrimental to the ancient necropolis in the nearby mountains. Quarrying continued and was intensified, destroying numerous tombs or parts of tombs.

In regards to this matter, the English politician, traveller and writer Henry Windsor Villiers Stuart (1827-1895) wrote the following in 1879:

We reached Siout and paid a visit to the bazaar, where we bought some daggers of native manufacture; they are of good design but of bad iron and practically worthless. We bought some pottery for which this district is famous. We then started for the tombs, which I found cruelly mutilated since our last visit … These interesting monuments are being rapidly destroyed for the sake of the limestone in which they are excavated. The whole mountain is a mass of limestone, and any quantity might be obtained without a single tomb being injured, but of course it is less trouble to carry away the walls and columns found in these tombs hewn ready to hand, than to quarry the mountain in fresh places. For the sake of this advantage, records of priceless value to the historian are ruthlessly destroyed for ever, after having escaped for 4000 years. If the work of spoliation goes on much longer the roofs will fall in, and their total destruction will be consummated. Even in their decay they are grand monuments.
(STUART 1879: 92-94)

This use of the mountain as a quarry is a major reason for the present calamity researchers are faced with. A good deal of things described by the French Expedition had already disappeared eighty years later, when Stuart wrote his account. The results of the French Expedition thus are one of the most important sources on Asyut. The illustrations in the *Description* are invaluable documents on the architecture and inscriptions of tombs which, in the meantime, have been destroyed (attempted reconstruction of the front inscriptions of Tombs III-V can be seen in EDEL 1970; EDEL 1984).

The reports of numerous travellers and scholars from the nineteenth and twentieth century are, next to the detailed account of the French Expedition, of high value for obtaining knowledge concerning ancient Asyut and its understanding. Apart from showing the changes and decay the monuments were subject to, they also inform about remnants that the French Expedition disregarded. Furthermore, they also display the particular preferences of the visitors in respect to their time.

This can especially be seen with regard to the high concentration of visitors to the tombs documented by the French Expedition, even though hundreds, not to say thousands, of tombs were hewn into the mountain. The various reports and illustrations of the French traveller and mineralogist Frédéric Cailliaud (1787-1869), who visited Asyut from 1819 to 1822, as well as those of the English Egyptologist and traveller John Gardner Wilkinson (1797-1875), who lived in Asyut during his twelve year stay in Egypt (1821-1833), and of the English architect and painter Francis Arundale (1807-1853), who saw Asyut in 1835, complement what can be known on the town and the necropolis during their specific times. The destruction of some of the tombs can be dated to a relatively precise degree by comparing the various reports (GRIFFITH 1889a: 247-248).

The growing publicity of the necropolis also attracted antiques dealers. For example the French painter Comte de Forbin, who visited Asyut from 1817 to 1818, reports of Italian antiques dealers, who brought their finds to Europe (cf. VOLKOFF 1979: 487).

Quarrying led to the continuous decay of the monuments, as statements such as those of the French draughtsman and archaeologist Nestor L'Hôte (1804-1842) show. The situation was especially dramatic around 1820. In 1839, L'Hôte wrote a letter stating that it was impossible to discover the whereabouts of the tombs documented by the French Expedition, with exception of Tomb I and a single neighbouring tomb (L'HÔTE 1840: 83). Even though Nestor L'Hôte's portrayal may have been a bit too pessimistic, it nonetheless goes to show the extent of the destruction and changes which the mountain to the west of Asyut must have experienced during the preceding forty years.

MODERN DAY EGYPTOLOGY'S EXPLORATION OF ASYUT

The work of the English Egyptologist Francis Llewellyn Griffith (1862-1934), who copied the inscriptions of Tombs I through V (cf. Chapter Four), is a cornerstone of the exploration of Asyut. Ladders were his most important tools, as he had to transcribe hieroglyphs from walls up to eleven metres high. Griffith wrote:

I ... had to tramp every evening to the town, leaving the precious ladders in doubtful security though hidden in the darkest recesses of Tomb I.
(GRIFFITH 1889a: 123)

Griffith presented the results of his epigraphic endeavor to the general public in 1889 (GRIFFITH 1889b). His copies have been the authoritative starting point for studying the texts of Tombs I through V.

The English Egyptologist Percy E. Newberry worked in Asyut around 1893, copying texts and making sketches in the tombs, aiming to publish corrections to Griffith's publication. However, Newberry did not complete his work (MAGEE 1998: 717-718).

The articles of the French Egyptologist Pierre Montet (1885-1966), who published the inscriptions after copying them himself in 1911 and 1914, are further publications of scientific value. Montet added a small paleography and three photographs to his publications as examples (MONTET 1928: 53-68; MONTET 1930-35: 45-111).

Reliable translations of Tombs III through V were attempted for the first time using the copies from the French Expedition (1799) and to Montet (1914) as a basis. The translations of the German Egyptologists Hellmut Brunner (BRUNNER 1937), Wolfgang Schenkel (SCHENKEL 1965: 69-89; SCHENKEL 1978: 29-35), and Elmar Edel (EDEL 1970; EDEL 1984) are substantial advancements for the exploration of Asyut, even though many details are still difficult to understand. Edel tried to reconstruct the fronts of Tombs III through V in 1970 and 1984 (cf. FRANKE 1987: 49-60), which had been destroyed after the French Expedition had transcribed them. He clarified some obscure passages although the find of some Roman papyri in Tebtynis has recently rendered a few particular reconstructions improbable (OSING 1998a: 55-100).

Archaeological excavations took place in the necropolis of Asyut at the end of the nineteenth century and at the beginning of the twentieth century. Unfortunately, these excavations produced no beneficial results, as their findings remained either entirely unreleased or only unsatisfactorily published.

The works of the French Archaeological Institute Cairo, for which Charles Palanque (1865-1910) worked in 1903 (PALANQUE 1903: 119-128), were published in the year 1911 by Émile Gaston Chassinat (1868-1948) (CHASSINAT/PALANQUE 1911). Twenty-six graves were published. Unfortunately, neither of the two archaeologists supplied a plan of the necropolis nor of the architecture of the individual tombs, due to their focus on inscriptions and statues.

Practically nothing is known about the results of other excavations. In 1889, the Director of the Antiquities Service, Eugène Grébaut (1846-1915), permitted Mohammed Halfawee to undertake "a considerable excavation, quite grandiose" (CAPART 1936: 528). This excavation took place in the courtyard of the Salakhana Tomb and seems to have concentrated on Tomb VI in particular. A man named Farag supervised another Egyptian excavation, which targetted the tomb of Mesehti. Models of soldiers were found in this tomb (cf. CHASSINAT/PALANQUE 1911: V). In 1897 Farag Ismail (it is not clear whether he is identical with the above mentioned man) and Yasser Tadros explored the ruins of the monastery Deir el-Azzam (MASPERO 1900: 109-119).

Not much more is known about the excavations of the Italian archaeologist Ernesto Schiaparelli (1856-1928; cf. FORBES 1996: 82-84), who worked in Asyut over the course of five campaigns between 1905 and 1913 (LEOSPO 1989: 188-194). Schiaparelli at first worked in the southern half of the necropolis, and later moved on to the northern half. Only a single anthropological article was published (MARRO 1913). To this day, thousands of finds are waiting in the Museo Egizio di Torino to be studied (CURTO 1976: 52, 105).

On behalf of the British Museum, the English archaeologist David George Hogarth (cf. RYAN 1996: 77-81) searched the northern half of the necropolis in winter 1906/07 "for virgin tombs," in order to deliver as many splendid finds as possible to the museum. The repeated use of dynamite (RYAN 1988: 79) and his failure to produce documents make his work appear highly dubious. Ryan reconstructed Hogarth's attempts in 1988.

The Egyptian Egyptologist Ahmed Bey Kamal (1851-1923) also acted as a contract excavator (cf. FORBES 2005: 82-84). Kamal worked for the private collector Sayed Bey Khashaba in Asyut, shortly before World War I broke out. Even now, some Egyptologists erroneously assign Kamal's discoveries to the neighboring village Deir Drunka, even though Kamal himself, and later on Henri Wild, explicitly pointed out that they originated in Asyut (KAMAL 1916: 66; WILD 1971: 307-309). Kamal published lists of the objects he found (KAMAL 1916: 65-114), however these do not seem to be complete (WILD 1971: 308, note 1). The numerous objects which entered into Khashaba's possession were scattered all over the world after the collection was disbanded. A small fraction of the collection is still located in the Coptic School in Asyut.

Archaeological activities in Asyut were brought to an end by the outbreak of World War I and larger excavations were not resumed until recently. The extensive excavations seem to have abated Egyptological interest in the town and its necropolis.

Nonetheless, there were exceptions to this lack of interest, such as the clearing activities of the English Egyptologist and archaeologist Gerald Avery Wainwright (1879-1964) in some of the larger tombs, especially in the court of Tomb I and in the so-called Salakhana Tomb (WAINWRIGHT 1926: 160-166; WAINWRIGHT 1928: 175-189; cf. DUQUESNE 2007), as well as the short surveys of the Egyptian archaeologist Moharram Kamal in 1931 and 1932 (KAMAL 1934a: 49-53; KAMAL 1934b:125-126), the Egyptian Egyptologist Ali Hassan in 1962 (HASSAN 1976: 93), the American Egyptologist Donald B. Spanel (SPANEL 1989: 301-314) and the English Egyptologist Diana Magee in the 1980s (MAGEE 1988).

Archaeological activities on site were rendered impossible during the most recent decades because the mountain was used as a military base. The situation has fortunately changed in the last years. Since 2003 a German-Egyptian joint mission of the University of Sohag and the Johannes Gutenberg-Universität Mainz (originally with the participation of the Westfälische Wilhelms-Universität Münster) has been working in Asyut (EL-KHADRAGY/KAHL 2004; VERHOEVEN-VAN ELSBERGEN 2004; KAHL/EL-KHADRAGY/ VERHOEVEN 2005a; KAHL/EL-KHADRAGY/VERHOEVEN 2005b; KAHL/EL-KHADRAGY/ VERHOEVEN 2006; KAHL/VERHOEVEN 2006; BECKER 2006; KAHL 2006; EL-KHADRAGY 2006a; EL-KHADRAGY 2006b; EL-KHADRAGY 2007; ENGEL/KAHL forthcoming).

REASONS AND AIMS FOR EXPLORING ASYUT

The reasons and goals for once more getting involved with the site are quite clear. Even though the inscriptions of Tombs III through V have been copied and worked upon, facsimiles still are not available. In view of their importance for Egypt's political history during the First Intermediate Period, this is quite a desideratum. There are no existing facsimiles for the inscriptions of Tomb I, nor are they available in a continuous translation. The paintings and decoration, set in relief, in these tombs have been entirely ignored, even though they convey valuable information about the art and culture of the First Intermediate Period and the early Middle Kingdom. Tombs I through V are not the only ones to have remained neglected since the French Expedition. A good example is Tomb I10.1 (cf. Chapter Four; Figs. 80-81), which, according to the reports of the participants of the French Expedition (JOLLOIS/DEVILLIERS 1821: 149-150), was one of the most marvellously decorated tombs in the area. However, neither the *Description de l'Égypte* nor later scholarly publications show a picture of the tomb's highly praised decoration. Other tombs were ignored by the French Expedition and by later scholars and are on the verge of destruction, or already have been ruined. Exposure to sunlight, wind, and rain has been highly detrimental to the reliefs and paintings, alongside excrement from bats and birds, the destructive work of grave robbers and graffiti from careless tourists.

A complete survey of Asyut's rock necropolis is by all means necessary. Surveying was first commenced in 2003 and has been continued since 2004. The survey is aimed at establishing a map of the necropolis, in which not only as many tombs as possible will be charted for the first time, but which will also document their architecture and decoration.

The survey is not limited to the tombs of the First Intermediate Period and the Middle Kingdom, as the subsequent reuse of the tombs, later tombs, quarries, Coptic monasteries, and the cells of anchorites will also be studied so that we can obtain a complete picture of the way the mountain had been used through the course of time. In so doing the landscape (i.e. the mountain) and its history can be reconstructed as well as the history of Asyut and the town's fate as a wounded city and border town.

SCHOLARLY LIFE IN ASYUT

Information about the habits and living conditions of scholars in Asyut is sparse, as almost nothing has been published concerning this matter. Tomb robbers surely must have been the main problem they were faced with. Both Chassinat (CHASSINAT/PALANQUE 1911: 1) and Hogarth noted the constant danger that portable antiquities faced, often disappearing from an excavation. Hogarth, who described Asyut as "a large town notorious for its illicit traffic in antiques" (HOGARTH 1910: 155), informs us about the daily life of his workers:

Dealers waited for my men at sunset below the hill and beset them all the way to the town, and one digger, a youth of brighter wit and face than most—he was half a Bedawi—gained so much in the few weeks before I turned him off that he bought him a camel, a donkey and a wife. The order of his purchases was always stated thus, whoever told the tale.
(HOGARTH 1910: 156)

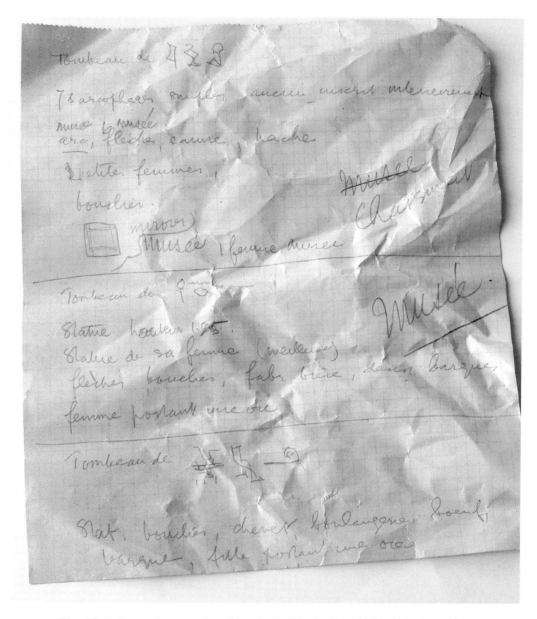

Fig. 13: Palanque's notes found in Tomb III, shaft 1 (S04/st313; © Kahl).

A further problem connected to this seems to have been security. Chassinat relates that his excavation team was threatened after discovering the still intact tomb of Nakhti in 1903 (cf. Chapter Four). Enraged antiquities dealers, who saw their lucrative income being diminished by the scientific excavations, even threatened to attack and pillage the excavation camp (CHASSINAT/PALANQUE 1911: 1-2). All antiquities were therefore brought into the tomb of Khety II (Tomb IV), which could be secured with iron bars. Traces of this relocation were recently unearthed during the excavations of the German-Egyptian mission. In 2004, notes written by Palanque concerning finds from the tombs of Nakhti,

Iw, Ankh-ef, and Wepwawet-em-hat (Fig. 13) were found in the neighboring Tomb III, which is connected with Tomb IV through a Late Antique corridor. The notes describe how the finds were to be split up between Chassinat (i.e. the French Archaeological Institute), whom Palanque worked for, and the Egyptian Museum in Cairo.

Adolf Erman (1854-1937), a German Egyptologist, also reports the threat the locals posed in the year 1886 (ERMAN 1929: 216).

The political situation still is a problem for the safety of researchers. During the French Expedition the French army and scholars worked together, thus exposing the latter to the risk of being attacked by enemy troops. This threat has nowadays been replaced by the spectre of worldwide terrorism, which the Egyptian government counters by placing the excavators under police protection. In other words, the team is escorted by the police day and night.

The elements also made things unpleasant for archaeologists. Hogarth set up his base camp in one of the large rock tombs, presumably Tomb IV, and spent the cold winter nights in front of his camp fire, which he fed using ancient coffin boards (HOGARTH 1910: 157).

Schiaparelli also seems to have lived in the mountain. Letters addressed to him and his short-lived assistant Virginio Rosa (1886-1912; cf. CURTO 1973-1975: 10) were found in the debris of Tomb III and recovered. The address used simply was "Asyut" or "Gebel Asyut" (Fig. 14).

It is also difficult to reconstruct how the excavators nourished themselves. The French mission had a penchant for white wine, whereas the Italian mission preferred

Fig. 14: Letter to Virginio Rosa (Tomb III; S05/st066; © Kahl).

Fig. 15: Cigarette packet (Tomb III; S05/st066; © Kahl).

cigarettes (Fig. 15). Dust was part of each and every meal, just as it is today. Hogarth wrote the following about eating in his base camp:

Not that our wide-mouthed grotto, however, proved much better than a tent. The north wind struck its farther wall, and was sucked around the other two in an unceasing, unsparing draught which dropped dust by the way on everything we ate or drank or kept.
(HOGARTH 1910: 157)

CHAPTER THREE

ASYUT: ITS SACRED LANDSCAPE

And they [i.e. the priests of the Wepwawet-temple] shall go forth following his *Ka*-servant, at his glorification, until they reach the northern corner of the temple, as they do, when they glorify their own noble ones, on the day of kindling the fire.
(Siut I, 278-279)

With respect to theology and the history of religion, Asyut had been of supraregional importance since the late Old Kingdom (KAHL 1999: 339-348). In the Pyramid Texts, the oldest transmitted corpus of religious texts at all, Asyut is mentioned for the first time at the beginning of the Sixth Dynasty (Pyr §§ 630 a-c, 1634 a-c). The town is described there as the place on which the goddesses Isis and Nephthys kept vigil over the dead Osiris (cf. Chapter One).

Also during later periods there are references to Asyut. Papyrus Boulaq III which dates to the first century AD relates a passage dealing with Asyut in the so-called *Rituel de l'embaumement* (SAUNERON 1952):

You speak with your mouth in Asyut,
Osiris comes to you in Asyut.
Your mouth is Wepwawet's mouth in the western mountain,
when Osiris is speaking to his son Horus.
(Papyrus Boulaq III, 4.23-5.1)

Copies of a manual dated from the second century AD record myths concerning Upper Egyptian nomes. However, the original composition of the mythological manual might have occured much earlier. The myths concern local religious features revolving round the Osiris myth. Also the 13th Upper Egyptian nome is included (OSING 1998b: 143-150) and the narratives broaden the knowledge about the sacred landscape of the regional capital Asyut. For example, a relic of Osiris, i.e. his fingers, was kept in Asyut according to the manual (Papiri della Società Italiana, inv. I, 72). Furthermore the manual reports on a statue made of gold and iron-ore depicting the contending gods Horus and Seth. It also mentions a hall of the sistrum, in which Isis-Hathor appears. Other narratives refer to an otherwise unknown temple called "House of the Eight Trees," sacred trees planted near Asyut, and a statue representing Wepwawet sitting on Isis' lap. It remains to be seen whether there was also an obelisk as mentioned in the manual (Papiri della Società Italiana, inv. I, 72, 3.12; cf. OSING 1998b: 147 note g).

Asyut's sacral importance as seen from religious texts is mirrored in temples and sanctuaries that once existed in the town. Varied texts provide evidence for this in ancient

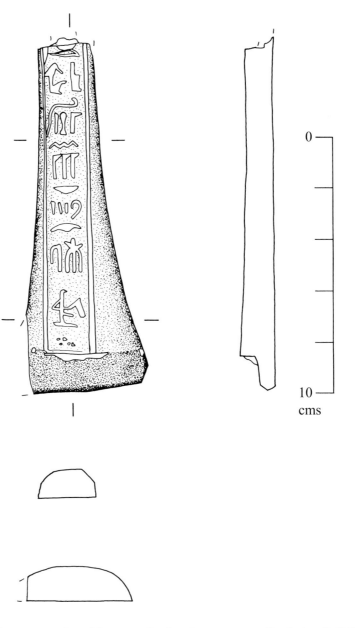

Fig. 16: Inscription on wooden object mentioning the overseer of priests of all the gods Ah-mose (S05/019; drawing: Eva-Maria Engel).

Asyut. The temples were not only of religious importance but they were also cultural and economic centers. They owned land (cf. Papyrus London BM EA 10591 rto. VII.13; THOMPSON 1934: 27) and economic installations (e.g. kitchens and bakeries; cf. the title "overseer of the house of fire of the Wepwawet-temple" in Papyrus London BM EA 10591 rto. VI.4, VIII.19 from the Ptolemaic Period [THOMPSON 1934: 23]), and they even had libraries (KAHL 1999: 290) at their disposal.

Asyut: its sacred landscape

Fig. 17: Stela London BM EA 1725: representation of Wepwawet as canid standing on a standard (BIERBRIER 1993: Pl. 83.1725).

Fig. 18: Stela London BM EA 1430: representation of Wepwawet as standing canid (BIERBRIER 1993: Pl. 81.1430).

In theory, cult practice in temples was a matter of the king; in practice, however, it was the local elite, who performed rituals in most temples, also in Asyut.

Various priestly titles are attested from Asyut. They point to the existence of temples or cults of the deities referred to in the texts and give an impression of Asyut's sacred landscape. In addition to those titles referring to particular deities, one has to mention one more title from the Late Period and the Ptolemaic Period: "the support of heaven and clothier of manifestations" (cf. the bibliographical references in GUERMEUR 2005: 376, note a and EL SABBAN 2005: 27-28). This title denoted originally the high priest of Asyut; later it was used as an honorific title for priests (Papyrus Cairo CG 50058 and 50059; KAMAL 1916: 94-95; cf. SOTTAS 1923: 40; BEINLICH 1976: 148-149). Another title, "overseer of priests of all the gods (of Asyut)," is known from the New Kingdom (Djefai[…]: Cincinnati Art Museum 1966.266, CAPEL/MARKOE 1996: 169-172; Ahmose: S05/016, S05/017, S05/019 [Fig. 16]).

Apart from the deities who had their own cults in the temples of Asyut (cf. infra), many more are known as mentioned especially in offering formulae on coffins, statues, and offeringtables. Some of them seem to have been restricted to the region of Asyut and its surroundings, for example Akhenitief ("Glorious one of his father"), Heritepsenuef ("Chief over his brothers"), and Merymutef ("Beloved of his mother") who most likely played the part of a pre-eminent deity of Manqabad, about 11.5 km downstream from Asyut (ZECCHI 1996: 7-14). Others seem to have had a limited field of activity, for example the violent goddess Hereret mentioned twice in the tombs of the nomarchs of the First Intermediate Period (Siut III, 33; Siut IV, 54), both times in connection with armed conflicts (EDEL 1984: 81-83; OSING 1998a: 78). Sporadically Middle Kingdom coffins mention a goddess called Sahet (e.g. GAUTHIER/LEFEBVRE 1923: 19). Her epithet, "she who presides over the house of the god's books," points to (sacral) knowledge as her scope of duties. Tatenenet, apparently a female counterpart to Tatenen, is exclusively known from Asyut (cf. LEITZ 2002: 349). Several Middle Kingdom coffin inscriptions invoke the gods of the Heliopolitan ennead as well as Ra-Atum and his hand (CHASSINAT 1912: 159-160; KAMAL 1916: 72, 75; KEES 1956: 326).

Ceramic sculptures (cf. EISSA 1994: 64, note 17; DUQUESNE 2000: 14) and about five hundred stelae of the New Kingdom found in the so-called Salakhana Tomb (cf. Chapter Four) furnish evidence of the private worship of gods in Asyut (cf. Chapter Seven). Apart from the chief deity, Wepwawet, stelae were dedicated to other deities such as Wepwawet-Ra (BRUNNER 1958: Pl. 3; DUQUESNE 2002a: 13, Pl. 2a-b), Amun, Amun-Ra, Amun-Ra-Kamutef, Osiris, Ptah, and Thoth (WAINWRIGHT 1928: 175, 182, Fig. 6), Hathor of Medjeden, Ra-Horakhti, Sobek, Taweret, and Harsaphes (DUQUESNE 2002b: 42, Pl. 2; DUQUESNE 2004: 47; DUQUESNE 2007: 28). The Pushkin Museum of Fine

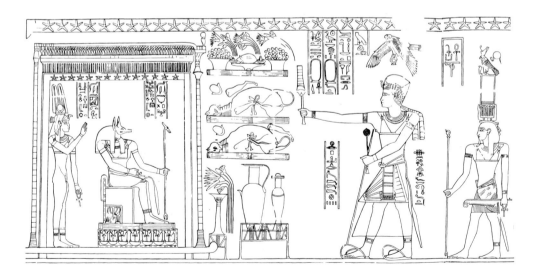

Fig. 19: King Darius I followed by the figure of his "living *Ka*" dedicates an offering to Wepwawet in a shrine with Hathor of Medjeden; temple of Hibis (El-Khargeh Oasis), Hypostyle M, North Wall, Register I (DAVIES 1953: Pl. 30, detail).

Arts, Moscow, houses a stela of the Nineteenth Dynasty on which Isis and Horus, son of Isis, are venerated among others (HODJASH/BERLEV 1982: 145-149 [89]).

These stelae were originally dedicated in the temple of Wepwawet and in other sanctuaries of Asyut. There is no certain clue as to the technique of their installation. Only two had a socle they could stand on freely. The others might have been fixed on the temple walls with cement (as is the case in the Serapeum at Saqqara) or they might have been erected in small offering chapels (as in Abydos). However, they might also have been stored in a chamber or been stuck freely in the ground. Eventually they were set up outside of the temple on either side of the processional road (EISSA 1994: 64, note 15).

The following pages give an overview of the gods whose temples or cults are attested in Asyut.

THE TEMPLE OF WEPWAWET

First of all, the temple of Wepwawet is worth mentioning. Wepwawet was the chief deity of Asyut. He was a funerary and protective deity (cf. GRAEFE 1986: 862-864; HOUSER-WEGNER 2001: 497; DUQUESNE 2005: 390-397) with a belligerent component (DURISCH 1993: 207-208, note 12). Most often he was represented as a canid (jackal or dog) standing on a standard (Fig. 17), but he was also depicted standing without a standard (Fig. 18) or as canid-headed man (Fig. 19). Occasionally he was shown recumbent (DURISCH 1993: 207, Fig. 1). Greek iconography depicted him as a young man (Fig. 20). His name means "the Opener of the Ways," for example the ways in the mountains and the roads to the oases. From this point of view, the attributes stated in his name are ideal for the chief deity of a town like Asyut, favorably situated with regard to major transportation routes. His most frequent epithets were *nb s3w.ti* ("lord of Asyut"), *sḫm t3.wi* ("power of the Two Lands," EISSA 1994: 61, note 5), *šmʿ.wi* ("the Upper Egyptian").

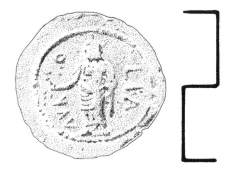

Fig. 20: Coin (Obol) from year 11 of Emperor Hadrian (AD 126/127), depicting Wepwawet in Greek iconography; verso: Wepwawet as young man, standing, dressed in chiton und himation. He wears a crown with ram horns and sun disk and holds a standing canid in his right hand (Cologne 3410; after GEISSEN/WEBER 2004: 304-305, Pl. 2.21).

A passage from the tomb of Djefai-Hapi I gives a good impression of the immense power attributed to Wepwawet during the Twelfth Dynasty:

Wepwawet,
the adorned one, who is upon his standard,
lord of the shedshed (i.e. the protuberance on the standard), exalted above the gods,
the one with sharp arrows, lord of Asyut,
who is upon the thrones of Atum,
who is stronger and more powerful than the (other) gods,
who took possession of the Two Lands being triumphant,
to whom the heritage was given forever,
Wepwawet,
the Upper Egyptian, power of the Two Lands,
controller of the gods.
(Siut I, 232-233)

The numerous personal names showing Wepwawet's name as an element reflect his extraordinary importance for the inhabitants of Asyut impressively (cf. the overview given by BECKER 2004: Pls. II-XXX). These names give concrete information on how the inhabitants of Asyut felt Wepwawet's power and efficacy:
- Wepwawet-nakht "Wepwawet is strong" (First Intermediate Period – Middle Kingdom)
- Wepwawet-em-hat "Wepwawet is foremost" (often attested for the Middle Kingdom)
- Wepwawet-hotep "Wepwawet is gracious" (Middle Kingdom, New Kingdom, Late Period)
- Wepwawet-mose, Wepi-mose "Wepwawet is the one who gave (him) birth" (New Kingdom)
- Wepwawet-iir-di-es "Wepwawet is the one who gave him" (Late Period)
- Pay-ef-tjau-em-awy-Wepwawet "His breath is in the hands of Wepwawet" (Late Period)
- Djed-Wepwawet-iu-ef-ankh "Wepwawet has said, he will live" (Late Period)
- Wepwawet-iu, Wepuy-iu "Wepwawet has come" (Ptolemaic Period)
- Pa-di-Wepuy "The one, whom Wepwawet has given" (Ptolemaic Period)
- Pa-di-Wepuy-iu "The one, whom Wepwawet has given, has come" (Ptolemaic Period; THOMPSON 1934: 69)
- Petophois "The one, whom Wepwawet has given" (grecized form; Ptolemaic Period)

Other personal names are composed of shortened forms of the god's name Wepwawet:
- Wepa (Middle Kingdom)
- Wepai (Middle Kingdom)
- Wepay (Middle Kingdom)

Wepwawet appears as the chief deity of Asyut in the White Chapel of King Senwosret I (in combination with the name of the 13th Upper Egyptian nome; LACAU/CHEVRIER 1956-1969: Pl. 3). A bronze vessel (Fig. 21) found in the tomb of King Tutankhamun probably came originally from the temple of Wepwawet in Asyut according to its inscription (RADWAN 1983: 118, Pl. 59; EISSA 1996: 85).

The temple of Wepwawet probably was the most important and largest in Asyut. Because of this, general statements like "the temple of Asyut" (Papyrus London BM EA 10591 rto., VII.13; THOMPSON 1934: 27) have to be related to the Wepwawet-temple.

The temple had been recorded for the first time in the First Intermediate Period: Presumably Siut V, 14 ("*I was one great in monuments for the temple*") refers to the Wepwawet-temple. During the reign of King Merikara, at the end of the First Intermediate Period, its name was "*The sky of the one, who made the sky*" (Siut IV, 21). The history of its foundation mentions the Memphite god Ptah as its builder and the god Thoth as its founder:

"The sky of the one, who made the sky" which Ptah built with his fingers, which Thoth founded, for Wepwawet, lord of Asyut, was protected by a decree of the king, the ruler of the Two Lands, the *nesu-bit*-king Merikara.
(Siut IV, 21-22)

Also the coffin Turin Museo Egizio Sup. 14439 (Wepwawet-em-hat) refers to the temple of Wepwawet (MAGEE 1988: II, 53).

Inscriptions of the First Intermediate Period and the Middle Kingdom reveal that there was a columned hall (*iunyt* [Siut IV, 24]; *wesekhet* [Siut I, 283-284]) in the temple. Apart from that, one may assume that the temple was composed—as other temples during that time—of a pylon, a court (perhaps a hypostyle), cult rooms, and a shrine for the statue of the deity. In addition to statues of gods, statues of private people were erected (presumably in the court); these people hoped to participate in the cult and to be near the god in this way (cf. Siut I, 290 for a statue of Djefai-Hapi I). On the statue of the royal herald Ankh-en-mer (Liverpool Museum 1966.178) from the Thirteenth Dynasty it is written:

Every priest and every *wab*-priest who enters the temple of Wepwawet, lord of Asyut, and sees this statue […]
(BOURRIAU 1988: 69-70)

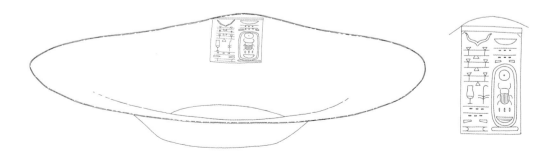

Fig. 21: Bronze vessel found in the tomb of King Tutankhamun (RADWAN 1983: Pl. 59 [333]).

Fig. 22: Illicit excavation of a house owner in Asyut (GABRA 1931: 237, Fig. 1).

Statues from the Wepwawet-temple are also known from the New Kingdom: The statue of the viceroy of Kush Meri-mose (Pl. 12; Vienna, Kunsthistorisches Museum ÄS 36; JAROŠ-DECKERT 1987: 92-98) from the reign of Amenhotep III (Eighteenth Dynasty) and the statues of the overseer of the double granary of Upper and Lower Egypt Si-Ese III (Pl. 13; Vienna, Kunsthistorisches Museum ÄS 34; Brooklyn Museum 47.120.2; SATZINGER 1978: 7-20, Figs. 1-10) from the reign of Ramesses II or Merenptah (Nineteenth Dynasty).

Visitors' graffiti from the Eighteenth Dynasty on the northern wall of Tomb N13.1 also mention the temple, which was surrounded by a wall of more than 15 m height during the reign of Ramesses III (Twentieth Dynasty; Papyrus Harris I, 59,2; cf. below).

At least during the Ptolemaic Period the *dromos* of the temple of Wepwawet was the place where temple business was conducted, oaths taken, and deeds of apportionment completed. Contracts were drawn up and witnessed there as well (THOMPSON 1934: 18, 23).

During the First Intermediate Period and the Middle Kingdom the nomarchs Khety II (Siut IV, 19-20) and Djefai-Hapi I (Siut I, 235-236) report on restoration work conducted in the Wepwawet-temple—both times presumably as consequence of the dam-

Fig. 23: Inscribed blocks of the Wepwawet-temple found during an illicit excavation (GABRA 1931: 239, Fig. 3).

age incurred during the civil wars of the First Intermediate Period and the beginning of the Twelfth Dynasty (cf. BUCHBERGER 1993: 375). Djefai-Hapi I wrote in his tomb:

Djefai-Hapi, he says:
I am a brave heir with enduring monuments, a protector, one, who restores ancient things.
I erected the walls, which had been destroyed.
I covered […] ancestors.
I rebuilt the house of my father.
I renewed all that was primeval in Asyut.
I was one who beloved of the king and one who was favored by his township, one who gave orders to the […]
(Siut I, 234-236)

The autobiographical inscription of the master builder Min-mose (HELCK 1956: 1441-1445, 1448; HELCK 1961: 98-102; ULLMANN 2002: 98-101), a stela of Haremhab (EISSA 1996: 84-85) and Papyrus Harris I (GRANDET 1994: I, 306, 311) prove that also during the New Kingdom restorations were made by order of the Kings Thutmose III, Amenhotep II, Haremhab and Ramesses III. Papyrus Harris I which lists benefactions made by Ramesses III to the principal shrines of Egypt reports that the king did not only restore the temple but that he also built two funerary temples for himself within the sacred area:

I restored the walls in the house of my father, Wepwawet, the Upper Egyptian, lord of Asyut. I built my house therein, of stone of *Ayan*, inscribed and engraved with the graver's tool in his august name. I completed him with the good things of every land. I assigned to him serf-laborers in great number. I made for him a store-house anew containing divine offerings, in order to present them for his provision daily. I hewed for him a great barge of the "First-of-the-River," like the morning-barque of Ra which is in heaven. I walled about his house with a wall, splendidly executed, with twenty courses in the ground foundation, and with a height of 30 cubits [= more than 15 metres]; having ramps, towers and battlements in its whole circumference; great doorposts of stone, and doors of cedar, fitted with mountings (of bronze) of a mixture of six parts, engraved with the great name of thy majesty, forever.
(Papyrus Harris I, 58,12-59,3)

Some decorated blocks from the reign of Ramesses II (Nineteenth Dynasty) furnish archaeological proof for the temple. They came to light during an illicit excavation for gold (Fig. 22) eight meters under the modern floor of a house (GABRA 1931: 237-243). The blocks were found together with those of King Akhenaten (Eighteenth Dynasty) (Fig. 23). Whether the latter are original or are brought in from elsewhere and reused in Asyut still remains open. The discovery of Late Antique columns under this house (GABRA 1931: 237-238) and in its vicinity (Fig. 24; KAHL/EL-KHADRAGY/VERHOEVEN 2005a: 165-166), as well as the knowledge about more illicit excavations in this area, which could be stopped by the police, leave no doubt that—from the Nineteenth Dynasty till nowadays—the Wepwawet-temple, a Late Antique sacred building and a modern Coptic church were erected on one and the same place in Asyut. This place is situated in the west of the modern Asyut (Fig. 5). In addition, the more ancient remains of the Wepwawet-temple of the First Intermediate Period and the Middle Kingdom also lie buried there under the modern city.

The Demotic Papyrus Cairo CG 50059 dating from the eighth year of the Persian usurper Cambyses (Twenty-seventh Dynasty), who conquered Egypt in 525 BC, gives a hint that the Wepwawet-temple was situated at the southwestern edge of Asyut during that time. The papyrus also mentions a pool between Asyut in the north, a suburb in the south and the Wepwawet-temple to the west of it (CG 50059, 4-5; SPIEGELBERG 1932: 42, 44), hence the ancient city can be located to the north of the Wepwawet-temple (Fig. 25). This corresponds very well to elevations that are still visible today in the modern city, and which may go back to the ancient strata of settlement.

Fig. 24: Late Antique column found in Asyut (© Kahl).

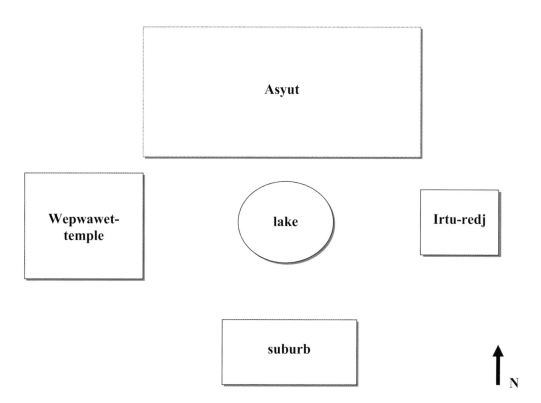

Fig. 25: The reconstructed position of the Wepwawet-temple during the reign of Cambyses according to written sources.

The census-register Papyrus Oxyrhynchos 984 from the first century AD, which probably refers to Asyut, names a quarter called Lykagogon; this could be interpreted as evidence that an image of Wepwawet was carried through this quarter during a procession (MONTEVECCHI 2000b: 146).

The third contract in the tomb of Djefai-Hapi I (cf. Chapter Four) informs us that the temple of Wepwawet was administered by staff known as the *qenbet* during the reign of Senwosret I (Twelfth Dynasty). The members of the *qenbet* who are not mentioned by name administered ten offices (Siut I, 283-284). The highest office was that of the "overseer of priests of Wepwawet, lord of Asyut." Further offices were those of a "herald," "master of secrets," "wardrobe keeper," "overseer of the magazine," "chief of the (broad) hall," "overseer of the *Ka*-house," "scribe of the temple," "scribe of the offering-table," and "lector priest." In addition *wab*-priests and the *wenut*-priesthood are listed in the contracts (Siut I, 273, 281-282, 299).

Documents from 175 BC (Papyrus London BM EA 10589,14; SHORE/SMITH 1959: 53, 55), 171 BC (Papyrus London BM EA 10597,16; THOMPSON 1934: 76), 170 BC (Papyrus London BM EA 10591 rto. I.2,7; II.14; IX.12; X.16; vso. IV.18; THOMPSON 1934: 12, 13, 30, 33, 56) and 157 BC (Papyrus London BM EA 10561; SHORE/SMITH 1960: 284, 288) refer also to priests of Wepwawet.

Title	Name	Date
Overseer of the priests of Wepwawet, lord of Asyut	Khety I (Siut V, 1, 41, 45)	First Intermediate Period
Overseer of the priests of Wepwawet, lord of Asyut	Iti-ibi (Siut III, 2, 57)	First Intermediate Period
Overseer of the priests of Wepwawet, lord of Asyut	Khety II (Siut IV, 45, 61)	Merikara (First Intermediate Period)
Overseer of the priests of Wepwawet, lord of Asyut	Iti-ibi-iqer (Tomb N13.1)	First Intermediate Period
True overseer of the priests of Wepwawet	Mesehti (Tomb N13.1)	First Intermediate Period/Middle Kingdom
Overseer of the priests of Wepwawet, lord of Asyut	Mesehti (Cairo CG 28118-9)	Eleventh Dynasty
Overseer of the priests of Wepwawet, lord of Asyut	Anu (Turin; ROCCATI 1974: 42, 44)	Beginning of Twelfth Dynasty
True Overseer of the priests of Wepwawet, lord of Asyut	Djefai-Hapi II (Siut II, 3)	Beginning of Twelfth Dynasty(?)
Inspector of priests in the house of Wepwawet	Djefai-Hapi I (Siut I, 217)	Senwosret I (Twelfth Dynasty)
Prophet of Wepwawet	Djefai-Hapi I (Siut I, 232)	Senwosret I
(True) Overseer of the priests of Wepwawet, lord of Asyut	Djefai-Hapi I (Siut I, 80-81, 150, 155, 157, 180, 218, 240, 260, 268, 330, 337, 345)	Senwosret I
Musician of Wepwawet	Djefai-Hapi I (Siut I, 335)	Senwosret I
First prophet of Wepwawet	Hori (PALANQUE 1903: 123)	New Kingdom(?)
First prophet of Wepwawet	Amen-hotep (S05/029)	Beginning of Nineteenth Dynasty
Chantress of Wepwawet	Renenut I (Berlin 2/63)	Sety I (Nineteenth Dynasty)
Chantress of Wepwawet	Renenut II (New York, MMA 33.2.1)	Ramesses II (Nineteenth Dynasty)
Chantress of Wepwawet	Ta-ket (Moscow, Pushkin Museum I.1.a 5636; HODJASH/BERLEV 1982: 145-149 [89])	Ramesses II or later
Chantress of Wepwawet	Wenep (Moscow, Pushkin Museum I.1.a 5636; HODJASH/BERLEV 1982: 145-149 [89])	Ramesses II or later
Chantress of Wepwawet	Nefret-Aset (Moscow, Pushkin Museum I.1.a 5636; HODJASH/BERLEV 1982: 145-149 [89])	Ramesses II or later

Title	Name	Date
Chantress of Wepwawet	Mehyt-khayt (Moscow, Pushkin Museum I.1.a 5636; HODJASH/BERLEV 1982: 145-149 [89])	Ramesses II or later
Chantress of Wepwawet	Tay-sen-nefret (Moscow, Pushkin Museum I.1.a 5636; HODJASH/BERLEV 1982: 145-149 [89])	Ramesses II or later
Chantress of Wepwawet	Iay (Yale Art Gallery 1947.81; CAPEL/MARKOE 1996: 174)	Ramesses III or later (Twentieth Dynasty)
Chantress of Wepwawet	Renenut (Cairo JE 68570; DUQUESNE 2000: 24, 36-37, Pls. 1a-b)	Ramesside Period
Chantress of Wepwawet	Ta-iay (Cairo, no number; DUQUESNE 2004: 42, Pl. 3)	Ramesside Period
Chantress of Wepwawet	Sat-Aset (MUNRO 1963: 49, Pl. 3.1)	Ramesside Period
Chantress of Wepwawet	Ta-weneshet (MUNRO 1963: 49, Pl. 3.1)	Ramesside Period
Chantress of Wepwawet	Iy(?) (Cairo JE 68576; DUQUESNE 2003: 38)	Ramesside Period
Chantress of Wepwawet	Sakhmet (CLÈRE 1969: 93-95, Pl. 14)	Ramesside Period
First prophet of Wepwawet	Wepwawet-mose (Cairo JE 68582; DUQUESNE 2000: 25, Pl. 2a-b)	Ramesside Period
Musician(?) of Wepwawet	I-kau(?) (Cairo, no number; DUQUESNE 2000: 29, 46-47, Pls. 6a-b; DUQUESNE 2003: 39-40)	Ramesside Period
Chantress of Wepwawet	Tay-wahet(?) (Cairo JE 47383; DUQUESNE 2003: 33, Pls. 1-4)	Ramesside Period(?)
Second prophet of Wepwawet	Nau-kau-mer Pa-si-en-metek(?) (London BM EA 10792; SHORE 1988: 205)	Amasis (Twenty-sixth Dynasty)
Third prophet of Wepwawet, lord of Asyut	Hor I (Cairo CG 50059; SPIEGELBERG 1932: 44; London BM EA 10792; SHORE 1988: 204)	Amasis

Title	Name	Date
Third prophet of Wepwawet, lord of Asyut; secretary of the house of Wepwawet, lord of Asyut; *setem*-priest of the house of Wepwawet, lord of Asyut	Wepwawet-hotep II (Cairo CG 50058; SPIEGELBERG 1932: 40; London BM EA 10792; SHORE 1988: 205)	Amasis
First prophet of Wepwawet, lord of Asyut	Menekh-ib-Ra (Cairo CG 50058; SPIEGELBERG 1932: 41)	Amasis
Third prophet of Wepwawet, lord of Asyut; scribe of *shen* of the house of Wepwawet, lord of Asyut	Nes-pa-met-shepes 1 (Cairo CG 50059; SPIEGELBERG 1932: 43; London BM EA 10792: SHORE 1988: 204)	Cambyses (Twenty-seventh Dynasty)
Third prophet of Wepwawet; scribe of *shen* of the house of Wepwawet, lord of Asyut	Nes-pa-met-shepes 3 (London BM EA 10792; SHORE 1988: 204-205)	Cambyses
Prophet of Wepwawet	Hotep (KAMAL 1916: 95)	Ptolemaic Period
Herold of Wepwawet	Djed-Djehuti-iu-ef-ankh (KAMAL 1916: 94-95)	Ptolemaic Period
Prophet of Serapis and Wepwawet of Asyut	Djed-Djehuti-iu-ef-ankh (Boston, MFA 54.993; RIGGS/STADLER 2003: 80-81)	Roman Period (first to second century AD)

Fig. 26: Priests and musicians of the Wepwawet-temple in chronological order.

Thirty-six priests and members of the Wepwawet-temple dating from the First Intermediate Period to the Roman Period are known by name at present (Fig. 26).

Also shipbuilders (Papyrus Cairo CG 50058; SPIEGELBERG 1932: 41), scribes (Pl. 2a; S04/171), gooseherds, and servants belonged to the personnel of the Wepwawet-temple (Papyrus London BM EA 10575,6; THOMPSON 1934: 43; cf. also Cairo JE 47384; DUQUESNE 2003: 36-37). Moreover musicians of the temple of Wepwawet are attested from the First Intermediate Period (Siut IV, 30).

Since, according to ancient Egyptian beliefs, the god Wepwawet could transform himself in canids, a pack of canids were associated with the temple. Probably only canids with salient features (e.g. a black coat) were selected. They were supposedly kept in an enclosure where they were also fed (cf. DURISCH 1993: 219).

The contracts of Djefai-Hapi I, who lived during the reign of Senwosret I (cf. Chapter Six), allude to official processions of the statue of Wepwawet through the streets of Asyut. Stelae from the New Kingdom depict these processions (DUQUESNE 2003), whose exact itinerary is still not known (DURISCH 1993: 219).

Title	Name	Date
Priest of Anubis(?), lord of Asyut, Imi-ut	Min-nefer (Leiden, RMO AMT 106)	Fifth Dynasty
Overseer of the priests of Anubis, lord of Ra-qereret	Khety I (Siut V, 42)	First Intermediate Period
Overseer of the priests of Anubis, lord of Ra-qereret	Iti-ibi (Siut III, 61)	First Intermediate Period
Overseer of the priests of Anubis, lord of Ra-qereret	Khety II (Siut IV, 53)	Merikara (First Intermediate Period)
Overseer of the priests of Anubis, lord of Ra-qereret	Iti-ibi-iqer (Tomb N13.1)	First Intermediate Period
Overseer of the priests of Anubis […]	Anu (Turin Museo Egizio; ROCCATI 1974: 47-48)	Beginning of Twelfth Dynasty
Overseer of the priests of Anubis, lord of Ra-qereret	Djefai-Hapi I (Siut I, 234)	Senwosret I (Twelfth Dynasty)

Fig. 27: Priests of the Anubis-temple in chronological order.

THE TEMPLE OF ANUBIS

Anubis, Egypt's principal funerary god (DOXEY 2001a: 97; DUQUESNE 2005: 367-384), was another deity most often represented as a canid. Unlike Wepwawet, he was mostly depicted in a recumbent fashion, rarely as a man with a canid's head. In Asyut, his principal epithets were "lord of Ra-qereret" denoting him as presiding over the necropolis of Asyut (GOMAÀ 1986: 270-272), "the one in the (place of) embalmment" (*Imy-ut*) and "lord of the holy land (i.e. the necropolis)."

The first of the ten contracts which Djefai-Hapi I made with the priesthood of the Wepwawet-temple points out that a procession took place going from the Wepwawet-temple to the Anubis-temple on the first of the five epagomenal days, that is on the fifth day starting from the end of year (Siut I, 273-274). Wepwawet, i.e. a portable statue representing the god, visited Anubis together with the inhabitants of Asyut. The Anubis-temple was situated in the immediate area of the rock necropolis, presumably directly at the foot of the mountain (Fig. 103; also cf. Siut III, 67; EDEL 1984: 48).

Several written sources mention the temple of Anubis, for example visitors' graffiti from the New Kingdom (Tomb N13.1), Papyrus Cairo CG 50058 (SPIEGELBERG 1932: 41) from the reign of Amasis (house of Anubis, lord of Ra-qereret), and Papyrus London BM EA 10591, rto. VIII.7 (THOMPSON 1934: 28) from the second century BC (house of Anubis). The latter reports on an altar dedicated to the goddess Isis in the Anubis-temple.

The Greek Papyrus Vindob. G 19769 (line 10-11) written during the reign of Emperor Alexander Severus (AD 229/230) hints at the continuation of the Anubis-temple into the Christian Era. It mentions the Anubieion, a quarter which was named after the Anubis-temple. The same quarter might also be referred to in SB VI 9310 A5 and B6 from AD 229 (HOOGENDIJK 1997: 128; MONTEVECCHI 2000b: 145-146).

Several nomarchs from the end of the First Intermediate Period and the early Middle Kingdom bore the title "overseer of the cattle of Anubis:" the well known Iti-ibi, owner of Tomb III (Tomb III, northern wall), Iti-ibi-iqer (Tomb N13.1), and Anu (beginning of Twelfth Dynasty; ROCCATI 1974: 43-44). The seventh and ninth contract of Djefai-Hapi I (Senwosret I, Twelfth Dynasty) mention a "great *wab*-priest of Anubis" (Siut I, 305, 312); the eighth contract refers to the *wenut*-priesthood of the Anubis-temple (Siut I, 307).

Seven priests of the Anubis-temple are known by name (Fig. 27; nota bene: Min-nefer could have been a priest of Wepwawet instead of Anubis; cf. BEINLICH 1976: 142).

THE TEMPLE OF OSIRIS

The first attested connection of Osiris, God of the Netherworld (GRIFFITHS 2001: 615-619), to Asyut dates from the Sixth Dynasty. According to the Pyramid Texts, Isis, and Nephthys kept vigil over the dead Osiris (Pyr §§ 630 a-c, 1634 a-c) who was designated as "lord of Asyut." Frequent epithets of Osiris in Asyut were "lord of the West" and "lord of Ta-ankh," but "lord of Busiris, great god, lord of Abydos" also occurs several times.

Occasionally Wepwawet was in a son relationship to Osiris as for instance on the stela of Ikher-nofret from Abydos, which designates Osiris as the father of Wepwawet (LICHTHEIM 1973: 124). This relationship between these two gods might have contributed to the special adoration of Osiris in Asyut.

The Osiris-temple is called "the house of Wennofer" in the tomb of Djefai-Hapi II (Siut II, 21). A visitor's graffito of the New Kingdom (northern wall of Tomb N13.1) reports also on the Osiris-temple. During the Twenty-sixth Dynasty a (*ra-per-*)temple of Osiris is attested. The god bears the peculiar epithet "who gives clothes" (SPIEGELBERG 1932: 41; BEINLICH 1976: 149, 162).

Priests of Osiris are known from the First Intermediate Period to the Late Period (Fig. 28). A shroud of a woman from the Roman Period called Ta-sheret-Hor-udja reveals Demotic inscriptions mentioning her father Djed-Djehuti-iu-ef-ankh, who was a prophet of Serapis and Wepwawet of Asyut. Because there is no evidence for a distinct cult of Serapis at Asyut, it seems probable that the town's Osiris cult may have persisted well into the Roman Period but used the god's additional name (RIGGS/STADLER 2003: 80-81, 86).

Title	Name	Date
Overseer of the priests of Osiris, lord of the west	Khety I (Siut V, 43)	First Intermediate Period
Overseer of the priests of Osiris, lord of the west	Djefai-Hapi II (Siut II, 11)	Beginning of Twelfth Dynasty(?)
Overseer of the priests of Osiris, lord of the west	Djefai-Hapi I (Siut I, 231)	Senwosret I (Twelfth Dynasty)
Chief of secrets of what only one hears in the house of Osiris	Djefai-Hapi (Worcester Art Museum 1938.9; DUNHAM 1937-1938: 13, Fig. 6, no. 3)	Mid-Twelfth Dynasty or later
Prophet of Osiris, lord of the west	Wepwawet-hotep II (Cairo CG 50058; SPIEGELBERG 1932: 40)	Amasis (Twenty-sixth Dynasty)
fekti-priest of Osiris, lord of Asyut	Nes-pa-met-shepes 1 (Cairo CG 50059; SPIEGELBERG 1932: 43); [London BM EA 10792; SHORE 1988: 204])	Cambyses (Twenty-seventh Dynasty)
fekti-priest of Osiris, lord of Asyut	Nes-pa-met-shepes 3 ([London BM EA 10792; SHORE 1988: 204])	Cambyses
Prophet of Serapis and Wepwawet of Asyut	Djed-Djehuty-iu-ef-ankh (Boston MFA 54.993; RIGGS/STADLER 2003: 80-81)	Roman Period (first to second century AD)

Fig. 28: Priests of the Osiris-temple in chronological order.

THE TEMPLE OF HATHOR

Hathor was the main female deity in Asyut and was venerated there at the latest from the Old Kingdom to the Roman Period. Till the New Kingdom, her priesthood was—as far as one can say—recruited from women (Fig. 29).

In the recently discovered Tomb N13.1 (cf. Chapter Four), several visitors' graffiti from the early New Kingdom refer to "the temple of Hathor, lady of Medjeden." For the most part Hathor is called "lady of Medjeden" in Asyut (cf. DURISCH 1993: 213-214). Medjeden is a toponym associated with the 13th Upper Egyptian nome. Its localization has not definitely been determined yet, but the earlier identification with Deir Drunka has to be dismissed; presumably Medjeden was situated directly near Asyut (GOMAÀ 1986: 276). Since the New Kingdom Hathor of Medjeden was venerated supraregionally all over Egypt (Fig. 19; CHADEFAUD 1982: 173, note 19).

Another epithet characteristic of Hathor in Asyut is "the mistress of 16." According to the mythological manual (second century AD) from Tebtynis, this epithet seems to refer more to the 16 secrets than to the 16 litanies or to an inundation of 16 cubits height (OSING 1998b: 144-145). "The mistress of 16" seems to have been the favorite epithet of Hathor in Asyut during the Graeco-Roman Period (BEINLICH 1976: 153-154).

Title	Name	Date
Priestess of Hathor	Khuit (London BM EA 46634; DAVIES 1995: 146)	Sixth Dynasty
Priestess of Hathor	Kait Idenit (London BM EA 46637; DAVIES 1995: 146)	Late Old Kingdom
Priestess of Hathor	Nebet-em-qis (Turin Museo Egizio Sup. 14378)	First Intermediate Period
Priestess of Hathor	Iti-ibi (Siut IV, 38)	Merikara (First Intermediate Period)
Priestess of Hathor	Senebet (Tomb N13.1)	First Intermediate Period
Priestess of Hathor	Senet-user (Cairo JE 44019; LEFEBVRE 1914: 9-18)	Early Middle Kingdom(?)
Priestess of Hathor	Idu (CHASSINAT/PALANQUE 1911: 21)	Eleventh Dynasty
Priestess of Hathor	Idy(?) (Tomb I, inner passage)	Senwosret I (Twelfth Dynasty)
Priestess of Hathor, lady of Medjeden	Nakht (Newberry Tomb 1/Tomb 8; MAGEE 1998: 720)	Senwosret III/Amenemhat III
Priestess of Hathor	Senebtisi (Newberry Tomb 1/Tomb 8; MAGEE 1998: 723)	Senwosret III/Amenemhat III
Great one of the women's company of Hathor, lady of Medjeden	Renenut II (New York MMA 15.2.1; KITCHEN 1975: 352.15)	Ramesses II (Nineteenth Dynasty)
Chantress of Hathor of Medjeden	Renenut II (New York MMA 33.2.1; KITCHEN 1975: 355.9)	Ramesses II
Prophet of the head of the magazine, the mistress of 16	Wepwawet-hotep II (Cairo CG 50058; SPIEGELBERG 1932: 40)	Amasis (Twenty-sixth Dynasty)
Prophet of the head of the magazine, the mistress of 16	Nes-pa-met-shepes 1 (Cairo CG 50059; SPIEGELBERG 1932: 43; London BM EA 10792; SHORE 1988: 204)	Cambyses (Twenty-seventh Dynasty)
[Prophet of the head of the magazine, the mistress of 16]	Nes-pa-met-shepes 3 (London BM EA 10792; SHORE 1988: 204)	Cambyses

Fig. 29: Priests and musicians of the Hathor-temple in chronological order.

Additionally the epithet "head of the magazine" denoted Hathor in Asyut (EGBERTS 1987: 27-28).

THE TEMPLE OF THOTH (HERMES)

Priests of Thoth, god of wisdom and justice (BOYLAN 1922; DOXEY 2001b: 398-400) often depicted as an ibis or baboon (Fig. 30, S05/022), are known from the Ptolemaic Period. The Demotic family archive of Tef-Hape mentions a prophet of Thoth named Shep-Min for 170 and 169 BC (Papyrus London BM EA 10598-10599; THOMPSON 1934: 77-79). Hermes was the Greek equivalent to Thoth. A priest of the temple of Hermes named Tothoes, son of Thothortaios, is recorded in a Greek papyrus from 125 BC (Papyrus Mediolanum inv. 47; DARIS 1958: 35-44; VANDONI 1976: 105-108). The temple was situated close to the Gebel Asyut and can be connected with a "feeding place of the ibis" (cf. Fig. 103), which is also mentioned in the Demotic family archive of Tef-Hape (Papyrus London BM EA 10591 rto. VIII.3, Papyrus London BM EA 10591 vso. VI.4, and Papyrus London BM EA 10575, 6; THOMPSON 1934: 28, 43, 60).

The late evidence of the Thoth-temple corresponds with personal names referring to this god, which are primarily attested in Asyut starting from the Late Period:

Twentieth Dynasty:
- Djehuti-em-hab (Yale Art Gallery 1947.81; CAPEL/MARKOE 1996: 174)

Twenty-sixth to Twenty-seventh Dynasty:
- Djed-Djehuti-iu-ef-ankh (Cairo CG 50058, 50060, 50061; SPIEGELBERG 1932: 41, 46; Papyrus London BM EA 10792; SHORE 1988: 205)

Ptolemaic Period:
- Djed-Djehuti-iu-ef-ankh (Papyrus London BM EA 10575, 10591, 10594; THOMPSON 1934: 71, 143; KAMAL 1916: 95)
- Djehuti-iir-di-es (Papyrus London BM EA 10575, 10591, 10592; THOMPSON 1934: 66, 143);
- Djehuti-heri (Papyrus London BM EA 10575; THOMPSON 1934: 40)
- Djehuti-setem (Papyrus London BM EA 10575, 10597; THOMPSON 1934: 40, 75)
- Pa-sher-Djehuti (Papyrus London BM EA 10593, 10594; THOMPSON 1934: 68, 71)
- Thothortaios (Papyrus Mediolanum inv. 47, I 31; VANDONI 1976: 106)
- Pa-heb (Papyrus London BM EA 10592; THOMPSON 1934: 66)

Roman Period:
- Djed-Djehuti-iu-ef-ankh (Boston, MFA 54.993; RIGGS/STADLER 2003: 80-81)
- Ta-na-hibu (Papyrus London BM EA 10575, 10591; THOMPSON 1934: 142)
- Thortaios (P.O. III 488,3; MONTEVECCHI 1998: 69)

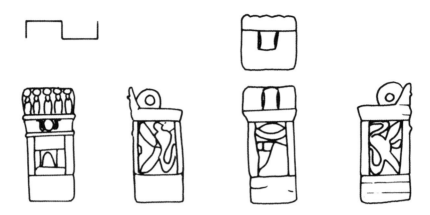

Fig. 30: Faience amulet (S05/022) showing Thoth as an ibis and baboon (drawing: Sameh Shafik).

However, there is some evidence for a cult of Thoth going as far back as the New Kingdom. A votive stela dedicated to Wepwawet mentions the personal name Baket-Djehuti (DURISCH 1993: 214); whether this woman came from Asyut, remains open. Another stela mentions a chantress of Thoth named A(p?)y-nofret (PALANQUE 1903: 125); perhaps the stela can be dated to the New Kingdom (PORTER/MOSS 1934: 265).

MAAT

Although references to priests of Maat (for Maat cf. TEETER 2001: 319-321) and thus to a cult or a temple of the goddess are rare (Fig. 31), they extend from the Middle Kingdom to the Ptolemaic Period. Papyri of a family archive of officials connected with the necropolis of Asyut mention several times a certain title of Pe-te-tum, son of Tuot. The editor of the *editio princeps* thought that Pe-te-tum was a scribe of the divine rolls in a temple of Maat in Asyut (THOMPSON 1934: 41 note 4). This interpretation corresponds with the title "prophet of Maat" born by the nomarchs Djefai-Hapi II and Djefai-Hapi I at the beginning of the Twelfth Dynasty. The offices allude either to a temple of Maat or to a cult of the goddess practiced in another temple in Asyut.

Title	Name	Date
Prophet of Maat	Djefai-Hapi II (Siut II, 13)	Beginning of Twelfth Dynasty(?)
Prophet of Maat	Djefai-Hapi I (Siut I, 358)	Senwosret I (Twelfth Dynasty)
Scribe of Maat	Pe-te-tum (Papyrus London BM EA 10591, VI.22, VIII.24; cf. THOMPSON 1934: 41 note 4)	181 BC

Fig. 31: Priests and scribes of Maat in chronological order.

ATEN

During an illicit excavation in the old city of Asyut, a house owner found blocks of an Aten-temple (Figs. 22-23; GABRA 1931). Even the name of the temple could still be read: Rudj-ankh-Aten "One who has a permanent life is Aten." It remains to be seen, however, whether these blocks were the remnants of a sanctuary built during the Amarna Period for the god Aten. Since additional blocks inscribed with the name of Ramesses II probably belonging to the Wepwawet-temple came to light in this context, the blocks from the Amarna Period could also have been taken to Asyut during the Ramesside Period, where they were reused to enlarge the Wepwawet-temple.

AMUN-RA AND AMUN

The title "chantress of Amun-Ra" (Renenut I: tomb-chapel of Amen-hotep; KITCHEN 1975: 351.10; Renenut II: New York, MMA 15.2.1; KITCHEN 1975: 353.7) attested in Asyut at the beginning of the Nineteenth Dynasty gives no certain proof for a cult of the god Amun-Ra in Asyut, because this title could also refer to the occupation of these two women in Memphis (KITCHEN 1993b: 244, 248). The same applies to the chantress of Amun-Ra Kha-nub (Cairo JE 47969; EISSA 1991: 47, Fig. 1) and the chantress of Amun Ty (CLÈRE 1969: 93-95, Pl. 14) on Ramesside stelae from the Salakhana trove (cf. Chapter Seven). These women could have also worked outside Asyut. Likewise the reference to a temple of Amun on an inscribed wooden staff (London BM EA 24388) of the New Kingdom (HASSAN 1976: 147) is not convincing proof for the existence of such a temple in Asyut.

The offering-litany to Min-Amun, however, recorded in the forecourt of the Luxor Temple and mentioning Amun-Ra in Asyut explicitly, provides unquestionable evidence for a cult of Amun-Ra in Asyut during the reign of Ramesses II. The liturgy reads:

Offering to Amun-Ra in Apu/Panopolis.
Offering to Amun-Ra in Asyut.
Offering to Amun-Ra in Asyut.
(KITCHEN 1979: 625.53-55)

During the New Kingdom Amun-Ra was venerated in Asyut in form of an (ityphallic) Nile goose or a bull (EISSA 1995: 33-34). A stela which mentions a prophet of Amun dates probably from the New Kingdom (PALANQUE 1903: 125; PORTER/MOSS 1934: 265). The base of a Late Period statuette can be attributed to a sistrum-player of Amun-Ra named Ta-sheret-Khonsu (KAMAL 1910: 154). A prophet of Amun-Ra-Ope in Asyut named Djed-Djehuti-iu-ef-ankh is known from the lid of a sarcophagus of the Ptolemaic Period (KAMAL 1916: 95; GUERMEUR 2005: 375-376).

Khonsu

There is only one attestation of a cult of Khonsu dating from the reign of Amasis (Twenty-sixth Dynasty): Nes-pa-met-shepes 2 was prophet of Khonsu in Asyut (Cairo CG 50058; Spiegelberg 1932: 41).

Sakhmet

Nes-pa-met-shepes 2 (Cairo CG 50058; Spiegelberg 1932: 41) points to a cult of Sakhmet in Asyut. He bore the title "prophet of Sakhmet in Asyut" during the reign of Amasis (Twenty-sixth Dynasty).

The title "overseer of the priests of Sakhmet" attested during the Nineteenth Dynasty (Amen-hotep and Iuny), however, does not produce evidence for a local cult of the goddess. Rather it points to the activity of the title bearer in the medical sector (von Känel 1984: 254).

Neith

The title "scribe of the ships of Neith" is attested during the reign of Cambyses (Twenty-seventh Dynasty) and hints to a cult of this goddess in Asyut (Papyrus Cairo CG 50059; Spiegelberg 1932: 45). Neith was primarily venerated as a goddess of war and hunting in Sais. The cult of Wepwawet in Sais (Houser-Wegner 2001: 497) could have promoted the cult of Neith in Asyut.

Isis and Isis-Hathor

The group statue of the overseer of the double granary of Upper and Lower Egypt Si-Ese III dating from the reign of Ramesses II indicates a cult of Isis in Asyut (cf. Münster 1968: 187; Kitchen 2000: 102-103), presumably in the Wepwawet-temple (Bohleke 1993: 363-364).

An altar in the Anubis-temple was dedicated to the goddess in the second century BC (Papyrus London BM EA 10591, rto. VIII.7; Thompson 1934: 28).

Worship of Isis might have occurred in Asyut as consequence of the cult of Osiris. Osiris was regarded as the father of Wepwawet, for that reason Isis was considered to be his mother.

Horus son of Isis and son of Osiris

The prophet of Horus son of Isis and son of Osiris Djed-Djehuti-iu-ef-ankh is known from a sarcophagus of the Ptolemaic Period (Kamal 1916: 94; Guermeur 2005: 375-376). Djed-Djehuti-iu-ef-ankh also bore the title "prophet of Amun-Ra-Ope in Asyut."

KHNUM

There is only one evidence for a cult of Khnum in Asyut. A Ramesside stela from the Salakhana trove (cf. Chapter Seven) mentions the chantress of Khnum Iyt-nofret (Cairo, no number; DuQuesne 2000: 28). Since the donors of those stelae could have come from outside the town itself, it remains to be seen whether the priestess belonged to a cult of Khnum in Asyut or whether she worked, for example, in the neighboring town Shutb, where Khnum was the chief deity.

PEPY I

The coffin London BM EA 46629 of the inspector of the priests of the *Ka*-house of Pepy Hetep-nebi gives inscriptional evidence for the *Ka*-House of King Pepy I (Sixth Dynasty; Davies 1995: 146, Pl. 31.1).

The *Ka*-house of Pepy I was part of a series of buildings, which the king founded throughout Egypt. *Ka*-houses of Pepy I were linked to the local temples in Bubastis, Memphis, Zawiyet el-Meitin, Qusiya, Akhmim, Naqada, and Elkab, eventually also in Hierakonpolis (cf. Franke 1994: 121-126). The *Ka*-houses were installed with personnel and land so that regional centers could develop from them, which were directly bound to the king and the residence. On the one hand, the *Ka*-houses served the funerary cult of the king, on the other hand, they increased the income of the local temples. The foundation of the *Ka*-house of Pepy I in Asyut might account for the rise of archaeological and inscriptional evidence for Asyut during the Sixth Dynasty. Since then the town and its temples had more resources and became a (supra)regional center.

The contracts of Djefai-Hapi I list an „overseer of the *Ka*-house" (Siut I, 283-284). Whether this *Ka*-house is identical with the *Ka*-house of Pepy I or it is the *Ka*-house of Djefai-Hapi I (so Franke 1994: 125) remains to be seen.

RAMESSES MERYAMUN, THE GOD IN ASYUT

The priest of an otherwise unattested statue of King Ramesses II (Nineteenth Dynasty) is mentioned on a stela (Moscow, Pushkin Museum I.1.a 5636) dating from the reign of this king or slightly later (Hodjash/Berlev 1982: 145-149 [89]): "the prophet of Ramesses Meryamun" Khonsu.

DJEFAI-HAPI

Visitors' graffiti on the walls of the recently discovered Tomb N13.1 prove that one of the nomarchs of the Twelfth Dynasty named Djefai-Hapi was venerated as a local saint (Kahl 2006: 27). Scribes report on their visit to the temple of Djefai-Hapi (Fig. 32). Paleographic features date these inscriptions to the end of the Second Intermediate Period or to the beginning of the New Kingdom.

OTHER TEMPLES

There is some inscriptional evidence for further temples. It is, however, not clear whether these temples were located in Asyut.

An inscription on the statue of Djehuti-em-hab (Yale Art Gallery 1947.81; CAPEL/MARKOE 1996: 174) refers to a temple of Mut:

Fig. 32: Visitor's graffito in Tomb N 13.1 mentioning the temple of Djefai-Hapi (© Kahl).

An offering which the King gives and Amun-Ra, king of the gods, Wepwawet, the Upper Egyptian, the power of the Two Lands, Mut, lady of heaven, Hathor, lady of Medjeden and the lord of heaven, that they may cause my name to remain in their temples.

The census register Papyrus Oxyrhynchos 984 of the late first century AD mentions cults for Ares (Onuris) and Apollo (Horus). It is debatable whether the register involved Asyut (BAGNALL 1998: 1097; MONTEVECCHI 1998: 49-76).

CHURCHES

The temples were replaced by churches in Late Antiquity. Some temples might have been destroyed, others were rebuilt as Christian churches. The continuity of the sacred can be proven in one spot of the city even up to today (Fig. 5): The Ramesside Wepwawet-temple is situated under or near Late Antique columns, which in their turn were found close to the modern Coptic church Alwet el-Nasara ("the mound of the Christians").

The writers Abu Salih, al-Maqrizi, Leo Africanus, and many others report on churches in and around Asyut (cf. TIMM 1984: 235-251).

CHAPTER FOUR

THE MOUNTAIN AT THE DESERT EDGE: FUNCTIONS AND CHANGES

There are more rock tombs here than in any other place I have seen. This may be due to various causes, the nearness of the cliff to the city, its suitableness and prominence, the size and importance of the ancient Siût, the special sanctity of its necropolis, consecrated to Anubis and Osiris. I believe also that a great consideration with the ancient Egyptian must have been the unrivalled view north, south, and east to the Nile and the opposite hills, and over fertile lands in which every operation of agriculture could be watched complacently by the ghost of the deceased.
(GRIFFITH 1889a: 125)

The ancient necropolis as well as the modern cemetery of Asyut are situated on the west bank of the Nile in the western mountains (Pls. 1b, 2b). The mountain ridge peaks at over 200 metres above sea level. The ancient necropolis extends over several kilometres along the cultivated land (KAHL/EL-KHADRAGY/VERHOEVEN 2005: 159). The mountain is called "Gebel Asyut al-gharbi" ("Western Mountain of Asyut") or "Stabl Antar" ("Antar's Stable") or "Gebel al-Koffra" ("Mountain of the Gravediggers;" cf. NORDEN 1784: 304; BAYLE 1852: 131-132; cf. Gebel el-Kafirin "Hill of the Unbelievers" [GRIFFITH 1889a: 245]). Geologically, the mountain is part of what is known as the Drunka Formation. This is a particular limestone formation which constitutes a special facies structure within the Upper Theban group of the Lower Eocene (KLEMM/KLEMM 2006).

Thousands of ancient tombs, and also quarries, ruins of monasteries, hermitages, places for prayers and military camps, have rendered the mountain into a landscape with an eventful history. Over a period of at least 4200 years (2200 BC to present) certain parts of the mountain and its function have been subject to change.

All available information from this time-span helps in reconstructing the ancient landscape on the one hand and the history of Asyut on the other—especially as some of its inhabitants are buried in the mountain, while others lived and worked there.

According to Dietrich and Rosemarie Klemm (KLEMM/KLEMM 2006; KAHL/EL-KHADRAGY/VERHOEVEN 2006: 242), the mountain can be divided into eleven limestone layers (Fig. 33). Each layer starts with a more massive limestone of 5-15 m thickness and grades at its top into marl and shale beds of 0.5-3 m thickness. Weathering has shaped these beds into gently inclined slopes, while the more massive limestones, relative to them, form steep cuts. This kind of rhythmic layering therefore forms morphological stages, which can easily be followed over a stretch of several kilometres due to their flat horizontal bedding. Nevertheless, the entire hill slope of the archaeological site of Gebel Asyut is in places so heavily covered with débris that it is hard to recognize these steps.

Fig. 33: The stages of Gebel Asyut al-gharbi according to Klemm & Klemm (© Klemm/Klemm).

The basal type of limestone occurs within stages 1 to 4. It is mainly of a light greyish colour and its weathered surface evokes the image of elephant hide. This type is generally strongly affected by karstification, which forms long extended karst holes and funnels becoming increasingly extensive in the lowest layers. Stages 1 to 4 have so many structural and fossil correspondences that they may be considered as a unity, the "Djefai-Hapi-unity" (the name derives from the tomb of Djefai-Hapi I, which is situated in stage 2).

A denser limestone forms stages 5 to 8, which has no macroscopically visible fossil remains and far fewer karst phenomena. Again, these stages are part of another geological unity, the "Khety-unity" (the name refers to the tombs of Khety I and Khety II in stage 6).

Finally stages 9 to 11 are composed of a somewhat coarser grained limestone with intensive secondary calcification, which gives the rock type a more porous structure and consequently a lower resistance to deterioration. These stages are summarized as "Upper tombs-unity" (KLEMM/KLEMM 2006), because many small tombs were cut into them.

The geological division of the mountain also mirrors its use as necropolis. Thousands of rock tombs were hewn into the mountain and make it look like a honeycomb (cf. Fig. 7). Stage 6 seems to have been the most appropriate for the construction of large tombs. The nomarchs of the late First Intermediate Period had their tombs built there. Tomb III especially is impressive in showing the quality of the stone. The ceiling of the 600 m² large inner hall is still able to support itself, although it was originally supported by four pillars and two architraves (FAUERBACH 2005: 166).

The situation in stage 2 is completely different. Here, the rock has been affected by karstification. The builders of the tomb of Djefai-Hapi I, the largest Middle Kingdom rock tomb of a non-royal person, made their work easier by following the karst fun-

Fig. 34: Quarry O17.1 (Middle Kingdom; © Kahl).

nels inside the hill. The remaining open caves in the tomb were then walled off and plastered, but over time these wall portions decayed, due to water damage from the karst systems (KLEMM/KLEMM 2006). Thus, geological circumstances facilitated the building of this monumental Twelfth Dynasty tomb, but numerous repairs followed. Nevertheless, the advantage of relatively easy construction work seems to have outweighed these flaws, because Djefai-Hapi III cut his large tomb (Salakhana Tomb) also into stage 2 some decades later.

The Old Kingdom tombs already excavated by Hogarth (cf. RYAN 1988) might be situated in stage 5, even if they have not yet been relocated.

During the First Intermediate Period and the Twelfth Dynasty, Gebel Asyut was a separate and thus sacred area (Ta-djeser). Huge gallery quarries (e.g. O17.1; Figs. 34-35), which might have been exploited chiefly for constructing buildings in the town, were situated to the south and did not interfere with the tombs of this period. This situation changed during the Eighteenth Dynasty at the latest. Some of the ancient tombs were now used as quarries: for example, Tomb II from the Twelfth Dynasty, which was extended as a quarry to the north and the south (N13.2; O14.5), and Tomb IV from the end of the First Intermediate Period, where quarrying activities of the

Fig. 35: Quarry O17.1 (Middle Kingdom), interior (© Kahl).

Amarna Period are visible. In addition new quarries (e.g. O15.1; Fig. 36) were hewn into the mountain (KLEMM/KLEMM are preparing a contribution to the quarries, which will replace the description in KLEMM/KLEMM 1993: 150-154).

There is no information about the exact position of the New Kingdom and Third Intermediate Period tombs. Both the finds of Kamal's excavations, as well as objects gathered and left behind in Tomb III and IV by other early twentieth century archaeologists, at least point to the fact that the mountain was still used as necropolis (KAHL/EL-KHADRAGY/VERHOEVEN 2005: 160, 163-164).

Tombs of the Late Period and the Ptolemaic Period seem to have been hewn into the existing free spaces of the mountain, especially in the northern part of the necropolis: traces of such constructions were observed under the modern cemetery (DARESSY 1917a: 95-96). In 2006, a burst water pipe uncovered a tomb of the Ptolemaic Period (L6.2) directly at the southern edge of the modern cemetery. The upper level of the northern part of the necropolis is also said to house tombs from the Twenty-sixth Dynasty and the Graeco-Roman Period (PALANQUE 1903: 121).

Furthermore, it was usual to reuse older tombs, at the latest from the New Kingdom onwards (e.g. Tomb III; probably also Tomb I10.1, where "yellow coffins" were found in burial chambers [personal communication by Inspector Mahmoud Osman in 2004]).

During the Pharaonic Period, the bodies of noble and rich people were buried in wooden coffins and/or stone sarcophagi. In the Old and the Middle Kingdoms, most of the Asyuti coffins were made from sycamore fig, some from tamarisk or imported cedar (DAVIES 1995: 146-147). Cedar had the distinct advantage that it could be easi-

The mountain at the desert edge: functions and changes

Fig. 36: Quarry O15.1 (New Kingdom or later; © Kahl).

Fig. 37: Reed box (length: c. 80 cm; inner height: c. 16 cm) used as coffin, First Intermediate Period (Tomb N13.1, shaft F11). The reed stalks were bound by nine cords on the long side and by five cords on the narrow side. A round pillow for the head was made of short sticks (© Kahl).

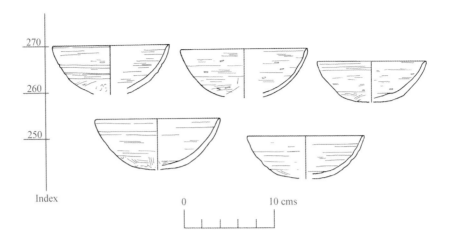

Fig. 38: Hemispherical cups of the First Intermediate Period (drawing: Eva-Maria Engel).

ly treated. Coffins were occasionally decorated with religious texts and ritual scenes. The Middle Kingdom coffins were sometimes inscribed with Pyramid or Coffin Texts. These are funerary texts which might belong to one and the same corpus and which were considered to facilitate the transition from this life to the next and augment the endurance of the deceased in the hereafter. A special feature of this period are the diagonal star clocks, which were sometimes painted on the inner side of the coffin lids (cf. Pl. 11a and Chapter Eight). Some workshops even produced coffins in stock and sold them when required (e.g. ROEDER 1929: 235-236).

Double baskets made of rushes (LEOSPO 1989: 190-191) and reed boxes (Fig. 37) were also used as coffins during the end of the Old Kingdom and the First Intermediate Period. Coffin planks made of palm fibre are known to have been made in the Late Period, and stone sarcophagi from Asyut are attested from the New Kingdom onwards. The granite sarcophagus of Si-Ese III with a lid weighing about 750 tons (SETTGAST 1972: 245-249) and the limestone sarcophagus of Te-nai-nefer from the Ptolemaic Period (DARESSY 1917: 95-96; BUHL 1959: 47, Fig. 14; 49) are good examples. Furthermore, it is likely that poorer people were buried in reed mats during all periods (cf. below).

The amount and the quality of grave goods varied due to social and chronological factors. Pottery, as tableware for eating and drinking, often belonged to the grave goods (Figs. 38-39). Sometimes, however, bodies were buried without any grave goods at all, or they were equipped only with a wooden headrest (Fig. 40). The Tomb of Nakhti, excavated by Chassinat and Palanque, provides a good example of a relatively rich and undisturbed burial of the Middle Kingdom (cf. below). During the Middle Kingdom typical grave goods included small wooden models representing a range of activities (boats, food preparation, offering-bearers, granaries and others; Fig. 41;

The mountain at the desert edge: functions and changes 65

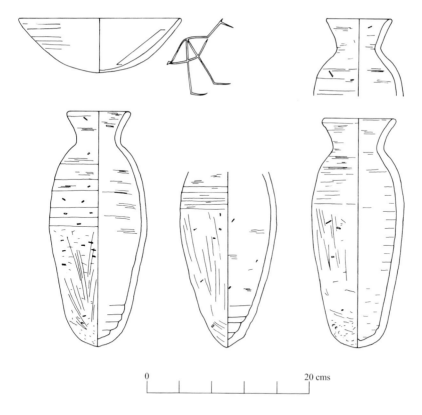

Fig. 39: Bowl and funnel neck jars (First Intermediate Period/Middle Kingdom; drawing: Eva-Maria Engel).

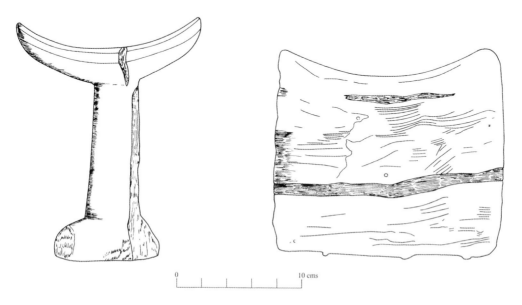

Fig. 40: Wooden head-rests S06/024-025; Tomb N13.1, shafts F5 and F8 (First Intermediate Period; drawing: Sameh Shafik).

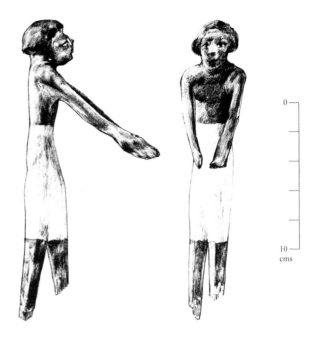

Fig. 41: Sailor from a model boat (S05/112; drawing: Ammar Abu Bakr).

cf. TOOLEY 1989: 68-72; ZÖLLER 2007). Statues (cf. e.g. Figs. 42, 77) and ushebtis (Fig. 43) were also deposited in the tombs.

The German-Egyptian Asyut Project found deepenings cut into the floor of Tomb III to make space for later burials; the different orientation of these deepenings point to the fact that the deceased were not Christians, but the exact date of these burials still remains unknown. Some of the bodies were wrapped in reed mats; a ball (Fig. 44) was among the grave goods, indicating the burial of a child.

From the Late Period onwards there were certainly also animal cemeteries in Asyut: mummies of canids in and near the Salakhana Tomb (GAILLARD

Fig. 42: Statue of a woman (First Intermediate Period/Middle Kingdom), Paris, Louvre E 12003 (© Musée du Louvre/Maurice et Pierre Chuzeville).

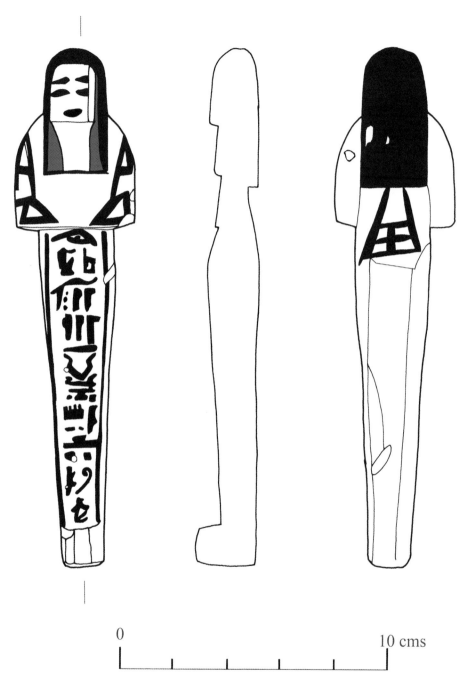

Fig. 43: Ushebti of Amen-hotep, New Kingdom, S05/029 (drawing: Eva-Maria Engel).

1927: 33-42) attest to this, as does the mention of "the Cats" on Ptolemaic papyri, which might denote a cemetery of sacred cats (THOMPSON 1934: 42, note 9; cf. GRIFFITH 1889a: 127). Finds of mummified calves (CHARRON 2002: 202), predatory

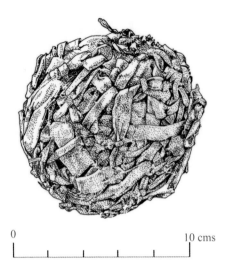

Fig. 44: Ball, palm fibre (Tomb III, shaft 4; S05/065; drawing: Ammar Abu Bakr).

birds, probably monkeys (JOLLOIS/DE-VILLIERS 1821: 153-154) and ibises (Tomb III) give a first impression of the—probably much higher—diversity of the buried animals. In addition, there is a currently inaccessible tomb called "Tomb of the Dogs" below the tombs of the nomarchs of the First Intermediate Period. The accumulation of canid bones at this spot points to a last resting-place for these animals.

The report of the excavation of Mohammed Halfawee in 1889 by the American businessman and traveller Charles Edwin Wilbour (1833-1896), gives a better idea of the beautiful jackal necropolis near the Salakhana tomb:

March 22, 1889 ... Omar told me of new work in the mountain and took me after noon to a considerable excavation, quite grandiose, which Mohammed Halfawee, with permission from Grébaut, was making. It is only a few rods north of the end of the causeway, perhaps one third of the way to the cemetery, and thirty or forty feet up. A narrow way cut through rock leads to an open place, on the north side of which are two rock chambers, the door of the farthermost being inscribed in the name of the same Hap-jef whose two tombs [i.e. Tomb I and Tomb II; J.K.] have been a wonder for many years ... Digging is only begun on the north side of the place. Above six feet of sand is a four or five foot layer of jackal mummies in pots, some of which are ornamented. Their shape and decoration is wonderfully

Fig. 45: The mausoleum of Sheikh Abu-Tug in the northern part of the necropolis (© Kahl).

Fig. 46: Statues in an Old Kingdom Tomb now destroyed (after PANCKOUCKE 1822: Pl. 46.9).

varied. One had a face with protruding tongue; many had raised work. I remember too, a hawk-headed Sphinx with the beginning of a Demotic inscription.
(CAPART 1936: 528)

The necropolis of Asyut was called Ta-ankh or Pe-djeser (cf. Chapter Five) and was administered by special personnel. Several writings give insight into the organization, the activities and the life of the workmen of the necropolis.

To establish his funerary cult, Djefai-Hapi I (Twelfth Dynasty) entered into two contracts (the ninth and tenth of the contracts inscribed on his tomb's walls; cf. Pl. 7b) with the overseer of the necropolis workers, the *tepiu-dju* necropolis-workers, the necropolis guard and the overseer of the desert (Siut I, 312-326). The latter title seems to have been the most important among the necropolis workers, because the overseer of the desert received more than twice as much as the other workers. It seems not to have been by chance that Djefai-Hapi I held this title and thus guaranteed a considerable income to his descendants who took over the office.

Demotic papyri from 181-169 BC (cf. Chapter Five: The Pe-te-tum/Tef-Hape-family) provide information about the life of a family of lector-priests of the necropolis.

Papyrus London BM EA 10561 (SHORE/SMITH 1960: 277-294) is dated to year 24 of King Ptolemy VI Philometor (157 BC). Its purpose appears to be how to regulate what should be provided in the case of a single hypothetical burial (SHORE/SMITH 1960: 286). Pet-Amen-ophis and On-nophris, two lector-priests of the necropolis of Ta-ankh at Asyut, gave certain undertakings to Pet-Amen-ophis, a third lector-priest of the necropolis of Ta-ankh at Asyut, who was associated with two other men of unspecified profession. The papyrus does not only mention lector-priests involved in a burial but also coffiners, winders (i.e. the men who actually wrapped the body), anointers and other groups of people whose exact function is unclear, for example, "the man who is brought from the town" or "the man who is turned over on the ground" (SHORE/SMITH 1960: 292).

The temple of Anubis may also have been in the necropolis or at its edge (cf. Fig. 103 and Chapter Three).

Fig. 47: Tomb V, ground plan (after PANCKOUCKE 1822: Pl. 47.8).

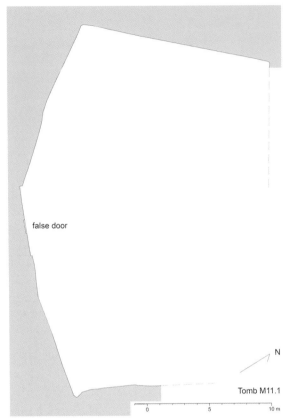

Fig. 48: Tomb V, preliminary ground plan (2004; © Fauerbach).

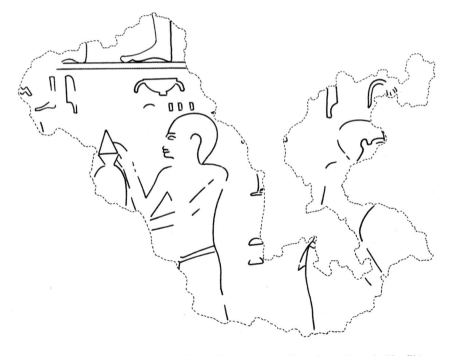

Fig. 49: Tomb V, metal working? scene (drawing: Sameh Shafik).

In the Christian Era, Coptic anchorites used the numerous tombs as cells or dwellings. They covered the tomb walls, which were decorated with pharaonic pictures and hieroglyphs, either with a rough mud plaster (e.g. in Tomb IV) or additionally white-washed the walls and decorated them with inscriptions and paintings. Today, most of the Coptic wall decorations have been destroyed, especially during the last century, when much of the substance was lost (cf. Figs. 90-93). Magical rituals and acts were also performed in the tombs: for example, a camel(?) bone, inscribed in red, was laid under a dead body in Tomb III with the intention of moving his spirit to take action against another living person (Pl. 2c).

Coptic people also sited their cemetery in the ancient necropolis. The corpses were often buried side by side and separated only by a small piece of rock: some bodies were laid to rest in simple coffins, while others were wrapped in mats made of reed stalks or palm trees (cf. infra Deir el-Azzam); some were laid on a litter or a matting of reed stalks and others on a bed of straw, with the head resting on a pillow. Dressed in long white garments, on which a cross was embroidered at chest level, they wore leather belts, some of which were decorated with crosses or figures. The burial of a child in a coffin, who was wrapped in a piece of cloth, was also recorded; the child's body was covered with a thick layer of honey inside the cloth (PALANQUE 1903: 126). Small children were also buried in vessels made of pottery (BOCK 1901: 91).

Coptic people erected at least two monasteries in the ancient necropolis: Deir el-Meitin (Figs. 87-88) and Deir el-Azzam (Fig. 83), which were abandoned during the fifteenth century AD at the latest (cf. infra).

Coptic installations are also attested everywhere in the pharaonic necropolis, yet only a few traces remain visible. For example:
- O13.2: A pharaonic tomb, which was later decorated with white plaster and red Coptic letters, where the word "Apa" is still readable.
- O15.1: The entrance area of this New Kingdom quarry shows white plaster and red Coptic letters on its walls.
- There is a tomb situated between O15.1 and O13.1, which was later decorated with Coptic paintings.
- Fragments of a red painted ground floor near the mausoleum of Sheikh Abu-Tug might also belong to the Coptic Period.

Proceeding on the assumption that the higher stages (5-11) of the mountain were built up with Coptic installations, one can imagine that, during Late Antiquity and Medieval times, the appearance of the Gebel Asyut al-gharbi was completely different from today. Once again, the report of the scholars of the French Expedition (cf. Chapter Two) gives an idea of how many Coptic remains were lost during the past two centuries:

Other rock-cut tombs have served as refuges for the first Christians of this country. On the walls of some of these are to be seen the figures of saints—drawn and painted in the worst taste. Some of the ancient tombs have also been inhabited by local people, who, as a consequence, have appropriated, removed and covered over—in effect have effaced—all traces of the ancient religion of the country.
(Russell 2001: 311)

There is also evidence of Islamic culture on the mountain. The mausoleum of Sheikh Abu-Tug (Fig. 45) was built in the northern part of the Gebel Asyut al-gharbi. At the foot of the northern part, the Islamic cemetery is situated (Fig. 4), which used to be called Gabaneh (Volkoff 1979: 484-485). Its origins have still to be determined as well as the exact date of the mausoleum.

Massive exploitation of limestone formed the appearance of the mountain from the eighteenth century at the latest to the mid nineteenth century (cf. Chapter Two). Vandalism and demolition through illegal excavations contributed to the change in the landscape (Palanque 1903: 121). In addition, the tomb's original decoration was destroyed by tourists who carved numerous graffiti (Pl. 3a). They came to Asyut predominantly since the 1850s, when a winter season on the Nile became popular and a stop of 24 hours in Asyut for food intake left enough time to visit the rock cut tombs in the western mountain (Walz 1978: 117). Francis Llewellyn Griffith remarked:

The inscribed portions of (Tomb) III and (Tomb) IV are covered with the names of tourists of all nations scrawled in pencil or too often cut with the knife.
(Griffith 1889a: 177)

The use of the mountain by the Egyptian military marks the last change in the history of the Gebel Asyut al-gharbi for the moment.

The following overview describes some of the installations in the western mountain (cf. Map 1).

Tomb of the Old Kingdom

Jollois/Devilliers 1821: 150; Panckoucke 1822: Pl. 46.9; Wilkinson 1843: 88; Griffith 1889a: 244, 246, 252; Porter/Moss 1934: 267; Magee 1988: II, 40

To the south of the mountain the savants of the French Expedition detected nine sculptures cut into the rock in very high relief (Fig. 46): eight standing women of 1.30 m height each and a child. An irregular excavation divided them into two groups. They are probably remains from the back of an Old Kingdom tomb which was already largely destroyed at that time. In 1843, Wilkinson saw five of the statues which were still extant, but Griffith observed none in 1888. Today the tomb is assumed to be completely destroyed.

The mountain at the desert edge: functions and changes 73

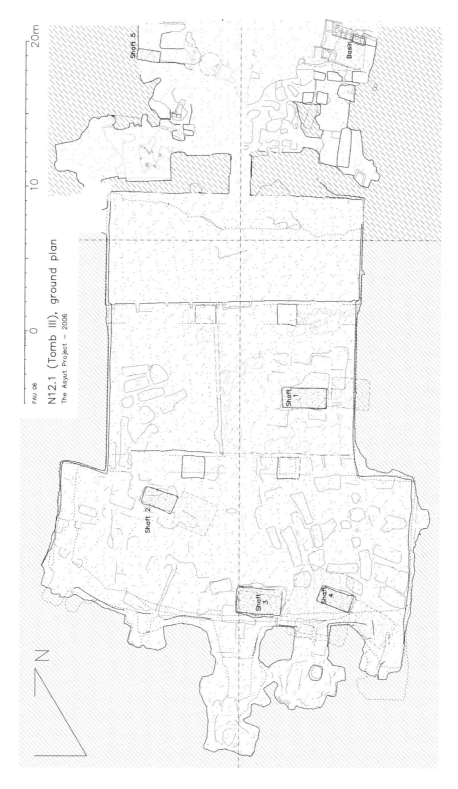

Fig. 50: Tomb III, ground plan (© Fauerbach).

Tomb V (Siut V; M11.1)

Khety I (First Intermediate Period)
    Jollois/Devilliers 1821: 144; Panckoucke 1822: Pls. 47.8-9, 49.6-7; Griffith 1889a: 122-127, 165-166; Griffith 1889b: 11, Pl. 15; Montet 1930-35: 107-111; Porter/Moss 1934: 264; Brunner 1937: 11-16, 64-69; Schenkel 1965: 69-74; Schenkel 1978: 29-35; Edel 1984: 157-177; Magee 1988: II, 22-24; Spanel 1989: 304-305; El-Khadragy/Kahl 2004: 241-243

    Tomb V is located north of Tomb IV and Tomb III. Like its neighbors, it was visited by the French Expedition, which was still able to record traces of two pillars on the floor of the irregularly shaped hall (Fig. 47). The façade, the entrance way and the large hall's roof were destroyed after the visit of the French Expedition (Fig. 48). A figure of the deceased stood on both sides of the façade holding a staff and a scepter. The interior of the hall is now filled with the debris of the collapsed roof and façade. There is a false door with an autobiographical text on the west wall of the hall and an autobiographical inscription on the south wall. In addition, fragments of painted decoration are still visible on the walls: for example, a metal working scene (Fig. 49).

Tomb III (Siut III; N12.1)

Iti-ibi (First Intermediate Period)
    Jollois/Devilliers 1821: 142-143; Panckoucke 1822: Pls. 48.9-11, 49.8-9; Griffith 1889a: 122-129; Griffith 1889b: 11, Pls. 11-12; Montet 1930-35: 89-98; Porter/Moss 1934: 263; Brunner 1937: 17-26, 42-51; Schenkel 1965: 74-82; Edel 1970; Edel 1984: 20-66; Magee 1988: II, 14-17; Spanel 1989: 305-306; El-Khadragy/Kahl 2004: 236-239; Kahl/El-Khadragy/Verhoeven 2005a: 160-163; Kahl/El-Khadragy/Verhoeven 2006: 243-244, Pls. 20-21; Kahl/Verhoeven 2006: 68-71

    Tomb III is situated on the southeastern part of the mountain on stage 6. Like the others, it is a rock-cut tomb and was built for the nomarch Iti-ibi during the late First Intermediate Period (Fig. 50). Between 2003 and 2007 archaeological information about this tomb has greatly increased. It is now clear that there were two side chambers in front of a large hall (Fig. 51). The façade of this hall was still visible during the time of the French Expedition, but it was later destroyed because of stone quarrying activities in the nineteenth century. Elmar Edel was able to reconstruct the inscriptions decorating the outer surface of the façade utilising the drawings of the French Expedition (Edel 1984; cf. Osing 1998a). The hall covers an area of about 600 m², making it the largest known tomb of its kind from the First Intermediate Period (Fig. 52). Two pairs of pillars divide the hall into three sections. Most of the pillars had already been destroyed before the scholars of the French Expedition arrived at Asyut, so that one pair of pillars has been overlooked by virtually every visitor to the tomb since the French Expedition. Consequently, the older plans of Tomb III are not correct.

Fig. 51: Tomb III, forecourt (© Kahl).

Fig. 52: Tomb III, inner hall (© Barthel).

The walls of the hall were once covered with plaster and painted, but today only small fragments of the decoration can still be seen. One fragment shows a part of a battle scene, presumably depicting the fighting between the Asyuti and Theban troops which lasted for several years during the First Intermediate Period (Fig. 53): An Egyptian warrior is seen raising a staff to strike another Egyptian soldier.

The long autobiographical inscription on the northern wall was carved in sunk relief, its hieroglyphs painted blue. It is partly incomplete and covered with plaster, on which a second inscription and the representation of the standing tomb owner were painted. The well-known autobiographical text reports on the military activities of the nomarch Iti-ibi against the Theban aggressors during the civil war of the First Intermediate Period: Iti-ibi first repels an attack by the southern nomes and sails, after another successful repulsion, against Upper Egyptian enemies. However, the autobiography was never completed; instead it was covered with plaster and a politically neutral inscription was painted on top of it. This was interpreted as a sign of Iti-ibi's subsequent defeat. Today, parts of both inscriptions are visible (Pl. 3b).

Fig. 53: Tomb III, northern wall, fighting soldiers (drawing: Ilona Regulski).

Four shafts are hewn into the floor of the hall, each leading to a burial chamber in the south. One of them, shaft 4, remained hidden to earlier Egyptologists and was cleaned, for the first time since Late Antiquity, in 2005 (KAHL/EL-KHADRAGY/ VERHOEVEN 2006). It can be presumed that this particular shaft was originally used as a burial ground for a member of the Iti-ibi-family, as were the other shafts. In the Late Period at least, it seems to have been reused for other burials (Pls. 4a-b). Still later, it was plundered, and during the Coptic Period it was used again.

In the rear wall of Tomb III some niches were hewn, which were also a result of later reuse.

Furthermore, some remarks written in the *Description de l'Égypte* point to a later reuse of the tomb: according to the *Description* there were reliefs on the entrance below the columns featuring inscriptions. These reliefs showed Isis suckling the Horus child (JOLLOIS/DEVILLIERS 1821: 143).

Two communicating passages join this tomb to Tomb IV in the north and the quarry of Tomb II in the south, these passages might date from the Coptic Period.

TOMB IV (SIUT IV; N12.2)

Khety II (temp. Merikara [First Intermediate Period])

JOLLOIS/DEVILLIERS 1821: 145-147; PANCKOUCKE 1822: Pls. 46.1-5, 48.3-5, 49.1-4; GRIFFITH 1889a: 122-127, 164-165; GRIFFITH 1889b: 11, Pls. 13-14, 20; MONTET 1930-35: 98-106; PORTER/MOSS 1934: 263-264; BRUNNER 1937: 27-35, 52-63; SCHENKEL 1965: 82-89; EDEL 1984: 67-156, 178-187; MAGEE 1988: II, 18-21; SPANEL 1989: 306-309; EL-KHADRAGY/KAHL 2004: 239-241; KAHL/EL-KHADRAGY/VERHOEVEN 2005a: 163-164; KAHL/EL-KHADRAGY/VERHOEVEN 2006: 244; EL-KHADRAGY 2006b

Separated by the same wall, Tomb IV (Fig. 54) adjoins Tomb III in the north. Tomb IV belongs to the nomarch Khety II and the priest-

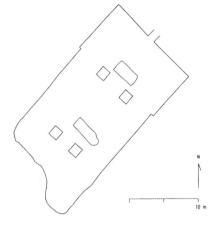

Fig. 54: Tomb IV, ground plan (2006; © Fauerbach).

Fig. 55: Tomb IV, inner hall (2004; © Kahl).

Fig. 56: Tomb IV, southern wall, marching soldiers, detail (© Kahl).

ess of Hathor Iti-ibi. Khety II was the successor of Iti-ibi as nomarch of Asyut. He was obliged to continue fighting against Thebes.

The façade and entrance of the tomb were destroyed after the documentation made by the French Expedition. A still-preserved large hall (Fig. 55) with two pairs of rectangular pillars is decorated, at the eastern end of the northern wall, with a representation of the tomb owner Khety II and a female relative, Iti-ibi (his wife?), as well as an autobiographical text in sunk relief, filled with blue paint. On the southern wall of the middle part of the large hall, there is a scene of soldiers in sunk relief (Fig. 56). The scene consists of three rows of soldiers carrying battle axes, although the third row is unfinished. The third row of soldiers and the condition of the second row of pillars in the rear part of the hall show that the tomb was not completed.

The tomb is now, amongst others, described as Kahf el-Asakir "Cave of the Soldiers" owing to the subject of the relief inside it (GRIFFITH 1889a: 175).

The aforementioned autobiographical text on the northern wall is a rich source of information about the battle for Asyut between King Merikara from Herakleopolis and Khety II on one side and the Theban troops on the other side. The text is one of the most extensive and informative sources for the history of the First Intermediate Period.

The Asyut Project detected two shafts in the southern part of the tomb, which seem to be original, although one of them might have been reused and extended in later periods.

Fig. 57: Tomb N13.1, entrance area (© Kahl).

In the entrance area the ceiling shows traces of a coloured decoration from the Coptic Period (EL-KHADRAGY 2006b: 90).

TOMB N13.1

Iti-ibi(-iqer) (late First Intermediate Period)
KAHL/EL-KHADRAGY/VERHOEVEN 2006; KAHL 2006

Tomb N13.1 was discovered during the 2005 season of fieldwork (Fig. 57). It is situated on geological layer 7 of the Gebel Asyut al-gharbi, 30 m above Tomb III, and consists of a c. 9 x 7 m large and c. 3 m high hall cut into the rock with two pillars supporting the roof (Fig. 58). In the western wall is a niche, in front of which a large shaft for the burial of the tomb owner was hewn. In front of the hall, an open court (Fig. 59) provides a space for several poor burials of subordinates of Iti-ibi(-iqer): small vertical shafts give access to roughly cut broadenings on their western or southern side which once contained the contracted bodies.

The tomb is important for several reasons: firstly, it belonged to the nomarch Iti-ibi(-iqer), who probably lived during the end of the First Intermediate Period. The tomb decoration is well preserved and is informative because of its motifs and scenes (Fig. 60) during a period which has not been explored very thoroughly. Secondly, its walls are covered with more than 140 graffiti, mainly from the early New Kingdom. These graffiti are either copies of literary texts (e.g. *The Loyalistic Teaching* and *The*

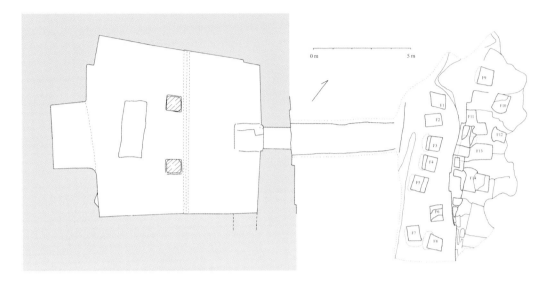

Fig. 58: Tomb N13.1, ground plan (© Becker/Fauerbach).

Fig. 59: Tomb N13.1, forecourt (© Kahl).

The mountain at the desert edge: functions and changes 81

Fig. 60: Tomb N13.1, eastern wall: marching soldiers (© Kahl).

Fig. 61: Tomb N13.1, graffito, *Teaching of Duaf's son Khety* (detail; © Kahl).

Fig. 62: Tomb N13.1, graffito, hippopotamus (© Kahl).

Teaching of Duaf's son Khety; Fig. 61), visitors' graffiti (Pl. 5a-b) or drawings of human beings and animals (Fig. 62; Pl. 14a). Some of the graffiti give evidence that Tomb N13.1 was used as a destination for school excursions (KAHL 2006). It can thus be hoped that Tomb N13.1 might shed further light on the ancient Egyptian educational system. Thirdly, those graffiti referring to Asyuti temples and gods inform us about the cults and topography of the early New Kingdom Asyut. Fourthly, the tomb decoration was covered with paintings showing a *mihrab*, giving further evidence for the mountain's change of function from a pharaonic burial ground to a place of prayer in the Islamic Period.

TOMB OF MESEHTI (HOGARTH, TOMB III)

Mesehti (Eleventh Dynasty)
GRÉBAUT 1890-1900: 30-36, Pls. 33-37; PORTER/MOSS 1934: 265; RADWAN 1983: 81; RYAN 1988: 13

The tomb of the nomarch Mesehti is located in the middle to northern part of the necropolis. It was partially excavated in 1893 by Farag, an otherwise Egyptologically unknown Egyptian, but had probably been plundered before. In 1907 Hogarth cleared the south side of the tomb, but did not record its plan. According to Chassinat and Palanque, the tomb was comparable in its dimensions to those of Iti-ibi and Khety I, but was anepigraphic (CHASSINAT/PALANQUE 1911: V).

Fig. 63: Tomb of Mesehti, models of soldiers (GRÉBAUT 1890-1900: Pl. 33).

Two coffins covered with numerous Coffin Texts come from this tomb (Cairo CG 28118, 28119). Orthographic criteria date the coffins (and Mesehti) to the end of the Eleventh Dynasty (cf. SCHENKEL 1962: 117-118).

The tomb is famous for its two models of soldiers (Fig. 63), which are now held at the Egyptian Museum, Cairo. One is composed of 40 Egyptian infantrymen carrying shields and spears (Cairo CG 258), the other of 40 Nubian archers (Cairo CG 257). The Nubian soldiers were probably members of the so-called C-group, who settled between the First and Second Cataract and served the Egyptian nomarch as mercenaries (BIETAK 1985: 87-97). The models show that orderly military formations, which were already practised by the rank and file, were in existence—probably in battle as well as in parades before their nomarch (BIETAK 1985: 87).

If the suggested dating is correct, Mesehti was nomarch after the end of the military conflict of the First Intermediate Period, but the two models of soldiers prove the importance troops still had at that time.

NORTHERN SOLDIERS-TOMB (MAGEE TOMB 13; H11.1)

Eleventh to Twelfth Dynasty
  MAGEE 1988: II, 36-38; KAHL/EL-KHADRAGY/VERHOEVEN 2005a: 164, Pl. 14.1; KAHL/EL-KHADRAGY/VERHOEVEN 2005b: 46-47; EL-KHADRAGY 2006a

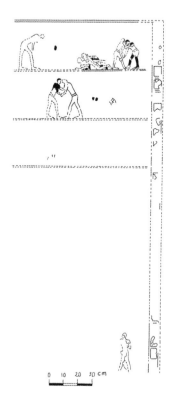

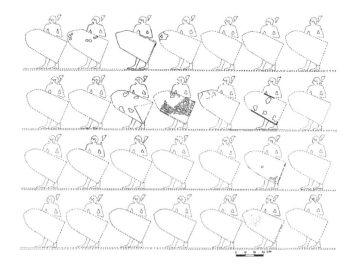

Fig. 64: Northern Soldiers-Tomb, southern wall, wrestlers (EL-KHADRAGY 2006a: 164, Fig. 8).

Fig. 65: Northern Soldiers-Tomb, southern wall, marching soldiers armed with shields and axes (EL-KHADRAGY 2006a: 162, Fig. 6).

There is some information in old reports about Asyut that Tomb IV was not the only tomb decorated with a scene showing marching soldiers (cf. KAHL/EL-KHADRAGY/ VERHOEVEN 2005a: 164 note 14). Other tombs existed which were decorated with the same motif. Diana Magee was able to relocate one of them in 1986.

The name of the owner of this tomb, which is situated in the southern part of the necropolis, is unknown, but the remaining decoration indicates that he might have been a nomarch. The tomb is for the most part destroyed: the northern wall of its inner hall has collapsed and the roof, weighing several tons, has also disintegrated, burying the rest of the tomb. Magee saw remains of decoration on the northern wall in 1986, which could not be relocated in 2003. Only a part of the southern wall has survived. Its decoration shows, amongst others, wrestlers (Fig. 64), marching soldiers (Fig. 65) and a deity.

TOMB OF SHEMES

Shemes (Eleventh to Twelfth Dynasty)
    LEOSPO 1990: 80

In 1908, the still intact tomb of Shemes was discovered by the Italian Egyptologist Ernesto Schiaparelli in the southern part of the necropolis. The exact location of the tomb remains unknown since Schiaparelli's excavation notes have not yet been examined. Unfortunately, the objects from the tomb of Shemes are also unpublished—as are practically all the other objects and findings of Schiaparelli's excavations in Asyut between 1905 and 1913.

The tomb of Shemes included two statues of the official, his coffin and that of his wife, three model ships (LEOSPO/FOZZATI 1992: 395), five staffs, a club and approximately one hundred jars and drinking cups (LEOSPO 1988: 102, Fig. 136; LEOSPO 1990: 80).

TOMB OF ANU

Anu (beginning of Twelfth Dynasty)
    ROCCATI 1974: 41-52; MAGEE 1988: II, 39

Ernesto Schiaparelli did not only bring numerous parts of burial equipment from different tombs to Italy, but also remains of wall paintings. Four fragments in the Museo Egizio in Turin come from the tomb of Anu, who was mayor and overseer of the priests of Wepwawet and Anubis. His tomb can not be relocated at present due to lack of documentation during the excavation. The wall fragments are decorated with painted hieroglyphs; the largest one is 8.5 cm long and 15 cm high (Fig. 66).

From the paleography and orthography, the inscriptions can be dated to the beginning of the Twelfth Dynasty. Oddly, Anu asserts that he wrote the tomb inscription himself, which is something no other Asyuti nomarch claims to have done.

Fig. 66: Tomb of Anu, wall fragment with painted hieroglyphs, detail (after ROCCATI 1974: 43).

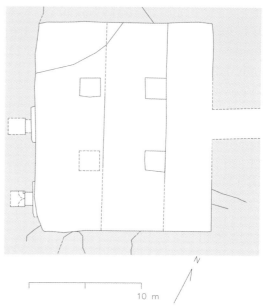

Fig. 67: Tomb II, ground plan (© Fauerbach).

Fig. 68: Tomb II, inner hall (© Kahl).

TOMB II (SIUT II; O13.1)

Djefai-Hapi II (beginning of Twelfth Dynasty)

JOLLOIS/DEVILLIERS 1821: 144-145; PANCKOUCKE 1822: Pls. 46.10, 47.1; GRIFFITH 1889a: 126-127, 174-175; GRIFFITH 1889b: 10, Pls. 10, 20; MONTET 1930-35: 86-89; PORTER/MOSS 1934: 262; MAGEE 1988: II, 12-13

The tomb is located on the same level (step 6) as Tombs III, IV and V of the First Intermediate Period. Therefore, and because of its ground plan (Fig. 67), which is more similar to those of the First Intermediate Period than to those of the large complexes of Tomb I and the Salakhana Tomb, a date at the beginning of the Twelfth Dynasty is quite likely. The tomb owner's name is Djefai-Hapi; although he is called Djefai-Hapi II in Egyptological literature, he might have lived earlier than the owner of Tomb I, Djefai-Hapi I. In modern times, Tomb II is sometimes called "Stabl Antar"

("Antar's Stable") (information of the local ghafirs in 2006; cf. GRIFFITH 1889a: 175). It is partially destroyed today (Fig. 7). Parts of the façade and the entrance, as well as the large hall, are still preserved. Of the four pillars that supported the roof in the hall, only truncated fragments attached to the floor and ceiling have survived (Fig. 68). Above the doorway, the members of the French Expedition noted two rows of inscriptions containing titles. Two vertical columns of inscriptions mentioning titles and epithets framed the doorway. Next to them was, on both sides, a representation of the tomb owner holding a staff and wearing a short kilt (Fig. 69). This representation and large parts of the façade were destroyed in 1885 or 1886 (GRIFFITH 1889a: 174).

The eastern wall shows the entrance to a sloping passage, probably leading to the burial chamber. At the back of the hall two doorways were sculpted, but the passages were never cut. To the south, there are two corridors leading to quarries. Another is located to the north, and this northern quarry (N13.2) can be dated to the New Kingdom. It connects Tomb II with Tomb III by means of another corridor.

TOMB I (SIUT I; P10.1)

Djefai-Hapi I (temp. Senwosret I [Twelfth Dynasty])
    JOLLOIS/DEVILLIERS 1821: 133-142; PANCKOUCKE 1822: Pl. 44; GRIFFITH 1889a: 166-168; GRIFFITH 1889b: 9-10, Pls. 1-10, MONTET 1928: 54-68; MONTET 1930-35: 45-86;

Fig. 69: Tomb II in 1799 (PANCKOUCKE 1822: Pl. 46.10).

The mountain at the desert edge: functions and changes 87

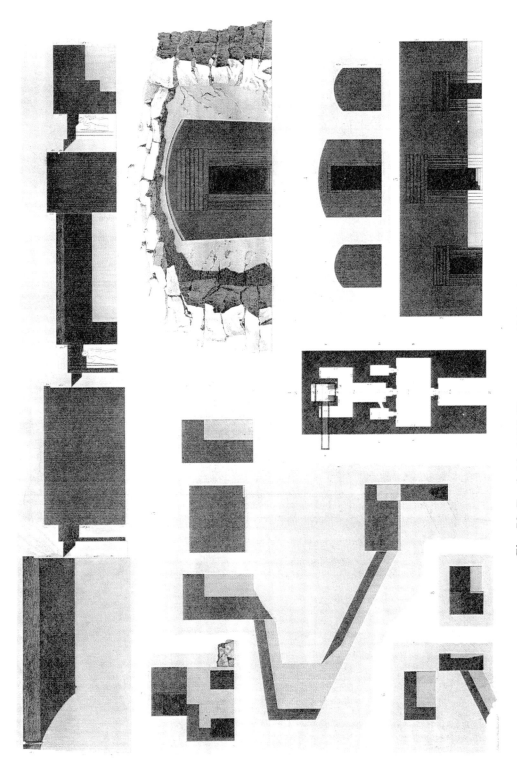

Fig. 70: Tomb I in 1799 (PANCKOUCKE 1822: Pl. 44).

PORTER/MOSS 1934: 261-262; MAGEE 1988: II, 3-11; KAHL/EL-KHADRAGY/VERHOEVEN 2005a: 164-165, Pl. 14; KAHL/EL-KHADRAGY/VERHOEVEN 2006: 244; KAHL/VERHOEVEN 2006: 70-72; EL-KHADRAGY 2007; ENGEL/KAHL forthcoming

Djefai-Hapi I was nomarch during the reign of Senwosret I in the Twelfth Dynasty and his tomb (Tomb I) was cut into the lower stratum of the mountain, into stage 2 (Pl. 6a). Thus, Djefai-Hapi I set himself apart from the elite of the First Intermediate Period and the early Middle Kingdom, who built their tombs higher up the escarpment. Tomb I is one of the largest rock cut tombs belonging to an individual in Egypt. A sequence of rooms hewn into the mountain and measuring more than 55 m length is still standing today. A further room was cut into the mountain; however today it lacks a roof. The inner rooms are up to 11 m high, their walls and ceiling decorated with reliefs and paintings. Djefai-Hapi I indicated in his tomb inscriptions that he received the means for construction and decoration of his tomb from the royal house: one of the lector priests was also "scribe of this tomb who gives from the royal house" (Siut I, 132).

Other appellations of the tomb are: "Stabl Antar" ("Antar's Stable"; GRIFFITH 1889a: 167), "Grotte de l'Estalle" (LUCAS 1719: 339-340), "L'hypogée principal" (JOLLOIS/DEVILLIERS 1821: 133-142), and "Hammâm" ("baths"; GRIFFITH 1889a: 175).

Thanks to its grandeur and easy accessibility, this monumental tomb used to be (and still is) the high point of any visit to the necropolis. Eighteenth century travellers like LUCAS 1719, NORDEN 1784, and PERRY 1743 mention Tomb I and Perry calls it the most famous of the Asyuti tombs.

Neither the modern state of the tomb nor the only measurement of the tomb by the French Expedition in 1799 show the building's original dimensions (Fig. 70). Back in the times of the French Expedition the tomb already was not preserved in its entirety. Quarrying activities between 1714 and 1799 might have caused the destruction of pillars mentioned by the French traveller Paul Lucas (LUCAS 1719: 339-340). Inscriptions in the tomb itself provide evidence that a causeway and a garden were included in the layout (cf. infra). Today, the still visible remains of the monumental tomb, its inscriptions and the reports of early travellers give a picture of its original layout (Pl. 6b).

The innermost part of the tomb consists of a transverse hall housing a large rock cut shrine (Fig. 71), which was closed with a double-winged door (a symbol for the door to heaven), which is missing today. There is a false door on the rear wall of the shrine, which originally housed a cult statue of Djefai-Hapi I. The northern, western and southern walls are decorated in relief. The northern and the southern walls contain offering lists. The eastern wall with the door is today destroyed, but there are descriptions and drawings of the French Expedition which enable the reconstruction of its decoration (EL-KHADRAGY 2007). A step led from the transverse hall to the shrine. The southern wall of the transverse hall gives access to the underground corridor system leading to the burial chamber, which is situated under the shrine.

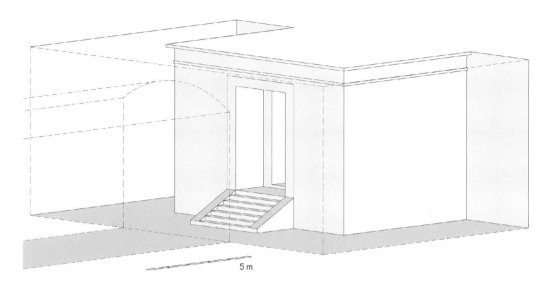

Fig. 71: Tomb I, shrine (after EL-KHADRAGY 2007: 56, Fig. 2 bottom).

A longitudinal passage, featuring a vaulted roof, leads directly into the aforementioned transverse hall. The passage's walls are decorated with paintings, which were first detected by the German-Egyptian Asyut Project in 2003 and will be published by Mahmoud El-Khadragy.

A great transverse hall is situated in front of this passage and measures 23.00 m (N-S) by 10.53 m (E-W). It was completely decorated with paintings and inscriptions in relief. A representation of Djefai-Hapi I, in front of the names of Senwosret I (Pl. 7a), a painting showing amongst others boys climbing in trees (cf. for the time being Fig. 72; SMITH 1957: 222) and the ten contracts (Pl. 7b), which Djefai-Hapi I made with the priests of the Wepwawet-temple (contract I-VI) and the Anubis temple (contract VII-VIII)—as well as with the workmen of the necropolis (contract IX-X)—to guarantee his funerary cult, are especially worth mentioning (cf. BREASTED 1906: 258-271; THÉODORIDÈS 1971: 109-251; THÉODORIDÈS 1973: 439-466).

The introduction to the ten contracts informs about the importance of the *Ka*-servants, their payment and how their professions were handed down to their sons. One of these texts reads:

The nobleman, count, overseer of the priests of Wepwawet, Djefai-Hapi, he says to his *Ka*-servant: "Behold, all these things, for which I have contracted with these *wab*-priests, are under your supervision. For, behold, it is the *Ka*-servant of a man who causes his possessions and his offerings to be perpetuated. Behold, I have brought to your knowledge these things which I have given to these *wab*-priests, as compensation for these things which they have given to me, take heed lest anything among them be lacking. Therefore, every word of my list, which I have given to them, let your son hear it, your heir, who shall act as my *Ka*-servant. Behold, I have endowed you with fields, with people, with cattle, with gardens and with everything, as for any exalted man of Asyut, in order that you may make offerings to me with contented heart. You shall stand over all my possessions which I have put under your hand. Behold, they are before you in writing. These things will belong to your particular son,

Fig. 72: Tomb I, great transverse hall, northern wall, boys climbing in trees (SMITH 1957: 222, Fig. 1).

whom you love, who shall act as my *Ka*-servant, before your (other) children, as consumer (of the revenues) who does not do mischief, without permitting him to divide them among his children, according to these instructions which I have given you."
(Siut I, 269-272)

The ceiling of the great transverse hall is decorated with delicate geometric patterns (Pl. 8a).

The hall's western wall gives access to two subsidiary chambers: one to the north and one to the south of the central axis. There is evidence in both chambers that they were originally decorated and the western wall of the northern side chamber features a false door.

A one-winged door separated the great transverse hall from the first corridor, which has a vaulted ceiling. This corridor (Pl. 8b) is about 11 m high and gives a good impression of the tomb as well as of the tomb owner. The ceiling is painted with blue stars,

Fig. 73: Tomb I, rectangular room in front of the first corridor (© Barthel).

whereas the walls are decorated with inscriptions and scenes. Some of the inscriptions are superimposed on earlier scenes; for example, the inscription Siut I, 380-417 substituted for a sculptured scene of either the tomb owner or his statue in a boat. The design in this corridor, as well as in the great transverse hall, seems to have been altered several times. The inscriptions in the first corridor contain the mortuary liturgy no. 7 (KAHL 1994; KAHL 1999: 53-186), which—according to Ancient Egyptian beliefs—helps to guarantee the existence of the tomb owner after death. This liturgy, containing spells from the Pyramid Texts, the Coffin Texts and other religious texts, is borrowed from the royal sphere.

A rectangular room, roofless today, is situated in front of the first corridor (for a possible reconstruction cf. ENGEL/KAHL forthcoming). The remaining parts of its northern and southern walls show rectangular openings leading to small side chambers (Fig. 73).

A steward called Heny was buried in this part of the entrance area of Tomb I (WAINWRIGHT 1926: 160-166; GUNN 1926: 166-171). Orthographic criteria (hieroglyph S 3 for *n*: GARDINER 1957: 27 note 4) as well as the pottery (cf. SEIDLMAYER 1990: 350-351) give strong evidence for his being a contemporary, probably a retainer, of Djefai-Hapi I. Some badly decayed pieces of boards from both an inner and an outer coffin were found in the debris. Astronomical inscriptions and figures painted on the inner side of the lid are especially worth mentioning (Fig. 74).

A causeway (cf. Pl. 6a, b) once led from the edge of the cultivated area to the rock cut tomb. The eighth contract mentions a statue which stood on the lower stairway, i.e.

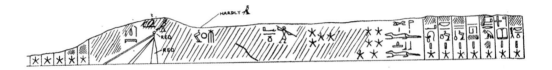

Fig. 74: Coffin of Heny, astronomical scenes (GUNN 1926: 171).

at the beginning of the causeway, and it was most likely stored in a lockable shrine. According to the ninth contract, a garden also used to be situated there.

The tomb was plundered during the Second Intermediate Period and statues were brought to Kerma in Sudan (cf. Figs. 99-100; Chapter One; SÄVE-SÖDERBERGH 1941: 103-116; HELCK 1976: 101-115; KENDALL 1997: 24-27).

In 2004 the German-Egyptian Asyut Project started to make facsimiles of the scenes and inscriptions in Tomb I, which was never entirely documented, even though its decoration is one of the most interesting and most completely preserved of private tombs of the Middle Kingdom. In addition, it is endangered by bat and bird excrement, which attack both the paintings and reliefs.[1]

TOMB VII (SALAKHANA TOMB)

Djefai-Hapi III (temp. Amenemhat II [Twelfth Dynasty])

LACAU 1922: 379-380; WAINWRIGHT 1928: 176-189; PORTER/MOSS 1934: 264; MONTET 1936: 134-135; CAPART 1936: 528; MAGEE 1988: II, 27-28

The tomb is known as the "Salakhana Tomb" because of its location behind the old slaughterhouse of Asyut and is cut into the same geological level as Tomb I (stage 2). It belongs to Djefai-Hapi III, an Asyuti nomarch who perhaps was a descendant of Djefai-Hapi I. It dates to the reign of Amenemhat II (MOSS 1933: 33). Today, the tomb is inaccessible to researchers as it is part of an Egyptian military base.

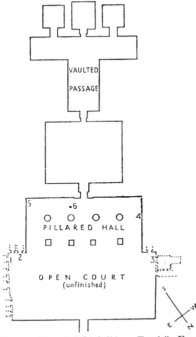

ASYÛṬ. Ḥepzefa III ('Salkhana Tomb'). From plan supplied by DR. STECKEWEH, who is not responsible for the dotted part, representing later subsidiary tombs, of which the details are only approximately correct.

Fig. 75: Salakhana Tomb, ground plan (PORTER/MOSS 1934: 260).

---

1 Unfortunately the local inspectorate was unable to install an impervious net on the modern tomb entrance, despite considerable investment by the Asyut Project.

The tomb consists of a court with four rectangular pillars and four papyriform columns (Fig. 75). The inscriptions include epithets of Djefai-Hapi III, an address to the living and a fragmentary contract text, which may be compared to those in Tomb I.

A doorway leads into a transverse hall, which gives access to a vaulted passage with a narrow transverse chamber. In the western wall, three niches are cut into the rock, the southernmost having a false door in its western wall.

Entrances to Tombs VI and VIII are to be found in the open courtyard (cf. MONTET 1936: 131-133, 135-137). In 1922, Gerald Wainwright discovered a large number of votive stelae covering the period from the New Kingdom through to the Twenty-seventh Dynasty, as well as small pottery sculptures showing canids, Demotic papyri and mummies of canids amongst the débris which filled the court (cf. Chapter Seven). For several years, Terence DuQuesne has been thoroughly documenting the more than 500 stelae and over 50 figurines. Nevertheless, it is still unclear whether the tomb functioned as a sanctuary from the New Kingdom or whether it was re-used as a cachette of the Wepwawet-temple (cf. DUQUESNE 2000: 18). The fact that the stelae refer to Wepwawet and not to the tomb-owner points to the second option.

TOMB OF NAKHTI (CHASSINAT/PALANQUE, TOMBEAU NO. 7)

Nakhti (Twelfth Dynasty)

CHASSINAT/PALANQUE 1911: 29-154; DESROCHES NOBLECOURT/VERCOUTTER 1981: 101-135; HARVEY 1990: 45-50; PODVIN 2000: 314-315

The tomb of the overseer of seals Nakhti was found intact. In contrast to most of the other tombs in Asyut, it was not plundered by tomb robbers, neither in antiquity nor during modern times. The position of the tomb can be inferred from a photograph published by Chassinat and Palanque (Fig. 87): it is located beneath the ruins of the Coptic monastery Deir el-Meitin. Chassinat and Palanque did not publish an architectural plan, and today the tomb is refilled again. Their descriptions nonetheless make it evident that it consisted of a rectangular hall, about 5 x 6 m wide, with a single pillar at the southern part of the hall supporting the roof (most likely there was originally a second pillar). The walls were not decorated. Four burial chambers were cut into the ground to receive the burials: two of them were accessible through shafts more than 5 m deep: burial chamber I (pit I) with the burial of Nakhti is situated in the southern part of the hall close to the western wall behind the pillar; burial chamber IV (pit IV) with burials of Nakhti's relatives (cf. CHASSINAT/ PALANQUE 1911: 142-143) is situated south of the entrance. The other two, with sloping corridors, are also placed at the southern part of the hall, but in front of the pillar (pit III) and in the northwestern part in alignment with the first shaft (pit II).

Nakhti's burial in chamber I (pit I) gives important insight into the burial customs of the Middle Kingdom (Fig. 76): the mummy rested on its left side on a bed with its head placed on a wooden headrest and covered by a mummy mask made of cartonnage, decorated with a collar and bracelets around the hands and feet. The mummy was placed inside a coffin, which was itself placed inside another coffin. Two models of quivers, two bows

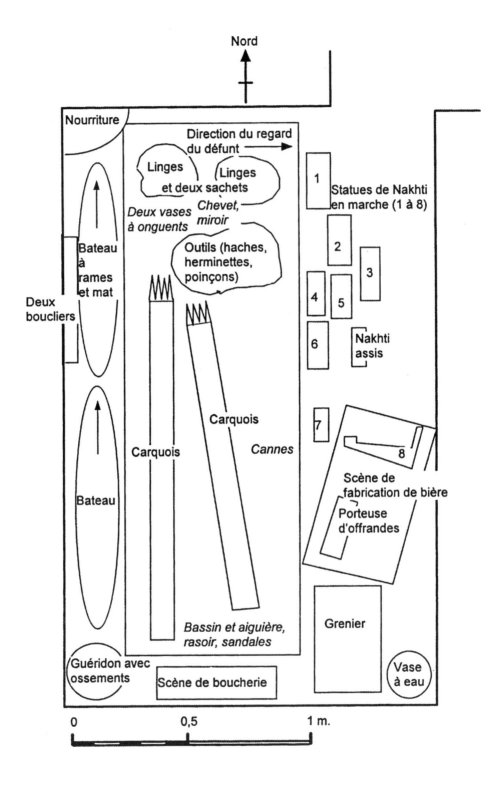

Fig. 76: Equipment of the Tomb of Nakhti (P‍ODVIN 2000: 315).

with arrows, as well as hand-axes and chisels with bronze blades, small handles and blades from model adzes and packages of cloth were placed on top of the outer coffin. The coffin was surrounded by eight wooden statues (cf. Fig. 77) of Nakhti (one of them made of ebony), a statue of Nakhti made of calcite-alabaster, a wooden statue of a female offering bearer, three wooden models with handicraft scenes (brewery, measuring of grain, butchery), an offering table with bones of a calf, two model boats with crew, two models of shields, a small heap of calf bones and a clay vessel. More constituents of the tomb equipment were inside the coffin: a piece of galena, a sceptre, staves, arrows, a bow, three vessels for ointments made of calcite-alabaster, two small cloth bags containing a red powder, a clay vessel, wooden models of *heset*-vessels, two pieces of cloth, a bronze mirror, wooden models of sandals, a bronze wash basin, and a razor blade.

Additionally, the entrance hall yielded parts of the tomb inventory, with eight statues among them (cf. HARVEY 1990: 45-47).

The tomb of Nakhti is often dated to the First Intermediate Period, but orthography (SCHENKEL 1962: 118) and pottery (SEIDLMAYER 1990: 350) point to a Twelfth Dynasty date.

TOMB M10.1

Middle Kingdom
PALANQUE 1903: 119-121; MAGEE 1988: II, 30-31

This large tomb lies on the same geological level (stage 6) as the tombs of the nomarchs of the First Intermediate Period, but further to the north. It is mostly destroyed, only parts of the architec-

Fig. 77: Statue of Nakhti (early Middle Kingdom), Paris, Louvre E 11937 (© Musée du Louvre/Maurice et Pierre Chuzeville).

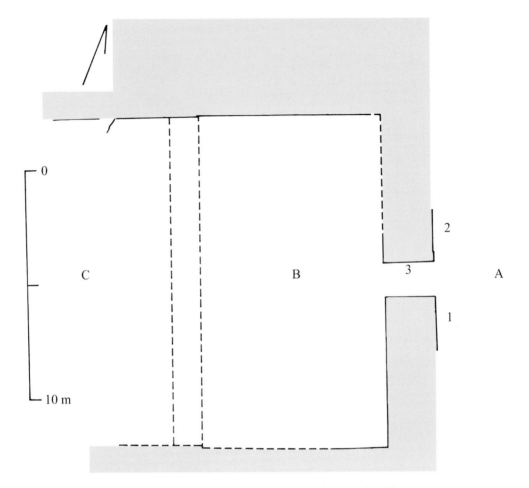

Fig. 78: Tomb M10.1, ground plan (© Fauerbach).

ture, of the representation of the tomb owner, and of inscriptions in sunk relief being preserved (Fig. 78).

TOMB I10.1

Middle Kingdom
  JOLLOIS/DEVILLIERS 1821: 149-150; PANCKOUCKE 1822: Pl. 48.6-8; GRIFFITH 1889a: 246-247
  The members of the French Expedition praised a tomb for its decoration, which must have been more extensive and excellent than those of the other Asyuti tombs they visited. But neither the *Description de l'Égypte* nor publications of later savants present a picture of the decoration. One can only read that the tomb consisted of a hall, a vaulted passage and another chamber. The hall's ceiling was painted with stars and ornaments, and all its walls were covered with light blue hieroglyphs. Inscriptions framed the doorway leading to the second chamber (JOLLOIS/DEVILLIERS 1821: 149-150).

Fig. 79: Tomb I10.1, vaulted passage (© Kahl).

After Griffith had described this report as "imaginary" or an "error" (GRIFFITH 1889a: 246-247), the tomb disappeared completely from Egyptological research. In 2003, however, the remains of a tomb were discovered, which may be identical with that mentioned by the scholars of the French Expedition: Tomb I10.1 is situated—as mentioned in the *Description*—in the northern part of the necropolis. It still shows the lateral walls of a large hall, a vaulted passage (Fig. 79) and a second chamber. In the passage, two sloping corridors branch off to the north and south, giving access to the burial chambers, as described by the *Description*. Blue hieroglyphs can be traced on the western wall of the large hall in addition to paintings at the northern wall. Tomb I10.1 can therefore probably be identified as the tomb mentioned in the *Description* (cf. Figs. 80-81).

TOMB OF AMEN-HOTEP (ERRONEOUSLY SAID TO COME FROM DEIR DRUNKA)

Amen-hotep (beginning of Nineteenth Dynasty)
    KAMAL 1916: 90-93; KARIG 1968: 27-34; WILD 1971: 307-309; KITCHEN 1975: 350-352; KITCHEN 1993a: 286-287; KITCHEN 1993b: 242-247; BERMAN 1999: 250-252; HOFMANN 2004: 111-112

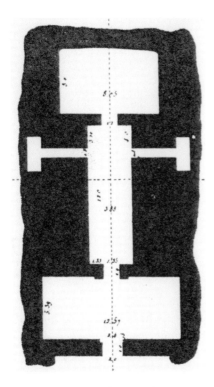

Fig. 80: Ground plan of a tomb (after PANCKOUCKE 1822: Pl. 48.6), presumably identical with Tomb I10.1.

In 1913/14 Ahmed Bey Kamal discovered the tomb of Amen-hotep in the northern part of the necropolis of Asyut, but did not record its exact position (cf. WILD 1971). The innermost cult-room was 1.53 m wide, about 3 m long and 2.40 m high with a vaulted roof. The walls of the cult-room were presumably made of mud bricks and covered with limestone slabs. Kamal had the slabs removed and brought to the private museum of his employer Sayed Bey Khashaba in Asyut. Today, the collection has been disbanded, only a few objects being still on exhibition in the school "Mathaf al-Salaam" in Asyut. The representations from the tomb of Amen-hotep are now scattered over four collections: Ägyptisches Museum Berlin, Inv. 31010/1; Zürich, Kunsthaus, Inv. 1963/36; Cleveland Museum of Art, Inv. 63.100, and Toledo (Ohio), Museum of Art, Inv. 62/64.

The reliefs from the cult chamber show the king's scribe, lector priest, chief, overseer of the *wab*-priests of Sakhmet and chief physician Amen-hotep (Fig. 82), his wife Renenut, his son Iuny, Iuny's wife, who was also named Renenut, and a further female member of the family. Amen-hotep

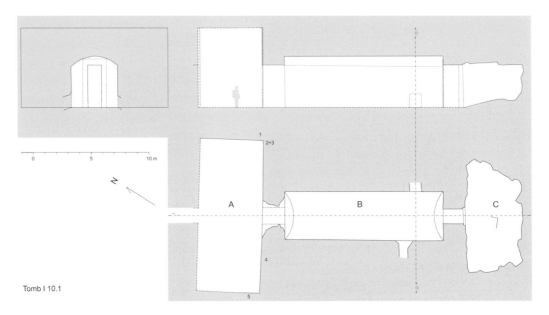

Fig. 81: Tomb I10.1, ground plan (© Fauerbach).

Fig. 82: Tomb of Amen-hotep, cult chamber (KARIG 1968: 33, Fig. 3).

is shown in presence of the gods Wepwawet, Ra, and Hathor. One scene depicts the last judgment (*Book of the Dead*, Spell 125); a tiny seated figure of the tomb owner is weighed against the figure of Maat, goddess of Truth.

All figures are carved in raised relief; some accompanying inscriptions are executed in sunk relief. The reliefs were originally polychrome.

Even though some features correspond to the late Eighteenth Dynasty, the figures are stylized in a fashion typical of the early Ramesside Period (beginning of the Nineteenth Dynasty). The quality of the reliefs is very high.

ROMAN MAUSOLEA

SAUNERON 1983: 90-94

In 1698, the French medical practitioner Charles Poncet observed the remains of an ancient amphitheatre and Roman mausolea, which were probably situated northwest of the town.

DEIR EL-AZZAM

MASPERO 1900: 109-119; BOCK 1901: 88-90; MEINARDUS 1965: 283; COQUIN/ MARTIN 1991a: 809; GROSSMANN 1991: 809-810

Deir el-Azzam ("The Monastery of Bones") is situated on top of the mountain plateau and only a ruin is left of this monastery today (Fig. 83). Some evidence indicates the exact attribution of the monastery's ruins: a jar (CRUM 1902: 33-34, no. 8104, Pl. 1) found *in situ*, bears a Coptic inscription dated 1156 and naming the site "Apa John of the Desert." Therefore Deir el-Azzam is often described as the hermitage of John of Lycopolis (cf. COQUIN/MARTIN 1991a: 809). However, it remains unclear

Fig. 83: Deir el-Azzam (2004; © Kahl).

where the three rooms were which served John for the rest of his life. If Deir el-Azzam is identical with the "Monastery of Seven Mountains" mentioned by al-Maqrizi (WÜSTENFELD 1845: 102), then it was raided and destroyed in AD 1418. Its remains suffered further destruction through heavy rainfall (information of the local ghafirs).

The monastery was surrounded by an irregular wall (Fig. 84), inside which were a church and a keep, in addition to a few insignificant residential buildings of the monks (GROSSMANN 1991: 810). The complex possessed a water reservoir. At the end of the nineteenth century, the mud brick buildings still showed parts of two stories, and some burials could be detected inside the church (MASPERO 1900: 110).

A cemetery of about 1,400 tombs surrounded the complex outside the wall on three sides (Fig. 85). They are partially cut into the rock, partially dug into the sand and usually about 2 m long, 70 cm wide and 70 cm deep. Each tomb contained one or two human bodies either bedded in a wooden coffin or wrapped in a mat made of palm branches. Some coffins had iron rings at each corner for easier handling (MASPERO 1900: 113) and were decorated with a painted cross with monogram on the lid, or on the upper part (BOCK 1901: 90). Some of the deceased were clad in white linen, embroidered with blue silk at the edges and decorated with a saffron painted cross. They wore a thinner cloth underneath the outer linen and were clad in a silken robe,

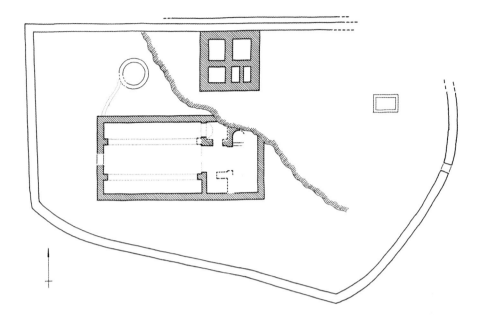

Fig. 84: Deir el-Azzam, ground plan (COQUIN/MARTIN 1991a: 809).

which had embroidered arms or Arabic inscriptions. They wore caps made from several layers of cloth, the outermost being blue, with a gold tip (MASPERO 1900: 114). The

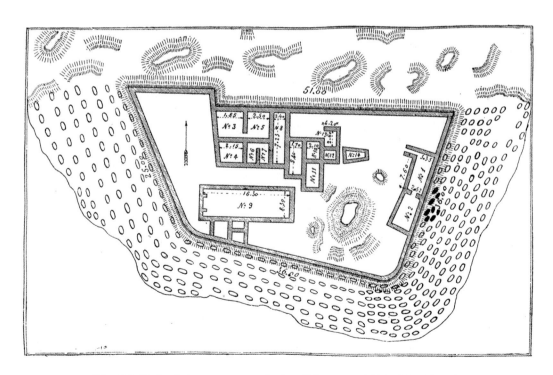

Fig. 85: Deir el-Azzam, ground plan (MASPERO 1900: 111, Fig. 1).

Fig. 86: Deir el-Azzam, cemetery, wooden comb (MASPERO 1900: 114, Fig. 4).

bodies wrapped in mats had similar linen cloths, but these were not embroidered. The women sometimes wore small earrings or had a wooden comb underneath their head (Fig. 86). Children formed a large proportion of the buried persons (BOCK 1901: 90). The graves were said to belong to Asyut's lower classes (MASPERO 1900: 114; BOCK 1901: 88, 90).

The mountain plateau is not only home to the ruins of this monastery, but also to a large area with kilns and huge layers of Coptic pottery called Kom el-Shukafa.

DEIR EL-MEITIN

BOCK 1901: 91; CLÉDAT 1908: 213-223; LEFEBVRE 1909: 50-55; CHASSINAT/PALANQUE 1911: 3, Pl. 1; JOHANN GEORG 1913: 76-78; MEINARDUS 1965: 282-283; TIMM 1984: 756-758; COQUIN/MARTIN 1991b: 842-843

Fig. 87: Deir el-Meitin and the entrance of the Tomb of Nakhti in 1903 (CHASSINAT/PALANQUE 1911: Pl. 1).

Following the name given by Chassinat and Palanque (CHASSINAT/PALANQUE 1911: 3), the name of this monastery can be translated as "The Monastery of the Dead;" it is also called Deir el-Muttin or Deir el-Mazall (TIMM 1984: 756-758). Al-Maqrizi (who died in AD 1441) mentioned it and reported that, although it was already deserted in his time, an annual festival was still celebrated there. Today, only some ruins of sun-dried brick are visible. The remains of the monastery have suffered during the last 100 years—not only through illicit excavation, but also through the French excavations in this area of the Gebel Asyut, as there was no documentation of the Christian remains (cf. CLÉDAT 1908: 214-215; CHASSINAT/PALANQUE 1911: 3, note 1).

The monastery's sun-dried mud brick ruins are situated in the southern part of the mountain, above the tomb of Djefai-Hapi I on geological layer 5 (Figs. 87-88).

The monastery was surrounded by a cemetery, which is now completely devastated. The interments usually took place without coffins: the bodies were merely wrapped in cloth and bound with cords. In the few cases where coffins were used, the cloth was inscribed. Young children seem to have been quite numerous, often being buried in clay vessels (BOCK 1901: 91). Glass bracelets and bone dolls were also found near Deir el-Meitin (BOCK 1901: 91).

The name Deir el-Meitin or Deir el-Muttin is also given to a cluster of Christian ruins situated in the northern part of the mountain (CLÉDAT 1908: 214; TIMM 1984: 757; COQUIN/MARTIN 1991b: 842). Today, the remains of two Christian chapels, which were inserted into pharaonic tombs and were already documented 100 years ago

Fig. 88: Deir el-Meitin in 2004 (© Kahl).

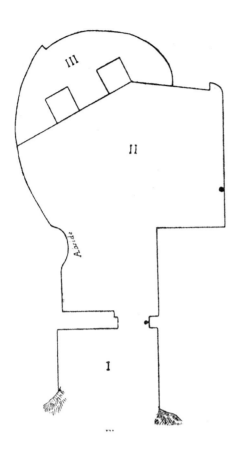

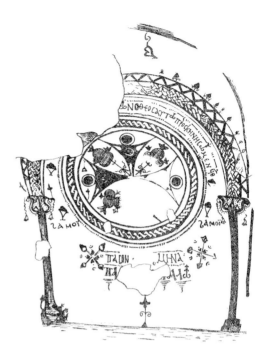

Fig. 90: Christian chapel, wall paintings in 1903 (CLÉDAT 1908: 219, Fig. 4).

Fig. 89: Christian chapel, ground plan (CLÉDAT 1908: 217, Fig. 1).

Fig. 91: Christian chapel, wall paintings in 2004 (© Kahl).

(CLÉDAT 1908), can be detected amongst others. Both the monastery and the chapels were demolished in the last century.

The first chapel was located near the mountain's centre, between Tomb M10.1 and Tomb I10.1, close to the tomb of Mesehti, and is divided into two rooms. A third room, which is incomplete, leads from the second one (Fig. 89). The first room was adorned with a wall-painting representing a young man carrying the Gospel and is covered with débris today. The walls of the second room show several wall paintings and graffiti (Figs. 90-91), perhaps dating back to the sixth or seventh century (CLÉDAT 1908: 217-221; MEINARDUS 1965: 283). A Coptic text of eleven lines refers to the evangelist Luke the physician (LEFEBVRE 1909: 50-55).

Fig. 92: Christian chapel G10.1, wall paintings in 1903 (CLÉDAT 1908: 222, Fig. 7).

Fig. 93: Christian chapel G10.1, wall paintings in 2004 (© Kahl).

The second chapel (G10.1) had two rooms, of which the first one is destroyed. Several wall-paintings decorated the second room: one of them originally represented an angel carrying a medallion of Christ (Fig. 92). The decoration of the second room is also damaged, as can be seen today. In his left hand, Christ holds a book on which is written "The Light" and "The Life" (cf. CLÉDAT 1908: 221-223; MEINARDUS 1965: 283). Only a small part is still preserved today (Fig. 93), yet the few remains show the lack of accuracy in Clédat's copies: he did not document the feet of the figure of Christ, which today form the best preserved part.

CHAPTER FIVE

LIVING AND DYING AT ASYUT

On the lofty mountains overlooking this richest valley of the Nile, and protecting it from the Libyan desert, is a long range of tombs, the burial place of the ancient Egyptians; and looking for a moment at the little Mohamedan burying-ground, the traveller turns with wonder from the little city he has left, and asks: "Where is the great city which had its graves in the sides of yonder mountain? Where are the people who despised the earth as a burial-place, and made for themselves tombs in the eternal granite?"
John Lloyd Stephens 1836
(MANLEY/ABDEL-HAKIM 2004: 122)

THE LOCATION

Asyut was the capital of the 13th Upper Egyptian nome, in Egyptian Nedjefet-khentet or later Atef (CLÉRE 1969: 93-95), which was restricted to the land west of the Nile. The southern border of the nome lay about 3 km south of Asyut, the northern border close to the modern village of Umm al-Qusur opposite Gebel Abu el-Foda (GOMAÀ 1986: 264). The location was the most dangerous passage for navigation north of the First Cataract: maps of the Nile Valley (Fig. 94) exhibit an area with large meandering bends in the river that have sections perpendicular to the valley (cf. GRAHAM 2005: 44).

THE NAME

The modern name of the town of Asyut probably derives from the Old Egyptian name *s3w.ti* (Sauti: "The Guardian") that refers to the strategically advantageous position of the town. Numerous different phonographic writings are attested since the Old Kingdom (Figs. 95-96).

A mythological manual of the Roman Period gives an etiological explanation of the town's name according to which it was decisive that a relic of Osiris was guarded here (OSING 1998b: 144-145).

Because of the—wrong—equalization of the god Wepwawet who was mainly worshipped at Asyut with a wolf, the town was called Λύκων πόλις (Lykonpolis: "Town of the wolves") by the Greeks. During Roman and Byzantine times the town was just called *Lycon* or *Lyco* (MONTEVECCHI 2000a: 139), and λαμπρά is also attested (CALDERINI 1980: 211). Its Coptic name was ⲤⲒⲞⲞⲨⲦ or ⲤⲒⲰⲞⲨⲦ (cf. GARDINER 1947: 74*-75*).

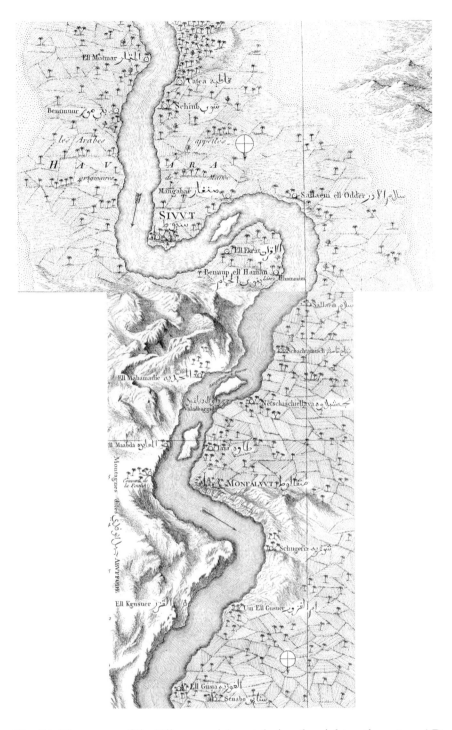

Fig. 94: The course of the Nile around Asyut during the eighteenth century AD (NORDEN 1795-1798: Pls. 80, 83).

The beginnings

At the beginning, the *Ka*-house of King Pepy I seems to have turned Asyut into a regional center (cf. Chapter Three). From that period, i.e. the Sixth Dynasty, single individuals are known from the town's necropolis for the first time (cf. Chapter Four). Only a few objects refer to earlier periods: there is a sarcophagus of the priest Min-nefer from the Fifth Dynasty (Leiden AMT 106) and two Early Dynastic vessels (Fig. 97), which were found in Tomb 13 of the French excavations (CHASSINAT/PALANQUE 1911: 162). They are probably heirlooms or were found by chance during the Middle Kingdom in the necropolis and then placed in the tomb. A copper vessel from the Third Dynasty probably comes from Asyut (RADWAN 1983: 38).

Quarters

Little now remains of the old town, except extensive mounds, and a few stone substructions, which are found in digging for the foundations of houses, or in cutting trenches on its site. It was under the mounds on the south side that the head of a statue was found in 1822, and the basement of a large stone building, both probably of Roman time; and here and there are seen the fragments of granite blocks. (WILKINSON 1843: 86).

This description of the old town by Sir Gardner Wilkinson is still valid today. Covered by the yearly deposits of the inundation of the Nile and completely hidden under the modern settlement, the ancient town of Asyut remains at a depth of several meters and is only sometimes brought to light, for instance in the shape of a probable Late Antique, 9.65 m high column which was seen in 1799 by the members of the French Expedition in the street that leads from the market (JOLLOIS/DEVILLIERS 1821: 130; RUSSELL 2001: 310-311). Another occasion occurred in the 1930s when a man attempted to find gold underneath his house and discovered blocks of the temple of Wepwawet instead (Figs. 22-23; GABRA 1931). Remains of the Late Antique town were detected some years ago during excavations in a cellar of a house in the old town of Asyut (Fig. 24). Also some years ago robbers of antiquities excavated a tunnel similar to those in a mine underneath the old town to reach the buried ruins of an ancient temple (probably the Wepwawet-temple). They were arrested by the police.[1]

Despite the deficiency of archaeological sources, information regarding the ancient town exists, particularly in papyri and tomb inscriptions. According to these, six "villages" (*tme*) existed during the Ptolemaic Period (THOMPSON 1934: 29, 147-148). They are either quarters of Asyut itself or outlying hamlets. Their names are:

- Merit
- The barn(?) of Djehuti-ir-di-es

---
[1] Personal communication from Mr. Hany Sadek Metri, 2005.

- The Valley of the necklace
- The double Fort(?)
- The (quarter?) of the swine
- The barn(?) of Pa-semtheus/Pa-setet(?)

Another village near Asyut was Pa-khyr (cf. Fig. 103; THOMPSON 1934: 28, note 142; SHORE/SMITH 1959: 54).

The ancient (and modern) necropolis of Asyut is situated close to the town at the steep slope of the mountain which is known today as Gebel Asyut al-gharbi or Stabl Antar (BAEDEKER 1929: 227; GOMAÀ 1986: 272). Names of the necropolis were Semit-nit-Sauti ("necropolis of Asyut") (GOMAÀ 1986: 269-270), Djeser/Pe-djeser/Pe-ta-djeser ("separated land," i.e. "holy land") (THOMPSON 1934: 148) and Ra-qereret ("opening of cave"). The last mentioned one is the designation of the mountain connected with Anubis (cf. Fig. 103). Anubis was called "Lord of Ra-qereret:" From far, the entrances to the tombs resemble caves so that the designation Ra-qereret was almost certainly chosen deliberately (Fig. 7).

Ta-ankh meant a certain part of the necropolis. It is that part that since at least the Middle Kingdom was thought to contain the tomb of the god Osiris (GOMAÀ 1986: 274-275). By the Late Period (if not earlier) this expression was used for the whole necropolis west of Asyut (SHORE/SMITH 1960: 283).

Medjeden was a cult place of Hathor close to Asyut. The goddess often has the epithet "mistress of Medjeden." Medjeden was for a long time wrongly identified as a site close to Deir Drunka, but today a location close to Asyut is favored (GOMAÀ 1986: 276) since the objects mentioning "Hathor, mistress of Medjeden" come directly from Asyut (cf. WILD 1971).

A bank building is attested for the second century BC (DARIS 1958: 44-46) and a number of churches are known for the Christian Era (ANTONINI 1940: 187-188; TIMM 1984: 240, 244-246; STEWART 1991: 296-297; cf. also MEINARDUS 1965: 281-282).

Northwest of the town was an "ancient and magnificent amphitheatre," the remains of which were observed by the French traveller Charles Poncet in 1698 (SAUNERON 1967: 157-160; SAUNERON 1983: 91). The amphitheatre probably dates back to the Roman Period. It can be related to a hippodrome and a bath that are mentioned in Coptic and Arabic manuscripts referring to the fourth century AD (JARRY 1964: 129-132; cf. Chapter Six).

The Armenian writer Abu Saleh mentions a "Gate of the Armenians" ("Bab el-Arman;" EVETTS/BUTLER 1895: 246) referring to a town-gate. This hints at the existence of an Armenian minority being present in Asyut during the Islamic Period (TIMM 1984: 244).

By the middle of the nineteenth century AD, Asyut was situated about 2.5 km from the western bank of the Nile, linked to its port, the village of el-Hamrah (Fig. 11), by a pleasant winding road lined with sycamores that escaped the annual flood (WALZ 1978: 113). Nothing is known about the harbor from antiquity but Asyut's location as a center of traffic leaves no doubt that the town must have had an important one. Inscriptions in the tombs of the nomarchs of the First Intermediate Period emphasize the fleets of ships and battles on the water (Siut V, 18; Siut III, 18; Siut IV, 15).

THE INHABITANTS

Although there are figures for the number of Asyuti inhabitants for modern times (Fig. 98), for antiquity only estimates can be given. The urban population of a provincial capital in the Pharaonic Period might have comprised 1,400-3,000 people (HASSAN 2001: 271). For the Roman Period a population of 25,000 seems to have been typical (BAGNALL/FRIER 1994: 55).

Names and professions during the Graeco-Roman Period are attested in papyri (collected for papyrological sources in CALDERINI 1922: 266-274; MONTEVECCHI 1998: 57-76; for Demotic papyri in THOMPSON 1934; SHORE/SMITH 1959). For the period between the third century BC and the sixth century AD the following trades and occupations are attested: bishops, deacons, presbyters, farmers, cattle-herds, camel-keepers, fishermen, bird-snarers, bakers, carpenters, dyers, wine-merchants, messengers, athletes, directors of a gymnasium (BILABEL 1950: 240), sculptors, scribes, keepers of archives (HOMBERT/PRÉAUX 1947: 123-125), doctors, employees of a bank (DARIS 1958: 45), poets, philosophers, boatmen, and soldiers. Additionally, slaves formed a considerable part of Asyut's population; during the first century AD it has been estimated that about 7% of the population consisted of slaves (SCHEIDEL 2001: 149). Slaves from Asyut are known by names in the third century AD (Tourbon and Aniketos the younger; HOOGENDIJK 1997: 126-127).

For the Pharaonic Period mainly the names of officials with different functions are preserved from written sources: mayors (e.g. Djefai-Hapi I), priests (cf. Chapter Three), overseers of the seal (e.g. CHASSINAT/PALANQUE 1911: 32) and sealers (e.g. STEINDORFF 1946: 24, Pl. 110[32]), scribes (MAGEE 1988: 52), legal officials (e.g. CHASSINAT/PALANQUE 1911: 135), overseers of troops (e.g. HABACHI 1977: 29) and great overseers of troops (SCOTT 1986: 128-131), overseers of the fleet (e.g. BRUNNER-TRAUT/ BRUNNER 1981: 209), and stewards (e.g. WAINWRIGHT 1926: 161). Physicians (BOURRIAU 1988: 87-88), soldiers (MUNRO 1963: 56), ladies-in-waiting, priestesses (e.g. LEFEBVRE 1914: 10-18), and ladies of the house (e.g. REISNER 1923: 509, 514) are also mentioned by name.

 [hieroglyphs]	Sarcophagus of Min-nefer; CT VII, 227i (Papyrus Gardiner II; DE BUCK 1961)
 [hieroglyphs]	Pyr. § 630b (T, P, M, N); § 1634a (Sq3C)
 [hieroglyphs]	Siut V, 1, 23, 33; Siut III, 1, 12, 28; Siut IV, 21, 61; N13.1, western wall; Tomb of Anu; Siut I, 2, 81, 155, 223; Siut II, 3
 [hieroglyphs]	Siut IV, 32
 [hieroglyphs]	N13.1, pillar
 [hieroglyphs]	CT III, 190b (S1C; DE BUCK 1947)
 [hieroglyphs]	Tomb of Anu
 [hieroglyphs]	Mastaba of Senwosret-ankh (HAYES 1937: Pl. 10 [486])
 [hieroglyphs]	Siut VIII, 1
 [hieroglyphs]	Deir Rifeh, Tomb VII (GRIFFITH 1889b: Pl. 19)
 [hieroglyphs]	Papyrus Reisner III suppl. verso 10, 20, 22-24 (SIMPSON 1969: Pl. 21)
 [hieroglyphs]	CT VII, 245c (Papyrus Gardiner II; DE BUCK 1961)
 [hieroglyphs]	Stela of Keky (Cairo, CG 20266; LANGE/SCHÄFER 1902)
 [hieroglyphs]	Coffin of Hetepi (Brussels, MRAH E. 3036; SPELEERS 1923: 21 [29])

Fig. 95: Ancient writings of the name "Asyut" (Old Kingdom to Middle Kingdom).

There are some indications on the life-expectancy, as indicated by a mortality and sex ratio study performed on both the osteological and the mummy collections from Gebelein and Asyut cemeteries in Turin. The results show a fairly low average age of death for adults of about 36 years for Dynastic Egyptians (the expected high mortality of children is neglected in this calculation). It can be observed that mortality in young adults was extremely high. The adult population appears to be reduced to one-half around 30 years. About 43 years the people from Asyut and Gebelein are reduced to about one-quarter. The number of elderly people represents an extremely low percentage (less than 5%). Young adult females had a higher mortality than the young adult males up to 30 years. This might correspond to their maximum fertility period, and it may be related to some of the difficulties and accidents of childbirth (MASALI/CHIARELLI 1972: 161-169).

	Statue of Min-mose (HELCK 1956: 1443, 3)
	Salakhana stela (EISSA 1996: Pl 17)
	Statue (Louvre A 73; KITCHEN 1980: 152.13)
	Luxor, temple of Amun, forecourt (KITCHEN 1979: 625.9)
	Luxor, temple of Amun, forecourt (KITCHEN 1979: 625.8)
	Salakhana stela (DUQUESNE 2004: Pl. 2)
	Salakhana stela (MUNRO 1963: 50, Pl. 3.3)
	Salakhana stela (DUQUESNE 2004: Pl. 3)
	Salakhana stela (DURISCH 1993: 207, Fig. 1)
sic!	Ostracon Golenischeff (GARDINER 1947: 74*)
	Temple of Hibis (DAVIES 1953: Pl. 4)
	Rituel de l'Embaumement (SAUNERON 1952: 4,23-5,1)
	Papyrus Louvre I.3079, col. 111, 76 (GOYON 1967: 151, Pl. 21.76)
	Temple of Dendara (CAUVILLE 1997: 410,1)
	Temple of Dendara (CAUVILLE 1997: 326,12)
	Temple of Dendara (CAUVILLE 1997: 156,11)
	Temple of Dendara (CAUVILLE 1997: 221,1)
	Temple of Dendara (CAUVILLE 1997: 283,8)
	Buch vom Ba (BEINLICH 2000: 44 [31])
	Papiri della Società Italiana inv. I 72, x+3,1-3 (OSING 1998b: Pl. 19B)
	Papiri della Società Italiana inv. I 72, x+3,15, 17-18 (OSING 1998b: Pl. 19B)

Fig. 96: Ancient writings of the name "Asyut" (New Kingdom to Roman Period).

Fig. 97: Early Dynastic vessel, Paris, Louvre E 11977 (© Musée du Louvre/DAE).

For the Roman Period the overall Egyptian life expectancy at birth was in the lower twenties, probably between 22 and 25 years (BAGNALL/FRIER 1994: 109). Once again one has to bear in mind the high mortality rate of children; it is to be expected that more than 50% of female deaths would include girls less than five years old (BAGNALL/FRIER 1994: 89).

The mortality of children might also have been high during the Coptic Period. There was a huge Christian cemetery on top of the mountain near Deir el-Azzam (cf. Chapter Four). Relatively many children were buried there.

In addition to illnesses, war and violence (cf. Chapter One) were always possible reasons for an early death, for instance during the civil war in the First Intermediate Period, during the revolt of Ankh-wennefer against Ptolemy V (CLARYSSE 1979: 103; PESTMAN 1995: 103, 121-122; McGING 1997: 299-310), during the persecution of Christians under Diocletian, or during Nubian raids (DELEHAYE 1922: 96, 101, 105; TIMM 1984: 238).

A papyrus kept today at the Trinity College in Dublin informs about the results of the revolt of Ankh-wennefer (Greek: Chaonnophris) for the area of Asyut:

From the time of the revolt of Chaonnophris it happened that most people (working on the land) were killed and that the land has gone dry. When therefore, as is regular practice, the land which did not have owners was registered among the ownerless land, some of the survivors encroached upon the land bordering their own and acquired more than was allowed. Their names are unknown since nobody pays for

Year	Total population	Source
1822	17,000	Walz 1978: 113
1843	20,000	Wilkinson 1843: 83
1872	27,470	Walz 1978: 113
1880	30,000	Ebers 1880: 201
1885	31,398	Evetts/Butler 1895: 245
1911	39,442	Budge 1911: 600
1921	51,431	Budge 1921: 365
1927	57,036	Baedeker 1929
1962	120,000	Brunner-Traut/Hell 1962: 412
2007	438,442	World Gazetteer; www.bevölkerungsstatistik.de

Fig. 98: Total population of modern Asyut (estimated value).

this land to the treasury. But of the cultivated area nothing has been overlooked, because the land-measurement of what is sown has taken place each year, and the taxes are being exacted.
(TCD Pap. Gr. 274, ll. 39-48)

The scarce remains of three letters belonging to a man named Spemminis probably also refer to military operations during the revolt (Clarysse 1979: 102; Hombert 1964: 204; Daris 1963).

During antiquity individuals aged 45 and upwards show evidence of osteoarthritis and dental problems, the two most commonly occurring disease conditions seen in archaeological human remains (Filer 1999: 24). Three individuals from the Twelfth Dynasty were examined anthropologically and show osteoarthritic changes as well. In addition, many of their teeth are missing, those remaining show signs of disease and attrition (Dawson/Gray 1968: 6-7; Filer 1999: 23-27).

In ancient Egypt marriage followed less juridical but more social parameters. It was mainly a matter between the spouses and their families. It appears that Egyptian women began to marry at or soon after age 12 (BAGNALL/FRIER 1994: 112). Male marriage before the later teens was probably rare (BAGNALL/FRIER 1994: 116). Brother-sister marriages did not widely occur before the Roman Period (ČERNÝ 1954: 23-29). Some documents from Asyuti family archives of the Late Period and Ptolemaic Period give details about marriages, for instance the financial support of the wives (THOMPSON 1934; JOHNSON 1994).

ASYUT AND FOREIGN COUNTRIES

The Libyan, Nubian, Assyrian, Persian, Greek, and Roman rulers in Egypt beginning with the tenth century BC make it likely that Asyut housed inhabitants from different ethnic groups. Military and trade concerns especially drew foreigners to the town. The presence of foreign soldiers is detectable again and again throughout its long history and might have led to mutual cultural influences: the wooden model of Nubian archers dating to the early Middle Kingdom (Cairo CG 257; cf. Fig. 63; BIETAK 1985: 87-97) already marks this influence. Greek mercenaries, Mauritanian horsemen (*Notitia Dignitatum Orient.*, no. XXXI: 17, 23; TIMM 1984: 240), and Persian soldiers (cf. RICHTER 2003: 229) are only some foreign troops probably stationed in Asyut in later periods.

Asyut was in constant contact with the Sudan through the 1,767 km long Darb el-Arbain ("the Forty Days Road"), the desert route leading from Kobbe (Darfur Province, Sudan) to Asyut. The Darb el-Arbain is one of the five main caravan routes that cross the deserts of North Africa from north to south. The desert road had several advantages compared to the more pleasant Nile route. The desert route was quicker, there were no porterages of goods at the cataracts, nor was a merchant's property subject to that constant attrition in the shape of bribes and presents then so widely demanded by the rulers of the countries which he transversed (SHAW 1929: 64).

This desert road seems to have been used as early as the Old Kingdom (EDEL 1955: 63). The removal of statues of Djefai-Hapi I (Fig. 99) and his wife Sennwy (Fig. 100) to Nubia might be connected with a use of the Darb al-Arbain, as are raids of Nubian tribes during the Christian Era. During the Islamic Period Asyut became a major trading center, especially for the slave trade, which was often conducted through the Darb el-Arbain until the nineteenth century. Caravans from and to Darfur in Sudan started and ended at Asyut. According to a report of the English traveller William George Browne, who accompanied a caravan in 1796 to Darfur and back, the following items were traded south:

Amber beads, tin in small bars; coral beads; cornelian ditto; false cornelian ditto; beads of Venice; agate; rings, silver and brass for the ankles and wrists; carpets, small; blue cotton cloths of Egyptian fabric; white cotton ditto; Indian muslins and cottons; blue and white cloths of Egypt called Melayes; sword-blades, straight (German) from Kahira; small looking-glasses; copper face-pieces or defensive armour for the horses' heads; firearms; kohhel for the eyes; coffee; silk, unwrought; wire, brass and

iron; small red caps of Barbary; light French clothes made into Benishes; silks of Scio; silk and cotton pieces of Aleppo; shoes of red leather; black pepper, writing-paper; soap of Syria.
(SHAW 1929: 64-65; VIVIAN 2000: 352)

The caravan brought other goods back north:

Slaves, male and female; camels; ivory; horns of the rhinoceros; teeth of the hippopotamus; ostrich feathers; gum; pimento; tamarinds made into round cakes; peroquets in abundance, and some monkeys and Guinea fowl; copper, white, in small quantity.
(SHAW 1929: 65; VIVIAN 2000: 352)

There are some literary testimonies for a longer presence of foreigners at Asyut. They mention people with their ethnic relation, for instance in Papyrus London BM EA 10591 vso. VI.11, a Greek woman, Aristion (?) the daughter of Agathokles, who sold a lake close to Asyut (THOMPSON 1934: 60). The brothers Tuot and Tef-Hape leased their land to a Greek cavalryman named Agylos son of Lysimachos in 172 BC (year 10 of Ptolemaios VI Philometor). One year later Tef-Hape leased his share of the land to another Greek cavalryman named Heraklides (THOMPSON 1934: XIV-XV).

A funerary stela of the Roman Period records the early death of a 16 year old boy from Asyut (BILABEL 1950: 240). The epitaph refers to Osiris of Abydos and to Hermes of Cyllene and Lethe. This stela is an example for the osmosis of Egyptian and Greek religious beliefs.

There are more foreign names known from Asyut. Although they are not necessarily a direct proof of the presence of foreigners, they attest at least to a multicultural society. The owners of some coffins dating to the Thirteenth Dynasty bore names compound with the Semitic gods Reshef and Baal (HASSAN 1976: 93). The number of foreign names increased in the first centuries before and after the beginning of the Christian Era. Examples are Dionysos, a Greek name, and Ouertes, a Persian or Armenian name, attested in second century BC (Papyrus London BM EA 10591 rto. I.24, III.8, VI.11; THOMPSON 1934: 14, 17, 24).

Archaeological evidence points to a direct or indirect contact with foreigners at Asyut as well, for instance, a golden earring probably dating to the fifth or fourth century BC. The Achaemenid (or Greek) form of this earring might point to a foreign woman as owner of this piece of jewelry (Pl. 9a; S05/073; for such earrings cf. MAXWELL-HYSLOP 1971: 214, Pls. 184-186; WILLIAMS 1924: 142-144, Pl. 17.81a-b).

Two hoards from Asyut attest to direct or indirect connections with the Mediterranean: The Asyut hoard of about 900 silver coins contains coins from Italy and Sicily, Macedonia and Thrace, Central Greece, Athens, Aegina, Corinth, the Greek Islands, Asia Minor, Caria, Sardes, Lycia, Cyprus, and Cyrenaica. The hoard dates from the early fifth century BC (PRICE/WAGGONER 1975). The whole hoard seems to have been

Fig. 99: Statue of Djefai-Hapi I, Kerma/Sudan, Boston, MFA 14.724
(© 2007 Museum of Fine Arts, Boston).

accumulated over a period of not more than fifteen years (c. 490-475 BC). The bulk of it was brought to Egypt about 480 BC. Who owned it—Greek or Egyptian—cannot be determined (PRICE/WAGGONER 1975: 121; cf. DUYRAT 2005).

Fig. 100: Statue of Sennwy, Kerma/Sudan, Boston, MFA 14.720
(© 2007 Museum of Fine Arts, Boston).

A stamp on an amphora handle from Rhodes dating to the Ptolemaic Period also points to contacts from abroad (Pl. 9b; S04/st307).

The hoard of Byzantine gold jewelry (Pls. 10a-c) from the fifth and sixth century AD (DENNISON 1918) indicates a connection to Constantinople. The enormous value of the high-carat gold and the precious stones—sometimes imported from places as far as Ceylon—suggest that commissioner, bearer, and goldsmith should be located in the capital of Byzantium. When and how the jewelry was transferred to Asyut remains unclear. The situation of the find spot of the nearly forty pieces of jewelry in a monastery close to Asyut—exact information is missing—points to an intentional hoarding of the jewelry. A connection with the Arabic conquest of Egypt (AD 639-642) is conceivable (PLATZ-HORSTER 2004: 286).

A connection between Asyut and Constantinople—this time going in the opposite direction—is attested in Papyrus Cairo Masp. 67032 dating to AD 551: an Asyuti notable of the Egyptian community in Constantinople was witness to a contract (CALDERINI 1922: 267). And already in the fourth century AD messengers of Emperor Theodosius came to Asyut to ask Saint John of Lycopolis about the emperor's fate (cf. Chapter Six).

EGYPTIANS IN ASYUT, ASYUTI PEOPLE IN EGYPT

The mobility of Asyuti people is attested not only outside of Egypt, but also inside. During the First Intermediate Period the nomarch Khety I had swimming lessons together with the royal offspring. That means that Khety I spend parts of his childhood at the court in Herakleopolis. His autobiographical inscription states

I was a favorite of the king ... He caused that I should be instructed in swimming along with the royal children.
(Siut V, 20-22)

In course of the military struggles of the First Intermediate Period between Thebes and Herakleopolis, numerous inhabitants of Asyut had also to leave their homes and escape from the town. The autobiographical inscription of Khety II says

He brought back the refugees into their homes. He buried his old people.
(Siut IV, 17-18)

The English Egyptologist Percy E. Newberry copied the inscriptions of a small Twelfth Dynasty tomb, whose exact position is unknown today. Newberry numbered the tomb as Tomb 1 as well as Tomb 8 (MAGEE 1998: 718). A biographical text records a visit to Shas-Hotep (modern Shutb) in the neighboring nome made by the tomb owner, the mayor of Asyut, Khety. Even if the exact purpose of the visit remains open, it was clearly of some importance to Khety as these references occur in what was probably the main biographical text in the tomb (MAGEE 1998: 729).

Iuny and his wife Renenut II lived at the beginning of the Nineteenth Dynasty. They belonged to an Asyuti family, but worked in the Memphite residence (see below). An

Asyuti physician named Hierax visited the Valley of the Kings at Thebes during the Roman Period (BAILLET 1926: 48, 254-256). During the Christian Era activities of Asyutis are attested in Memphis, Antinoe, and Abydos (CALDERINI 1922: 266-267). A stela of Apollonios from Asyut (Lycopolis) was probably erected at Abydos during the first century AD (KOEMOTH 2001: 217-233).

Visitors from other sites came to Asyut as well. Stelae found in the Salakhana Tomb (cf. DUQUESNE 2000: 19) point in this direction although the pilgrims' provenance can not be defined exactly; Asyut's strategically advantageous location probably attracted traders and soldiers. Of interest in this regard is an order for the delivery of chicken from Edfa near modern Sohag to two wine-merchants at Asyut during the reign of Emperor Alexander Severus (AD 229) (BOYAVAL 1965: 67, no. 49).

The reference of a mid-Twentieth Dynasty papyrus, which was purchased in the necropolis of Asyut in the early 1880s, to the town is unclear. The papyrus contains the record of a grain transport and other texts connected with grain transports (Papyrus Baldwin and Papyrus Amiens: JANSSEN 1995: 53-60; JANSSEN 2004). Asyut is not directly mentioned in the papyrus but the papyrus' provenance points to a connection with the town, perhaps such that the papyrus went to a granary in that town (JANSSEN 2004: 33) or that an official buried in the necropolis of Asyut had to deal with the transports.

According to Coptic tradition, the Holy Family reached Asyut on their flight to Egypt and found refuge in a cave near Drunka. The Monastery of the Holy Virgin was founded next to this cave, a former quarry (GABRA 2001: 115-120).

Papyrus Oxyrhynchos 984, which was drawn up in AD 91/92 from declarations for the census of AD 89/90, refers to Ptolemais or to Asyut. In either case, the census register mentions a process that was also valid for Asyut: the migration of people from various neighboring nomes and the establishment of their cults in their new residence (BAGNALL 1998: 1101).

People who came to Asyut during the fourth century AD to ask John of Lycopolis for advice and help deserve special mention (cf. Chapter Six).

THE LANGUAGE

Dialectic differences in the language are clearly distinguishable for the Coptic Period; a so-called Lycopolitan dialect was used in the area of Asyut (KASSER 1991: 139; NAGEL 1991: 151-159).

These differences existed already earlier. During the Ptolemaic Period several dialectal forms of common Egyptian names such as Amenaphis (for Amenophis) and Onnaphris (for Onnophris) are attested (CLARYSSE 1979: 105).

The religions

During the Pharaonic Period the religious beliefs of the population had been determined by ancient Egyptian concepts of the gods and the afterlife (cf. Chapter Three), but representatives of other religions came to Egypt, and also to Asyut, at least at the start of the Late Period. In Ptolemaic and Roman times it was primarily foreign soldiers and officials of the administration who practiced other, non-Egyptian, religions.

The spread of Christianity lead to a relatively high number of Christians among the Asyuti population. During the prosecution of Christians under Emperor Diocletian (AD 284-305), the Christian community of Asyut suffered from a difficult fate, as Arianus, *praeses* of the Thebaid during this period, located Christians in Asyut and tortured them. Martyrs who found their death in Asyut or were connected with the town were, among others, Phoibammon, Arsenophis, and Claudius (cf. TIMM 1984: 236-237; STEWART 1991: 296). Arianus had also Thekla, daughter of Kyros, decapitated after her refusal to acknowledge the gods of the Roman emperor (TILL 1936: 132). The earliest known bishop of Asyut was Apollonios, who lived during the Diocletian persecutions. During the Byzantine Period Asyut was one of the most important centers of Christianity in Egypt (cf. TIMM 1984: 235-251). The most important bishop of Lycopolis/Asyut in Late Byzantine Period was Constantine II (cf. Chapter Six). He lived during the third Persian conquest of Egypt (AD 619-629).

The influence of Christianity is reflected in the increasing use of Christian personal names in Asyut during the fifth and sixth centuries: Athanasia, Aleet, Apalos, Areion, Viktor, Viktorine, Georgios, Danielios, Ioannes, Kyriakos, Martha, Maria, and Petros are opposed by non-Christian names such as Akakios, Akoris, Apollos, Aphous, Iobinos, Konon, Kyros, Menas, Valentinos, Pakoris, Parresia, Plousammon, Sois, Phoibammon, Psois (cf. the onomasticon of Asyut in MONTEVECCHI 1998: 65-76).

During the nineteenth century there was a tendency among Asyuti Copts to trace their ancestry back to well-known Coptic personalities or even to eponymous pharaonic ancestors (WALZ 1978: 116).

The economy

The autobiography of Khety I in Tomb V mentions the seemingly ideal measures he took to care for the population during the First Intermediate Period, when, after the collapse of the centralized government at the end of the Old Kingdom, only the nomarchs were responsible for the prosperity of the inhabitants of their sphere of influence. Khety I reports in his autobiographical inscription on buildings and irrigation projects (cf. SCHENKEL 1978: 29-35). He wrote:

I was rich in barley, when the land was in need. I was one who nourished the city by apportioning with the Medjat-measure.
(Siut V, 9)

This abundance of grain and the wealth resulting from it were probably one of the determining factors for Asyut during her history as a whole. The Ramesside papyrus mentioned above that was bought at Asyut reports on grain transport south and north of the town (JANSSEN 2004).

Around AD 1200 Abu Salih, the Armenian, described the fertile landscape of Asyut as follows:

There is no finer bed of river-slime on the face of the earth than that found here, nor any that has a sweeter smell; it is enclosed by mountains and is deposited by the water of the Nile; its extent is 30,000 feddans, all in one plain; and if a little of it were rubbed in the fingers it would spread out evenly, and some of it would extend beyond the sides; in it they sow flax and wheat and clover and other crops. It is said that there is nowhere in Egypt anything like this level unbroken expanse of cultivated fields, or any more delightful place where the beauties of the country can be better enjoyed than this, when its crops are in full luxuriance, and when the flowers appear; they say there is nothing more admirable to be seen.
(EVETTS/BUTLER 1895: 246)

As late as 1844 Asyut was ranked as being one of the most extensively cultivated provinces in the whole of Egypt, furnishing the highest land revenues to the government and supporting the largest rural population in the country (WALZ 1978: 117).

During the eighth to eleventh centuries AD fine textiles were exported that were manufactured at Asyut (DESROSIERS 2002: 164). Whether the town produced textiles of high quality already during the Pharaonic Period has to remain open.

FAMILY ARCHIVES

Two family archives tell us about life in Asyut during the Twenty-sixth and Twenty-seventh Dynasties and the Ptolemaic Period respectively.

The Wepwawet-hotep/Hor-family
   SOTTAS 1923: 34-46; SPIEGELBERG 1932: 39-53; SHORE 1988: 200-206; JOHNSON 1994: 113-132
   In 1922 the British archaeologist Gerald Awery Wainwright discovered inside the so-called Salakhana Tomb a number of Demotic papyri of Saite and Persian date. The papyri were found without any observable context (cf. SHORE 1988: 200). Today they are kept in Cairo and London, and consist of a series of accounts and contracts. The following papyri were found (in chronological order):
   - Papyrus Cairo CG 50058 (year 28 of Amasis = 543 BC)
   - Papyrus Cairo CG 50061 (year 43, probably of Amasis = 528 BC)
   - Papyrus Cairo CG 50060 (year 5 of Cambyses = 525 BC)
   - Papyrus Cairo CG 50062 (year 7 of Cambyses = 523 BC)
   - Papyrus Cairo CG 50059 (year 8 of Cambyses = 522 BC))
   - Papyrus London BM EA 10792 (year 8 of Cambyses = 522 BC)

The documents contain information on two Asyuti families and their priestly activities from year 7 of King Amasis (564 BC) to year 8 of King Cambyses (522 BC). They are part of a series of written transactions that can be traced over three generations and forty-two years (SHORE 1988: 200). The archive is an example of annuity contracts as deeds containing a settlement pertaining to the law of matrimonial property drawn up in order to settle the matrimonial property (JOHNSON 1994: 125). The genealogy of the family of the priests Wepwawet-hotep and Hor can be reconstructed from the different papyri (Fig. 101). Wepwawet-hotep II had the titles of: "support of heaven and clothier of manifestations" (a honorific title), "third prophet of Wepwawet," "secretary of the house of Wepwawet," "*setem*-priest of the house of Wepwawet," "prophet of the head of the magazine, the mistress of 16 (i.e. Hathor)," and "prophet of Osiris;" Hor I was third prophet of Wepwawet.

The Pe-te-tum/Tef-Hape-family
　　THOMPSON 1934; SHORE/SMITH 1959: 52-60; VLEEMING 1989: 31-45

　　The British Museum houses thirteen Demotic papyri that come from Asyut or from the immediate vicinity. These papyri are part of an archive concerned with the affairs of a family of lector-priests of the necropolis of Asyut (Fig. 102). The central figure of the archive is a lector priest named Tef-Hape, who worked in the first half of the second century BC in the necropolis of Asyut. Tef-Hape was the son of a man called Pe-te-tum and his second wife Ta-wa. Tef-Hape had a sister named Te-te-im-hotep and a second sister, whose name is unknown. In addition there were the children from the first marriage of his father Pe-te-tum with a woman called Sen-Ese: Tef-Hape's half-brother Tuot and his half-sister T-shen-tuot.

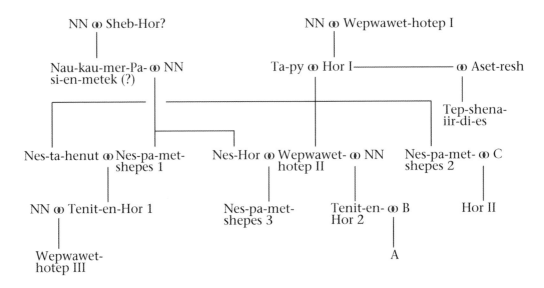

Fig. 101: The Wepwawet-hotep/Hor-family (according to JOHNSON 1994: 118).

The archive comprises papyri from the space of time 181-169 BC. The documents inform about family matters that took place between 208 and 169 BC. Three of the documents belonged to Tef-Hape's sister Te-te-im-hotep. The following are the different papyri of the archive:
- Papyrus London BM EA 10575 (year 25 of Ptolemy V Epiphanes; 181 BC; donation of a one-third share of property made by Pe-te-tum to his son Tef-Hape)
- Papyrus London BM EA 10589 (year 6 of Ptolemy VI Philometor; 175 BC; an undertaking by Tef-Hape and Wepwawet-iu to Ta-wa not to hinder her from building operations on a house and a court in a village of Asyut)
- Papyrus London BM EA 10591 (year 11 of Ptolemy VI Philometor; 170 BC; recto: report of the trial between Khrati-ankh and Tef-Hape; verso: other documents (cf. the remarks of SHORE/SMITH 1960: 280)
- Papyrus London BM EA 10592 (year 25 of Ptolemy V Epiphanes; 181 BC; Pe-te-tum makes a gift of one-eighth of a house and grounds near Asyut to his daughter Te-te-im-hotep)
- Papyrus London BM EA 10593 (year 9 of Ptolemy VI Philometor; 172 BC; marriage of Te-te-im-hotep to Pekusis)
- Papyrus London BM EA 10594 (year 9 of Ptolemy VI Philometor; 172 BC; acknowledgement by Pekusis of the receipt, made out to his wife Te-te-imhotep, of a sum of 21 silver pieces)
- Papyrus London BM EA 10595 (year 10 of Ptolemy VI Philometor; 172 BC; a tender of farming lease made by Aiglos to Tuot and Tef-Hape)
- Papyrus London BM EA 10596 (year 10 of Ptolemy VI Philometor; 171 BC; a receipt for barley given by royal scribes to Tuot)

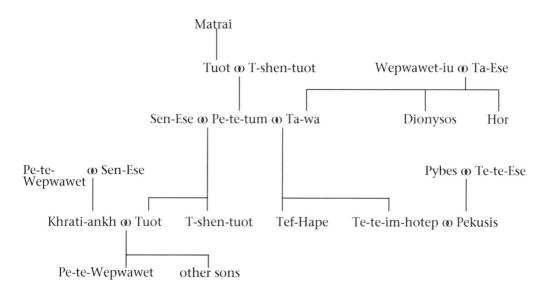

Fig. 102: The Pe-te-tum/Tef-Hape-family (according to THOMPSON 1934: X).

- Papyrus London BM EA 10597 (year 11 of Ptolemy VI Philometor; 171 BC; farming lease made by Tef-Hape to Heraklides)
- Papyrus London BM EA 10598 (year 11 of Ptolemy VI Philometor; 170 BC; petition made by Tef-Hape to Spemminis (Shep-Min), who was prophet of Thoth and royal overseer)
- Papyrus London BM EA 10599 (year 12 of Ptolemy VI Philometor; 169 BC; petition of Tef-Hape to Spemminis)
- Papyrus London BM EA 10600 (year 12 of Ptolemy VI Philometor; 169 BC; petition of Tef-Hape to Miusis)
- Papyrus London BM EA 10601 (year 9 or 10 of Ptolemy VI Philometor; c. 172/171 BC; a receipt given by Tuot to Tef-Hape for the third part of 17 artabas of wheat)

The documents of the archive of Tef-Hape concern a trial about the inheritance of Tef-Hape's father Pe-te-tum. The principal document is a papyrus, 2.85 m long and 32 cm wide

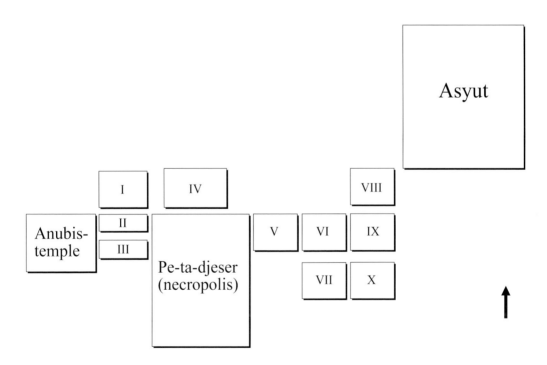

Fig. 103: The reconstructed Position of the Anubis-temple according to written sources.

I - village of Pa-khyr
II - quay of Pahe
III - dyke of Pharaoh
IV - the cats (necropolis?)
V - highland in the divine endowment of Wepwawet
VI - the lands of Pet-Amen-ophis, son of Tef-Hape
VII - the lands of Pet-Amen-ophis, son of Ber
VIII - feeding place of the Ibis
IX - highland in the divine endowment of Wepwawet
X - the lands of Pet-Amen-ophis, son of Tef-Hape

(BM EA 10591), containing the protocol of a judicial hearing from June 22, 170 BC. All other documents in Tef-Hape's archive refer directly or indirectly to this great lawsuit:

In 185 BC Pe-te-tum had a deed drawn up, endowing his first wife and her children with his entire property. In 181 BC Pe-te-tum endowed his second wife and her children with one third of his property: Tuot, son of Pe-te-tum by his first wife, Sen-Ese, inherited two-thirds of all his father's property, while Tef-Hape, son of Pe-te-tum by his second wife, Ta-wa, inherited one third. The preference given to the eldest son was common in ancient Egypt since he traditionally was responsible for the father's burial. In 173 BC Tuot agreed to this altered contract and he made out a deed of apportionment of one-third of the inheritance to Tef-Hape. Tuot's wife Khrati-ankh first also consented, but later Khrati-ankh complained that Tuot was forced to leave a third of the inheritance to Tef-Hape. She said:

Dionysos, who was a herd of Theomnestos [i.e. the Strategos of the Thebais], together with Hor, his camel keeper, the brothers of the mother of Tef-Hape aforesaid, were those who caused Tuot son of Pe-te-tum, my husband, to be put in the stocks, they causing him to make the apportionment deed under compulsion, they causing me to confirm it on account of the fear of the breath [i.e. of my life].
(Papyrus London BM EA 10591 rto. V.1-2; cf. THOMPSON 1934: 21)

Tef-Hape replied in 170 BC in court:

These (things) ... they are all falsehoods. Tuot son of Pe-te-tum was not put in the stocks. He never made for me an apportionment deed till the year 8 Pachons 2 of the ever-living Pharaoh. (It was) Theomnestos whom she addressed here in the territory of Asyut when they were completing the said deed with witnesses on the dromos of Wepwawet (and) exhibiting the apportionment deed which my father had already made for me thereon, together with the endowment deed which he made to Ta-wa my mother ...
(Papyrus London BM EA 10591 rto. V.26-VI.2; cf. THOMPSON 1934: 23)

During this lawsuit in 170 BC, the struggle for the inheritance was solved to the advantage of Tef-Hape. Since Tuot had agreed to the changed contract three years before (and it was impossible to prove that this agreement was produced by force), Tef-Hape was destined to inherit a third of this father's property. The following judgment was pronounced:

We have given judgment that the said Tef-Hape son of Pe-te-tum be put in possession of everything and all property, which is described in the apportionment deed of which the copy is written on the verso hereof (and) which exhibits there his 1/3 share of his father's property. We have told Har-im-hotep the bailiff (of) Andromachos the Eisagogeus to put Tef-Hape son of Pe-te-tum in possession of the property which is described in the apportionment deed, which Tuot son of Pe-te-tum made to him as aforesaid in the year 8 (for) the 1/3 share of the property of his father, which was confirmed by Khrati-ankh daughter of Pe-te-Wepwawet aforesaid, and that he (Tuot) give the said deed of cession as a declaration of title in consequence of the claim made by her.
(Papyrus London BM EA 10591 rto. X.13-15; cf. THOMPSON 1934: 33)

A CENSUS REGISTER FROM ASYUT?

Papyrus Oxyrhynchos 984 recto contains a register drawn up in AD 91/92 from declarations for the census of AD 89/90 (BAGNALL/FRIER/RUTHERFORD 1997). The papyrus' editors first thought that the Upper Egyptian town of Ptolemais had been the source of the census register, but in the meantime doubts have arisen (BAGNALL 1998: 1101). Personal names compounded with Wepwawet, Anubis, and Herakles as well as the designation of an area probably referring to a procession of Wepwawet might point to the fact that the census register mentioned on the papyrus described the population of Asyut (MONTEVECCHI 1998: 49-76; SCHEIDEL 2001: 147-151). Should Montevecchi's assumption prove to be true, then further important information about first century AD Asyut might be available, for example personal names, indication of migration of people from various neighboring nomes and the establishment of cults in their new residence (BAGNALL 1998: 1101).

CHAPTER SIX

MEN OF INFLUENCE AND POWER

The townships … were the basis of Egyptian territorial administration, and local rulers … probably exercised considerable individual authority and responsibility.
(Doxey 1998: 186)

Khety I

(cf. Chapter Four: Tomb V)

Khety I was Asyuti nomarch during the First Intermediate Period (cf. Fig. 8). As reported in his autobiography, which was written on the walls of his tomb (Tomb V; M11.1), Khety describes how well he served his hometown Asyut. He provided security, a stable food supply, and irrigation, and he built in the temple and increased its offerings. The civil war between Herakleopolis and Thebes was not yet a topic of his autobiography, so that one can assume that the war had not yet reached Asyut during his life. Furthermore Khety I mentions in his autobiography that he learned to swim together with the royal children.

Iti-ibi

(cf. Chapter Four: Tomb III)

Iti-ibi, owner of Tomb III (N12.1), was the successor to Khety I as Asyuti nomarch (cf. Fig. 8). He was a supporter of the Herakleopolitan kings. His autobiographical inscription (Pl. 3b) gives a graphic picture of the civil war during the First Intermediate Period. Iti-ibi narrates how he repelled the southern aggressors. It may be assumed that Iti-ibi became a victim of war because his autobiography was never completed and painted over with a neutral text and scene.

Khety II

(cf. Chapter Four: Tomb IV)

Khety II followed Iti-ibi as nomarch of Asyut (cf. Fig. 8). Supported by King Merikara, he continued the war against Thebes and expelled the Theban troops from Asyut after they had seized the city (cf. the autobiographical inscription in Tomb IV; N12.2). Khety II restored the temple of Wepwawet.

Finally, however, either he or his successor Iti-ibi(-iqer) lost the war against the Theban aggressors.

Fig. 104: Wooden statue of Djefai-Hapi I, height: 2,05 m (© Musée du Louvre/DAE).

DJEFAI-HAPI I

(cf. Chapter Four: Tomb I)

Asyut flourished culturally during the reign of Senwosret I (Twelfth Dynasty). The legacy of the then nomarch Djefai-Hapi I gives sufficient evidence of this. Djefai-Hapi I governed Asyut and introduced changes in the areas of art, literature, and architecture, which would last in the *cultural memory* of the ancient Egyptians for more than two thousand years. His monumental rock-tomb survived (Tomb I; cf. Pls. 6-8). On the one hand Djefai-Hapi I borrowed texts and architectural designs from the royal domain. At the same time he furthered the development of local traditions. Excerpts of his tomb inscriptions were still copied during the Roman Period (OSING 1998a; KAHL 1999). Statues of Djefai-Hapi I and his wife Sennwy (Figs. 99-100; REISNER 1923a: Pl. 7.1-2; REISNER 1923b: 34, 509, 513-516, Pl. 31; REVEZ 2002: 245-249) were taken to Kerma, in modern Sudan, where they seem to have been esteemed as prestige goods. Today, the Louvre in Paris and the Egyptian Museum in Turin also house larger than life-size wooden statues of Djefai-Hapi (Fig. 104).

The find of the above-mentioned statues at Kerma led to the assumption that Djefai-Hapi worked there as governor and that he also died there (REISNER 1918: 79-98). Archaeological circumstances, however, disprove a burial of Djefai-Hapi at Kerma (SÄVE-SÖDERBERGH 1941: 103-116; DUNHAM 1982: IX-X; KENDALL 1997: 24-27; OBSOMER 1995: 340-342). Rather one may suppose that the statues were taken to Kerma during the Second

Intermediate Period, a period of Egyptian disorganization (cf. HELCK 1976: 101-115; VALBELLE 1998).

The name of Djefai-Hapi's own father is not known; he designated himself as being the "offspring of Wepwawet" in his tomb (Siut I, 183). His mother was Idy, the elder, while his two wives were named Sennwy and Wepay. His daughter was also named Idy. His brother, as well as his both sons, bore the name Djefai-Hapi.

Djefai-Hapi rebuilt the temple of Wepwawet, which was presumably destroyed during outbreaks of violence at the beginning of the Twelfth Dynasty (cf. Chapter One). He did not report on other individual or singular events of his life. Instead he recorded an unparalleled catalogue of more than 50 titles and 180 epithets on his tomb walls. His life consisted of his excellent behavior and his loyalty to the king according to these inscriptions. For example, he describes himself as

One whose lord loves his actions (Siut I, 214)
One who is obedient of the one who established him (Siut I, 221)
One who accompanies his lord on his journeys (Siut I, 222)
Favorite of the king in all his plans (Siut I, 241)
One whose lord caused that he be great (Siut I, 338)
A king's favorite (Siut I, 214)
One whom the king distinguished more than his peers (Siut I, 152, 212)

As a consequence of his loyal behavior Djefai-Hapi I seems to have built his tomb with resources of the royal court (cf. Chapter Four).

Djefai-Hapi as well as the other local rulers of Asyut played an almost royal role in their town during the First Intermediate Period and the Middle Kingdom. Cult practice in the temple setting was officially portrayed exclusively as a royal responsibility. However, in actual practice it was the local elite who performed rituals in most temples, and statues of the elite may have served as intermediaries through whom the majority of the population could communicate with deities who they would otherwise have no direct access to. The local rulers, like Djefai-Hapi I of Asyut, thus cast themselves in a royal role, taking an active role in cult practice and implying that they could perform ritual actions on behalf of the larger population in exchange for public support and labor (DOXEY 1998: 104). Djefai-Hapi I referred to his role in cult practice and to his restricted access in cultic context when he said that he was "one who clothes the god in his clothing" (Siut I, 245), "one who clothes the bodies of the jackals, the gods, and the followers of Horus" (Siut I, 173, 238), and "one who sees the beauty of Wepwawet" (Siut I, 4).

Djefai-Hapi I established his own funerary cult and bound the priests of the Wepwawet-temple and the Anubis-temple, as well as the workmen of the necropolis, by contracts (Pl. 7b) to maintain his cult after his death (cf. Chapter Four; cf. BREASTED 1906: 258-271; THÉODORIDÈS 1971: 109-251; THÉODORIDÈS 1973: 439-466).

The words of the first contract run as follows:

Contract which the count, overseer of the priests Djefai-Hapi, justified, made with the hour-priests of the temple of Wepwawet, lord of Asyut.
There shall be given to him: A white loaf by each individual *wab*-priest for his statue which is in the temple of Anubis, Lord of Ra-qereret, on the first of the five intercalary days, when Wepwawet, lord of Asyut, proceeds to this temple. What he has given to them for it: his share of the bull offered to Wepwawet, lord of Asyut, in this temple, when he proceeds to it, consisting of his meat-offering which is due to the nomarch. Then, he spoke to them, saying: "Behold I have given to you this meat-offering which is due to me from the temple, in order that this white bread may be established which you give to me." Then they gave to him a portion of the bull for his statue, (which is) in charge of his *Ka*-servant, out of what he had given to them of this meat-offering. Then they were satisfied with it.
(Siut I, 273-276)

The funerary cult and its inclusion into religious feasts guaranteed to Djefai-Hapi a fixed position in the memory of Asyuti people. Therefore it is tempting to assign visitors' graffiti of the late Second Intermediate Period or the early New Kingdom mentioning "the beautiful temple of Djefai-Hapi" to Djefai-Hapi I (Fig. 32). However, conclusive evidence for this identification is still missing. Also Djefai-Hapi II (owner of Tomb II) and Djefai-Hapi III (owner of the Salakhana Tomb) are possible candidates for the deified Djefai-Hapi.

Personal names of the Ptolemaic Period bearing the element "Djefai-Hapi" show how long and how profound the Middle Kingdom nomarchs remained in the memory of Asyuti people (BECKER 2006).

THE AMEN-HOTEP/IUNY-FAMILY

HAYES 1959: 349-353; KITCHEN 1975: 350-357; KITCHEN 1976; KITCHEN 1993a: 286-292; KITCHEN 1993b: 242-251

A family of physicians and priests (Fig. 105), living at the end of the Eighteenth Dynasty, is known to have had its roots in Asyut. The scribe of the king, lector, chief and overseer of the *wab*-priests of Sekhmet Amen-hotep and his son Iuny left their traces in Asyut as well as outside of the town. In 1913/14 Ahmed Bey Kamal partially removed Amen-hotep's tomb, which was situated in the Gebel Asyut al-gharbi (cf. Chapter Four). Today scattered in museums all over the world, the tomb chapel, statues, stelae, and an ushebti of Amen-hotep's son Iuny, tell us about about the family and their activities.

Amen-hotep apparently came from Asyut, practiced medicine and worked for the temple, as some of his titles demonstrate. His title "lector" designates someone who carried the scrolls of the rituals, and his title "overseer of the *wab*-priests of Sekhmet" provides an association to the primary health care (NUNN 1996: 135). His son Iuny called him "chief physician."

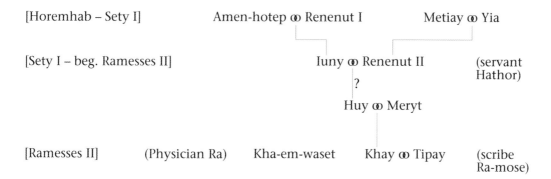

Fig. 105: Genealogical tree of the Amen-hotep/Iuny-family (according to KITCHEN 1976: 158).

Amen-hotep can be dated to the transition period of the Eighteenth to the Nineteenth Dynasty thanks to the style of his tomb decoration and his statues as well as some administrative documents. Hence, his son Iuny lived during the reign of Sety I and Ramesses II (KITCHEN 1976: 156-158).

Amen-hotep's wife Renenut was chantress of Wepwawet and chantress of Amun-Ra. Her last mentioned title is indicative that she was in the musical service of the Memphite Amun. Therefore Amen-hotep's and Renenut's lives might have centered around Memphis. This would explain why no tomb of Amen-hotep's son Iuny was found in Asyut, but only statues that might have been erected in his father's tomb.

Iuny was also concerned with religious writings and medicine according to some of his titles. Other titles, however, refer to the administration of the palace and show that Iuny worked in the king's personal surroundings. Additionally, Iuny executed royal orders in the Delta.

Iuny's wife bore the same name as his mother: Renenut (II). She was chantress of Hathor of Medjeden (in Asyut) and chantress of Amun-Ra (probably in Memphis; KITCHEN 1993b: 248) according to a double statue of Iuny and his wife (New York, MMA 15.2.1). Also her father Metiay worked in the administration. Her mother's name was Yia, and her servant's name was Hathor.

Two stelae mention Iuny, two other physicians named Huy and Khay, and their wives (Oxford, Ashmolean Museum 1883.14 and Louvre C89). The exact relationship of Huy and Khay to Iuny remains open, but they worked as physicians for the queen. Their common depiction on a stela confirms once again Iuny's medical background and his close connection to the royal house of the Nineteenth Dynasty.

THE OVERSEERS OF THE DOUBLE GRANARY OF UPPER AND LOWER EGYPT

BOHLEKE 1993

We know several high-ranking officials from the end of the Eighteenth and the beginning of the Nineteenth Dynasty who held the economically important office of "overseer of the double granary of Upper and Lower Egypt". This title designated them as heads of the royal grain administration. Some of these officials bore a relation to the god Wepwawet and hence to Asyut. Therefore Brian Bohleke comes to the conclusion that, perhaps with the rise of the "military" pharaoh Horemhab and his Ramesside successors, branches of a larger Asyut family with close connections to the cult of Wepwawet gained influence and key positions in the royal hierarchy (BOHLEKE 1993: 295). The following officials may have reference to Asyut: Wepwawet-mose I under Thutmose IV (BOHLEKE 1993: 194-196); Si-Ese I at the end of the Eighteenth Dynasty; Wepwawet-mose II, Si-Ese II, Qeny, and Si-Ese III during the Nineteenth Dynasty.

Si-Ese I

Si-Ese I, son of Khaa, is known from two stelae (Vienna KHM 126 and Leiden AP 8). He was the overseer of the double granary of Upper and Lower Egypt at the end of the Eighteenth Dynasty (BOHLEKE 1993: 260-280). Several members of his family were chantresses of Atum and Wepwawet. Chantresses of Wepwawet were his mother Taweret and his daughter Iserikh. Also his brother's theophoric name, Wepwawet-mose, shows a close relation of his family to Wepwawet, the chief deity of Asyut. An ancestral home in Asyut, followed by a move to Thebes or Memphis, both administrative capitals, would account nicely for the deities to whom Khaa's descendants showed devotion, but since not even the provenances of the stelae are known, no firm conclusion pertaining to this conjecture can be drawn (BOHLEKE 1993: 274).

Wepwawet-mose II

Wepwawet-mose was overseer of the double granary of Upper and Lower Egypt during the reign of King Sety I. He is known from several stelae (BOHLEKE 1993: 288-297). Wepwawet-mose was married twice; Nofret-Ptah and Sakhmet were his wives. The *wab*-priest of Wepwawet Wia was his father, the scribe of the royal harem Panehesi was his grandfather.

Si-Ese II

Si-Ese II served Ramesses II in his early decades (BOHLEKE 1993: 324-341).

Qeny

Qeny is not attested through any documents of his own, only through those of his son Si-Ese III and son-in-law, the high priest of Osiris Wen-nefer (BOHLEKE 1993: 342-349). As overseer of the double granary of Upper and Lower Egypt he was in office during the reign of Ramesses II.

Si-Ese III

Si-Ese's III career as overseer of the double granary of Upper and Lower Egypt spanned two reigns: from Ramesses II to Merenptah. His family originated at Asyut and was buried there (BOHLEKE 1993: 356-368). He was also buried at Asyut—and not at Deir Drunka (cf. WILD 1971: 307-309)—in a rose granite anthropoid sarcophagus, whose lid is now displayed in the Egyptian Museum of Berlin (SETTGAST 1972: 245-249). Further monuments of high quality are assigned to Si-Ese III, for example a wooden standard-bearer statue (New York, Brooklyn Museum 47.120.2), which most likely was donated by Si-Ese III to the temple of Wepwawet (SATZINGER 1978: 19-20, Figs. 9-10). The back-pillar records an invocation offering (cf. KITCHEN 1980: 153.11-12; KITCHEN 2000: 104):

An offering which the king gives (and) Wepwawet, the Upper Egyptian, power of the Two Lands, great god, lord of heaven that he might grant my name to endure because of what I have accomplished;—for the *Ka*-spirit of the royal scribe, overseer of the double granary in the temple of Usermaatra-setepenra in the estate of Amun, Si-Ese, justified.
(New York, The Brooklyn Museum 47.120.2)

An excellent statue group made of limestone represents Wepwawet and Isis-Hathor (New York, Metropolitan Museum of Art 17.2.5; HAYES 1959: 348-350). It records a speech from Si-Ese III to Osiris (KITCHEN 1980: 152.3-9; KITCHEN 2000: 102-103), and the genealogy of Si-Ese III:

O Osiris, Wennefer, the restored ram, lord of […] great of respect—may you grant my *Ba*-spirit to be divine in the necropolis, and I being divine in the land of the just men, because I am a servant of Abydos […] the great waters in Tanenet. I have fixed the twin plumes upon the Abydos-fetish, within the sarcophagus. I bound the bandage on your body, while the heart of the enemy was placed under your feet. May my soul go forth and take pleasure on earth in all the forms it desires. May I go forth from heaven and descend to earth without being turned back on the way;—for the *Ka*-spirit of the royal scribe, overseer of the double granary of the Two Lands, Si-Ese, justified, son of the dignitary, royal scribe and overseer of the double granary of the Two Lands, Qeny, justified, son of the dignitary, royal scribe, and overseer of the double granary of the Two Lands, Si-Ese, justified.
(New York, Metropolitan Museum of Art 17.2.5)

Pa-Ra-hotep

The Asyut Project found evidence for another hitherto unknown head of the royal grain administration called Pa-Ra-hotep. His titles "royal scribe" and "overseer of the double granary of the lord of the Two Lands" are inscribed on a wooden object (Fig. 106). Pa-Ra-hotep can presumably be dated to the reign of Ramesses II thanks to a paleographical analysis of the inscription by Jan Moje.

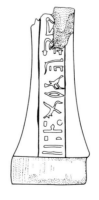

fig. 106: Wooden object mentioning the royal scribe and overseer of the double granary of the lord of the Two Lands Pa-Ra-hotep (Tomb III, S04/231; drawing: Sameh Shafik).

Pa-di-Nemti

WEILL 1950: 57-65; LEAHY 1999: 230-232

Papyrus fragments mention the name of an otherwise unknown king: Pa-di-Nemti "The One whom (the god) Nemti has given." Pa-di-Nemti is represented with skull-cap and a broad diadem with fillet (Fig. 107). Both are typical for the royal iconography of the Twenty-fifth Dynasty.

The papyrus was purchased near Asyut and is inscribed with chapters 18-24, 142, 145, and 146 of the *Book of the Dead*. This proves that the papyrus was produced as part of Pa-di-Nemti's funerary equipment.

Since Pa-di-Nemti is only attested in this papyrus, it is a reasonable assumption to consider him as a local ruler of the region of Asyut (LEAHY 1999: 230-232). It remains to be seen, whether he reigned over Asyut at the end of the Twenty-fifth Dynasty (LEAHY 1999: 231) or slightly earlier. At any rate, he can be considered as one of several local dynasts who ruled small kingdoms during the Third Intermediate Period.

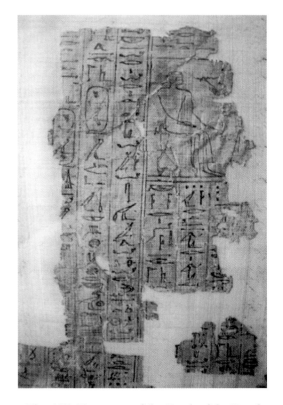

Fig. 107: Fragment of the *Book of the Dead* papyrus of King Pa-di-Nemti. The partially preserved vignette depicts Pa-di-Nemti himself (© James Ede).

The position of Pa-di-Nemti's tomb has been unknown up until now, and also other tombs of the Third Intermediate Period have not yet been localized. However, finds of this epoch show that people continued in using Gebel Asyut al-gharbi as burial ground.

Djed-Hor

KITCHEN 1986:397; ONASCH 1994: 36, 55, 118-119

During the Twenty-fifth Dynasty Asyut seems to have had a hard time. According to the Victory Stela of the Kushite (Nubian) invader Piye (728 BC), Asyut was part of the Theban, and thus Kushite, sphere of influence. Less than sixty years later, during the reign of the Kushite King Taharqa, the Assyrian ruler Assarhaddon seized Memphis in 671 BC and reorganized Egypt. Assurbanipal's annals (*Prism A*) refer to Egyptian local rulers, whom the Assyrian king had personally installed.

A man called Sikhâ (Djed-Hor) ruled over Asyut during this period. There has been no archaeological evidence for this man and his family up until now.

PLOTINUS

CALDERINI 1922; MONTEVECCHI 2000a; HALFWASSEN 2004

The Graeco-Roman philosopher Plotinus (AD 204–270) is the founder and most important thinker of Neo-Platonism. He left an impressive stamp on the philosophy of Late Antiquity as well as the philosophers of the Renaissance and the early Period of the Enlightenment.

Asyut is said to have been Plotinus' hometown, even if nothing is known for certain about his origin. Plotinus studied philosophy in Alexandria with the Platonist philosopher Ammonius Saccas. In 244/245, he settled in Rome and taught there. He left Rome in 268 and died at Minturnae in 270.

Plotinus enjoyed the support of many prominent people, including the Emperor Gallenius and his wife. His chief pupils were Ammenius and Porphyry. The census register Papyrus Oxyrhynchos 984, which eventually refers to Asyut in AD 89/90 (MONTEVECCHI 1998: 49-76; SCHEIDEL 2001: 147-151), mentions a gymnasion and Greek military personnel. It is imaginable that Plotinus experienced here his first intellectual and cultural education, before leaving his hometown (MONTEVECCHI 2000a: 142).

MELITIUS, BISHOP OF LYCOPOLIS/ASYUT

HARDY 1952: 56-69; TIMBIE 1991a: 1584-1585; TIMBIE 1991b: 1585

Melitius, bishop of Lycopolis at the beginning of the fourth century AD, was opposed to the instructions of Peter I, bishop of Alexandria, concerning the readmission of apostate Christians. Melitius became the leader of a schismatic group which adopted a stricter policy. Melitius was excommunicated in 306 and exiled. Upon his return from exile (sometime after 311), he began to organize a schismatic church (TIMBIE 1991a: 1584) that ordained its own bishops in many cities and towns in Egypt. Melitius was strongest in the least-Greek parts of the country. In 327, there were Meletian bishops in every sixth or seventh city of the Delta and in every second or third city of Middle and Upper Egypt (HARDY 1952: 53). The Melitians went on to oppose Athanasius I, bishop of Alexandria, in the fourth century. The twenty-fifth Canon ascribed to Athanasius said:

Whoso saith that the Meletians have a church, the same is accursed.
(CRUM 1927: 22)

Melitius died presumably before 332, but the Melitian movement prospered during the fourth century and a Melitian monasticism arose. However, the Melitians were looked upon as heretics (cf. CRUM 1927: 21-24). For example the sixth–seventh century encomium by Constantine of Asyut on the martyr Claudius records that these heretics practiced various abominations, such as using defiled animals for food. It was also said that Melitius should have tried to carry with him the martyr Claudius' body, when he went northward. Melitians were accused of sorcery during the eighth century AD (CRUM 1927: 22), after which traces of Melitianism disappear (TIMBIE 1991a: 1584).

JOHN OF LYCOPOLIS

BUTLER 1898: 100-106; TILL 1935: 138-154; TILL 1936: 137-140; JARRY 1964; DEVOS 1969a; DEVOS 1969b; DEVOS 1969c; DEVOS 1970; DEVOS 1976; DEVOS 1978; RUSSELL 1981: 52-62; DEVOS 1988; DEVOS 1991; DEVOS 1994; GROSSMANN 2002: 208-210; LUISIER 2004

During the fourth century AD John of Lycopolis (310/320–394/395), an ascetic and recluse, achieved fame due to his abilities as seer and prophet. Men from the Thebaide area as well as from all over Egypt, and even from outside, visited Asyut to consult him, who called himself a "poor man." Even Emperor Theodosius is said to have consulted John. In the *Historia Monachorum in Aegypto* (cf. Chapter Two) is written:

These are the wonders which he (John) performed before strangers who came to see him. As regards his own fellow-citizens, who frequently came to him for their needs, he foreknew and revealed things hidden in the future; he told each man what he had done in secret; and he predicted the rise and fall of the Nile and the annual yield of the crops. In the same way he used to foretell when some divine threat was going to come upon them and exposed those who were to blame for it.
(*Hist. Mon.* I, 11; RUSSELL 1981: 53)

John Cassian described John's impact on his contemporaries as follows:

...first of all Abbot John who lived near Lycon which is a town in the Thebaid; and who was exalted even to the grace of prophecy for his admirable obedience, and was so celebrated all the world over that he was by his merits rendered famous even among kings of this world. For though, as we said, he lived in the most remote parts of the Thebaid, still the Emperor Theodosius did not venture to declare war against the most powerful tyrants before he was encouraged by his utterances and replies: trusting in which as if they had been brought to him from heaven he gained victories over his foes in battles which seemed hopeless.
(John Cassian, *Institutiones coenobiticae* 4.23; SCHAFF/WACE 1995: 226)

Several sources written in Greek, Latin, and Coptic provide information on John, his life, and his work. He was born in Asyut and his parents were Christians. According to the *Historia Lausiaca*—one of the principal documents about Egyptian monasticism written by Palladius at the beginning of the fifth century—he had learned the carpenters' trade while his brother was a dyer. After his parents' death he went to Sketis (the Wadi al-Natrun) and became a monk. From the age of twenty-five to thirty years he was educated in different monasteries, studying with Apa Isidor and Apa Poemen. John's name became famous in far-away monasteries because of his intensive fasting and praying. The angel of the Lord appeared to him and instructed him to return to his hometown and to teach the way of righteousness there.

Therefore John came back to Asyut and, according to the principles of early monasticism, he lived as a hermit in the western mountain on a desert escarpment (*Hist. Mon.* I, 6). The building had no door. Therefore John did not leave his monastic quarters for forty (*Hist. Mon.* I, 4) or forty-eight years (*Historia Lausiaca* XXXV). Disciples gave him food and drink through a window. John did not eat anything apart from fruit. As a result the ascetic life wore down his body and, at the age of ninety years, his beard no longer grew and he fell into a state of decline (*Hist. Mon.* I, 17).

The exact location of John's hermitage is still disputed. Deir el-Azzam (ZUCKERMAN 1995) is a possible site, but the tripartite complex Tomb II (later quarry)/Tomb III/Tomb IV (N13.2/N12.1/N12.2) with its Late Antique corridors connecting the single tombs should be considered as well.

Through the window John stayed in touch with the world outside and he received visitors on Saturday and Sunday. The visitors had to be male; John refused to receive any women. There were a small church (DEVOS 1969: 194) and a rest house (*Hist. Mon.* I, 16; RUSSELL 1981: 54) for the visitors in the vicinity of John's cell.

Some of the visitors seeking John's advice were a tribune (John appeared the man's wife in a dream during night), seven foreign monks, and among them the anonymous author of the *Historia Monachorum in Aegypto* (the conversation with the seven dealt with spiritual matters), an officer (John told him that his wife had given birth to a son whom the officer should send to the monks at the age of seven), a senator asking for help for his wife (John cured her of blindness by giving her healing oil), and a general (John prophesied for him victory and honor in the service of the emperor). Poimenia, a "servant of god" and relative of Emperor Theodosius, traveled with numerous attendants and her own ships to Asyut so that John could cure her of a disease. John cured Poimenia by giving her healing water and oil. Before departure, he warned her about going to Alexandria, but she ignored his words. On their way back, the travellers were attacked by locals near Zawiyat Razin. One man died, others were wounded, Bishop Dionysios was thrown into water and Poimenia was derided.

John was consulted by Emperor Theodosius to whom he prophesied a victory over the usurper Maximus (AD 388) as well as success against Eugenius in AD 395. John's intervention on behalf of Asyut is also connected with Emperor Theodosius (cf. Chapter One).

The *Historia Monachorum in Aegypto* describes John's death:

We then went to see a number of other fathers, and while we were with them, some brothers came to tell us that the blessed John had died in a wonderful manner. He gave orders that for three days no one

would be allowed to visit him, and then, bending his knees in prayer, he died and departed for God, to whom be glory for all eternity. Amen.
(*Hist. Mon.* I, 65; RUSSELL 1981: 62)

CONSTANTINE, BISHOP OF LYCOPOLIS/ASYUT

GARITTE 1950: 287-304; COQUIN 1991: 590-592; SAMIR 1991: 592-593; SCHMELZ 2003: 732-734

Constantine was bishop of Asyut at the end of the sixth and the beginning of the seventh century. Between 578 and 605, the patriarch Damian ordained him bishop of Asyut and vicar for Upper Egypt. Especially the previously mentioned office secured great influence for Constantine.

The Arabic incipit of a nineteenth century manuscript tells us about Constantine's episcopal consecration:

The sun of justice has shone forth for us, and healing is beneath his wings and in his intercession. So now hear, o people who love Christ. It came to pass, when our father Damianos the Archbishop of Alexandria sent for me, me the wretched Constantine, and consecrated me a bishop, without my being worthy of it, for the see of the city of Assiut.
(Paris mss. Arabe 4893; SAMIR 1991: 592).

Constantine also experienced the third Persian occupation of Egypt (AD 619–629). He is said to have transported the body of Saint Elias to Asyut after the destruction of Qusiyyah (GARITTE 1950: 302). He attacked heretics (cf. above: Melitius, bishop of Lycopolis/Asyut) and sorcerers by virtue of his office (COQUIN 1991: 591; SCHMELZ 2003: 732-733). He composed a great number of writings (GARITTE 1950: 287-297):
- Two panegyrics (encomia) on Saint Claudius the Martyr (Coptic, Arabic, and Ethiopic).
- The panegyric (encomium) on Saint George (Coptic and Arabic).
- Two panegyrics (encomia) on the martyr John of Heraclea (Arabic).
- The homily "On the Fallen Soul and Its Exit from This World" (Arabic).
- The panegyric (encomium) on Saint Isidorus of Antioch (or of Chios) (Arabic).
- Two panegyrics (encomia) on Saint Athanasius of Alexandria (Coptic).
- The homily on Lent and the feast of Easter (Coptic).
- The panegyric (encomium) on Shenute (mentioned in the catalogue of the library of the monastery of Apa Elias)

Constantine is said to have been buried in the monastery al-Hanadah, in the Gebel Asyut (cf. COQUIN 1991: 591).

CHAPTER SEVEN

POPULAR RELIGION IN ASYUT

by Meike Becker

They [the Egyptians] are religious to excess, far beyond any other race of men.
(Herodotus, History, II, 37)

This chapter aims to deal with the question of "popular religion" and to find examples for this kind of religiosity in the city of Asyut (cf. BECKER 2004).

The phrase "popular religion" describes the piety and religiousness of the people which is not directly linked with the official religion and state theology. Above all, popular religion includes individual piety, which is an important part of religion in general. To further understanding of the entire complexity of religious thought and acting, which both play an essential role in Egyptian culture, it is necessary to gain an impression of the personal relationship between an individual and a deity.

However, most of the time Egyptological studies focus on the official theology instead of the religious means of expression of the people. This is most probably due to the fact that there are plenty of objects and finds belonging to the official cultic aspects, whereas objects concerning private forms of religion are very rare. Artifacts that are connected to the state theology or the kingship are made from a very durable material and survived the years in a better condition than relics which come from lower social classes and are thus made simpler.

The official religion however serves only to maintain the cosmic order and is not able to give the individual hope, consolation and mercy (cf. SATZINGER 1989: 15).

It seems to be very difficult to grasp the piety or religiosity of an individual or a special group of people in any scientific way, as it is mainly based on feelings and experiences of these individual persons. As all great religions have their roots in some kind of individual experiences (cf. GOLDAMMER 1960: 116), it is possible to work out individual tendencies and to try to combine these with the complexity of religion.

As the kinds of expression of religious life differ in every social class or group, it would be quite interesting to study a religion in view of its "internal pluralism". The expression "internal pluralism" was first used by Günter LANCZKOWSKI (1971: 50-55; 1980: 30-38; ALBERTZ 1978: 3) and it divides the different social classes and professionally orientated religious expressions that are all a place for acting and living religion.

Egyptian society can also be divided into several overlapping social strata, depending on e.g. age, sex, or status and power, which all have a different "religious daylife" (FINNESTAD 1988: 74). It should be very interesting to get an impression of popular religion and different forms of expression in Egypt in general and especially in the city of Asyut.

Aspects of daily life like marriage, birth, illness or death touch every man or woman deeply and cause them to search for divine closeness. They often want to put their lives under the protection of a special deity. Such means of expression of popular religion should be existent during the whole pharaonic history. There is less evidence for such expression during the stretch between the Early Dynastic Period and the Middle Kingdom than in the later periods. In spite of this there are small hints that give proof of a religious initiative which is not identical with the official religion (BAINES 1991: 173). The personal names e.g. give an impression of individual relationships between man and deity during all periods, because they show that the bearer of the name belonged to a special deity or his manifestations (BAINES 1987: 95). Votive offerings from the Early Dynastic Period and the Old Kingdom also attest religious activity follows personal interests (cf. DREYER 1986). Some objects from private households e.g. in Illahun provide evidence for familiar religiosity in the Middle Kingdom (PETRIE 1891: 11). One can also find references in the literature and the biographies of the Middle Kingdom that the life of an individual is completely dependent on a deity. BLUMENTHAL (1998: 213-231) shows the religious influence in the stories of *Sinuhe* and the *Shipwrecked Sailor*. The nomarch Khety II of Asyut from the First Intermediate Period tells in his autobiography (Siut IV, 19-20) that his local god Wepwawet caused him to build and rebuild temples.

The amount of evidence for popular and private religion during the New Kingdom has been continuously growing. People had lots of possibilities to express their personal fondness of a deity. Votive offerings (see e.g. PINCH 1993) and ostraca with prayers (cf. POSENER 1971: 59-63; POSENER 1975: 195-206) show e.g. that individuals not only looked for hope and mercy, but rather that they laid their fate into the hands of their personal deity. People also used oracles to establish a connection with the divine. The deified King Amenhotep I has been the most important oracle deity in the village of Deir el-Medineh. Another way to express this relationship are stelae which a devotee dedicated to a deity out of a special motive. Well known examples are the stelae from Deir el-Medineh (for translation see ASSMANN 1999: 148-168). However, there are more than 500 stelae found in Asyut in the Salakhana Tomb, Siut VII (see below).

The possibilities to express popular religion constantly increased after the New Kingdom. This development was probably influenced by the unstable political situation, when several foreign sovereigns ruled over Egypt. If the living conditions are not safe the need for divine affection and protection will grow stronger and stronger. Oracles and magic successively grew in popularity, disseminating a sense of security and hence helping people cope with their lives. The cults of divine animals which must have been supported by the mass of people increased in a spectacular fashion.

Returning to the "internal pluralism of religions", several strata within the popular religion can be determined that differ in their social embedding, their personal interests and the way religiosity was put into practice.

The local characteristics of religion which strongly influence people have to be mentioned first. Local cults often form the foundation for popular religious practices because e.g. an individual can far better conceptualize a regional deity than one from a remote area, thus making it highly probable that a local god will be favored over a non-regional deity. The people stand under the protection of the god of their city, because "the god, who is in the city, is the one, life and death of the inhabitants depend on" (Papyrus Insinger 28,4).

Special religious groups form the next tier, because "in its formal expression devotion is often communal or congregational and arises from, or is even dependent upon, the coming together of a group of people for a common devotional purpose" (KINSLEY 1986: 232) It is likely that people belonging to the same profession congregate to pray to a deity. People who carry out the same work often share the same interests and motives that are applied to a specific deity, which serves as a patron saint to this "trade group". The small chapels in the north of the village of the workmen and next to the paths to the Valley of the Kings and the Queen's Valley in Deir el-Medineh (cf. BRUYÉRE 1948: 104-105; SADEK 1988: 59; ANDREU 2002: 33) or the chapels in Amarna which are located in the N.E.-edge of the village and have been misconstrued by the first excavators as tomb chapels, although none contain a shaft (cf. PEET/ WOOLLEY 1923: 92-108) show that only a handful people met to perform the same service to a deity and even carry out the duties of a priest (ČERNÝ 1927: 194-95).

Religion also plays an important role within the families. Part of the family-religion was e.g. the ancestor cult that worshipped dead members of a family through stelae and busts as *Akh-iker-n-Ra* (DEMARÉE 1983: 284).

The term individual piety refers to a single person that has built up a relationship to his personal saviour-god. The personal relationship is not solely limited to a certain social class, but existent in all classes. This phenomenon has often been misinterpreted as belonging to a very low social group, owing to the self-humiliation of the pious people who use e.g. the expression *s:nmḥ*—"*to make oneself poor*" (ERMAN/GRAPOW 1926-31: IV, 165, 12) to describe the word "*pray*." The relation between man and deity is based on reciprocal acts. The individual cries for help in sorrow, the deity rescues him and receives the thankfulness of man; or the individual worships the deity with prayers and offerings to be in the favour of the deity.

As already mentioned several hints are known of in Asyut, that show acts of popular religion. In 1922 Wainwright discovered a large quantity of votive stelae from the New Kingdom in a layer of gravel in the Twelfth Dynasty tomb of Djefai-Hapi III (Siut VII). These stelae are known by the name of "Salakhana-stelae," because the tomb is located behind the old slaughterhouse of Asyut. The number of stelae is staggering and is somewhere about 500 to 600 (DUQUESNE [personal communication] reports that there are more than 500 stelae in the Egyptian Museum in Cairo; WAINWRIGHT 1928: 175; BEINLICH 1975: 493; EISSA 1994: 59, n.1). Most of the stelae share a similar iconography. The worshipper is shown standing in front of Wepwawet, who is represented standing on a standard and which in turn is followed by several stout, small canids. Nonetheless, also stelae in which Anubis, Osiris and Hathor of Medjeden are worshiped exist.

Undecorated stelae as they were found during season 2004 by The Asyut Project in the tomb of Khety II (Siut IV; S04/008; S04/020; cf. Fig. 108), suggest that simple limestone stelae existed that perhaps were merely colour decorated. These stelae could be manufactured without actual need and stored and, after the devotee made a choice, the colour decoration was completed. This theory can be supported by several of the Salakhana-stelae which only show the inscription *Wp-w3wt Šmʿ.w sšm t3.wj*— "Wepwawet from Upper Egypt, Power of the Two Lands." One can assume that the stelae were produced earlier and the name of the devotee could be added later with color or ink.

Another stela from Asyut, which was probably also found in the tomb of Djefai-Hapi III (MUNRO 1963: 51, Pl. IV, no.7), is made out of clay and it seems as if it was made by pressing a model into the clay. And one stela shows a short hieratic inscription (DUQUESNE, 2000: 28, Pl. Va-b) and states a rough and fast production. It is also possible that they were cheaper to produce, so that they were affordable for people from lower social classes. The undecorated stelae (Fig. 108) date without a doubt to the New Kingdom because of the chisel-marks with a fishbone design (cf. KLEMM/KLEMM 1993: 261-262).

In the following, two limestone stelae from the Ramesside Period will be described and translated to give a general impression.

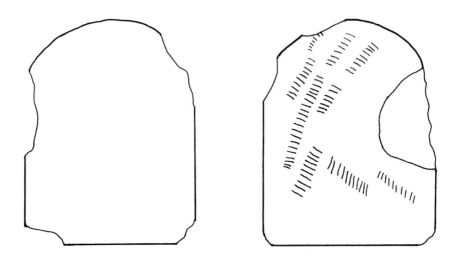

Fig. 108: Undecorated stela (S04/020; drawing: Meike Becker).

The stela London BM EA 1632 (Fig. 109; cf. BRUNNER 1958: 5-19, Pl. III; BRUNNER-TRAUT 1974: Fig. 52; SADEK 1988: 41-42; BIERBRIER 1993: Pls. 82-83; VAN DIJK 2000: 312; KESSLER 2001: 162-168; DUQUESNE 2003: 42, Pl. 9) tells the story of an official called Pa-ta-weret:

Fig. 109: Stela London BM EA 1632 (Ramesside Period; after BIERBRIER 1993: Pl. 83).

Fig. 110: Stela London BM EA 891 (Ramesside Period; after Bierbrier 1993: Pl. 81).

Pa-ta-weret (the devotee). The *wab*-priest Amen-mose. Wepwawet, the divine power, the power of the Two Lands, the great god, the lord of heaven. An offer that the king and An<ubis>, with good teeth (?),[1] the good god, give to the *Ka* of the praised of the good god, Pa-ta-weret. Wepwawet-Ra, lord of adoration, the saviour, <lord of> Asyut, against the crocodile and all fishes (?). Amun, very strong for the youth. Don't let (it) bite you!
(London BM EA 1632)

---
1 Sadek suggested *nfr bj3*—"with good miracles" (cf. Sadek 1988: 41, n. 3).

The stela is divided in four register. A procession scene is presented in the uppermost register. On the right side the devotee Pa-ta-weret is standing, with his arms in the adoration gestus. He bears a bouquet of flowers in his left hand. Next to him is a *wab*-priest carrying a vessel and a fan. They are standing on the opposite side of the standard of Wepwawet, which is carried by eight standard-bearers. Four corpulent canids are in the rear of the worshipper and the priest.

On the left side of the second register, a man is kneeling and giving a libation offering. In the middle of the scene one can see an offering table with breads placed on it. Next to the table a deity with the head of a jackal is shown squatting. On the right side a larger jackal is lying on a shrine.

In the third register an offering table stands in between two deities. The one on the left side is wearing the head of a ram and a feather-crown and holds a *was*-scepter and an *ankh*-sign in his hands. On the other side Wepwawet-Ra, a jackal-headed deity, stands in front of four canides, carrying a harpoon. With this harpoon he is stabbing a crocodile in the lowest register, that is following an escaping man. The upright going man is breaking through the register line. This probably means that both scenes belong together.

The stela seems to bear witness to the thankfulness of Pa-ta-weret, who was rescued from a dangerous crocodile by his saviour Wepwawet-Ra. If this is correct, the procession in the upper register would probably represent the moment of the donation of the stela. Pa-ta-weret's very personal reason for offering this stela shows that religion played a very important role in the life of people. People like Pa-ta-weret used religion in a very private sphere to come into contact with the divine in order to utter their wishes, hopes and thanks.

The stela London BM EA 891 (Fig. 110; cf. MUNRO 1963: 51, Pl. V; BIERBRIER 1993: Pl. 81; DURISCH 1993: 215, Fig. 5) also belongs to the group of objects that show several expressions of personal piety. On the left side the dedicator Hori—a soldier—is praying in front of the Wepwawet-standard, which is followed by four canids. The text reads:

Wepwawet/The soldier of the garrison made it. The soldier of the garrisons of pharaoh—may he live, prosper and be healthy—Hori made (this stela). Show mercy to me, Wepwawet. (Because) I am a servant of your house.
(London BM EA 891)

He asks for the mercy of Wepwawet. He shows his faith in Wepwawet by giving himself and his own life to the deity. One can also find the expression *ḥtp n=j*—"show mercy with me" on the stela of Neferabu from Deir el-Medineh, who seems to regret a faux-pas (ASSMANN 1999: 150).

It is also interesting to observe that there are lots of soldiers among the dedicators of the stelae, probably because of the warlike character of Wepwawet (GRAEFE 1986: 863). Asyut is also situated at a very strategic important place. It is hence obvious that more soldiers lived there than in the other cities of Egypt.

During the Late Period, private and unofficial forms of religion were popularly expressed through the offering of votive mummies. Early visitors already reported that lots of votive mummies could be found in the necropolis of Asyut. The members of the Napoleonic expedition describe in the *Description de l'Égypte*:

In all of the tombs of Asyut one sees a large number of caskets that formerly encloud the mummies. We have even found in several [tombs], fragments of the mummies themselves, particularly wolves, jackals, young cats and also birds of prey still retaining their plumage.
(JOLLOIS/DEVILLIERS 1821: 153; RUSSELL 2001: 314)

John Gardner Wilkinson writes in 1837:

The tombs in the mountain above Lycopolis, the modern E'Sioot, contain the mummies of wolves, many of which I have examined, and ascertained to be sacred animals of the place.
(WILKINSON 1837: 27)

And also the German Georg Ebers mentions canid mummies (EBERS 1886: 162-63). All three scholars from the nineteenth century suggest that mainly mummies of canids (jackals, dogs) were buried in Asyut. Lots of mummies are said to be from the tomb of Djefai-Hapi III (Siut VII). The two main deities of Asyut, Wepwawet and Anubis, are very well known because of their theriomorphic appearance as canids, so such a huge number of canid mummies seems to be usual. Numerous mummies were already discovered during the excavations of Schiaparelli and Hogarth (LORTET/GAILLARD 1903-1909: 259). Several of these mummies show strangulation marks (CHARRON 1990: 211; cf. LORTET/GAILLARD 1903-1909: 259, 283-286, 294; DURISCH 1993: 219, n. 32). This could indicate that the canids were murdered on purpose to produce a great number of offering mummies.

However, other animals such as ibises, falcons, baboons, bulls (for an illustration of a bull mummy from Asyut see CHARRON 2002: 203, no. 92) or cats were also mummified in Asyut (KESSLER 1989: 22; IKRAM 2005: xvii-xviii; bull mummies: London BM EA 47615, BM EA 47622, BM EA 47623; for the baboons see: JOLLOIS/DEVILLIERS 1821: 153; RUSSELL 2001: 314). Lots of mummies of birds were found by the Asyut Project during the season 2005 in the gravel in the tomb of Iti-ibi (Siut III). All of these mummies belong to the group of votive mummies, which were dedicated as offerings in the temples of certain deities. The mummies were "purchased by pilgrims, performed the same function that a lighted candle does in a church; they acted as a physical manifestation of a prayer addressed by the pilgrim to the divinity for eternity" (IKRAM 2002: 235).

The Salakhana-stelae from the New Kingdom portray several small canids. These stelae could prove the existence of a pack of canids which belonged to the temple. It could be interpreted as a Ramesside precursor of the animal cult of the Late Period. During the Late Period, "breeding stations" existed in the surroundings of a temple where animals were raised to serve as votive mummies in order to become a mediator between man and deity. However, inscriptional evidence has yet to give support to this hypothesis of long lasting animal worship.

It seems that private religious activity was very high in Asyut. One can find lots of objects that are related to "popular religion" such as the Salakhana-stelae or the votive mummies. Although the examples for popular religion are directly linked to the official theology (e.g. stelae or the dedication of mummies in a temple), one has to differ between both layers of religious expression, because different motives and conditions form the basis for popular religion or official theology. The finds from Asyut indicate that the people addressed themselves to their local deities Wepwawet, Anubis, Osiris and Hathor. At the moment, it is still questionable if the tomb of Djefai-Hapi III (Siut VII) was a special sacred place where the people came to pray, or if another comparable place exists anywhere in the necropolis. In Tomb N13.1 in the necropolis of Asyut, which was discovered by the Asyut Project during the season 2005, several hieratic graffiti mention a temple of Djefai-Hapi (Fig. 32). This probably refers to one of the nomarchs of the Middle Kingdom.

CHAPTER EIGHT

ATELIERS, SCHOOLS, AND KNOWLEDGE

Toward the end of the First Intermediate Period the workmanship at Assiut was well ahead of anything else being produced at any other site except at Thebes.
(SMITH 1957: 223)

During the early Nineteenth Dynasty the ancient Upper Egyptian town of Si'ut (modern Asyut) was the home not only of several well-to-do officials of the national administration, but also of an accomplished atelier of sculptors, to whose able hands we owe ... admirable pieces of private tomb statuary.
(HAYES 1959: 347-349)

Chapter One already dealt with Asyut's impact on Egypt's *cultural memory*. Texts from First Intermediate Period and Middle Kingdom Asyut were valued even during the Roman Period. They were copied in libraries and tombs all over Egypt as if they had been part of an encyclopedia of the Egyptian culture (VERNUS 1996: 557; KAHL 1999). Still the copies in the library of Tebtynis—the final known destination of Asyuti texts—transmit the names of those Asyuti people, for whose tombs these texts were intended more than two thousand years earlier: Khety I, Iti-ibi, Khety II, and Djefai-Hapi I. These nomarchs had not only such highly esteemed texts at their disposal, but also other masterpieces produced by Egyptian artists and architects. Tomb III with its large inner hall (Fig. 52), and Tomb I (Pls. 6-8) with its immense size, belong to the most impressive buildings of the First Intermediate Period and Middle Kingdom, respectively.

Texts and architecture of the tomb of Djefai-Hapi give evidence of an interplay between residential and local forces in its execution. The designation of a scribe in this tomb indicates that it was built with means of the royal house (Siut I, 132; cf. Chapter Four).

This explains the use of originally royal mortuary texts (mortuary liturgy no. 7: KAHL 1994; KAHL 1999: 53-186) on the tomb walls and reminiscences of royal funerary architecture in the ground plan (ENGEL/KAHL forthcoming). Recording the ten contracts and presenting a lengthy catalogue of epithets, however, seems to be a local feature (fragments of a contract are also preserved in the Salakhana Tomb).

Statues of Djefai-Hapi I establish a similar result, namely the combination of residential and local features (cf. LEOSPO 1988: 102). Two wooden statues, which are assigned to Djefai-Hapi I (Turin; Paris, Louvre E 26915), tower above all other Middle Kingdom private statuary. Their height of more than two meters is unsurpassed for this period and demanded a well trained craftsman. Some physiognomic features of the Louvre statue (Fig. 104), for example the elongated body, point to a local style, while others, such as the geometrical interpretation of the curls, find their parallels in a relief from the royal temple at Lisht (DELANGE 1987: 77). The latter feature is also traceable in the curls of one of the wooden statues of Nakhti (CHASSINAT/PALANQUE 1911: Pl. 5); the high quality of Asyuti workmanship is also reflected in his statues. They are of such a high quality (cf. Fig. 77) that manuals of Egyptian art refer to them again and again.

Vivid examples of the high esteem of Asyuti statuary are the finds of statues abroad. Presumably during the Second Intermediate Period statues of persons named Djefai-Hapi were brought to Sudan and the Near East (HELCK 1976: 101-115). They were valued as prestige objects in the Sudan at Kerma (Fig. 99-100; KENDALL 1997: 24-27) and Gebel Barkal (REISNER 1931: 80; DUNHAM 1937-1938: 14, Fig. 7) and at Tell Hizzin, Lebanon (CHÉHAB 1969: 22, Pl. 4.1).

Sporadically diagonal star clocks (Pl. 11a) were painted on the inner side of Middle Kingdom coffin lids (NEUGEBAUER/PARKER 1960: 1-21; 1969: 8-10; LOCHER 1983: 141-144; LOCHER 1992: 201-207; KAHL 1993: 95-107; LEITZ 1995: 58-116; KAHL 1999: 197-205). These star clocks could help in dividing the nocturnal hours and determining the seasons (SCHRAMM 1981: 219-220). On the coffins, however, they were depicted canonically. They had a long tradition and did not represent the firmament at the time of the deceased's funeral, but were rather an idealized tool for the deceased's orientation in the hereafter.

At present about twenty coffins with representations of diagonal star clocks are known. Most of them come from Asyut. Presumably they were composed in Asyut (KAHL 1993: 95-107).

These star clocks were the prototype for astronomical texts and depictions of the New Kingdom, the Late Period, and the Ptolemaic Period (KAHL 1999: 201-205). From the Roman Period fragments of decan lists are preserved, which were transmitted from Asyut to Tebtynis (OSING 1998a: 92-94).

Orthographical peculiarities, as well as the exclusive attestation of many Coffin Texts spells in Asyut, illustrate the existence of a local intellectual school (SCHENKEL 1996: 124-125; KAHL 1999: 338-339; cf. LESKO 1979: 77-88). Not only coffins, but also Asyuti tomb walls and papyri (Papyrus Berlin 10480-10482; KAPLONY-HECKEL 1986: 52-53) inscribed with Coffin Texts are known.

In addition, most of the Asyuti Middle Kingdom coffins represent local types of decoration that differ markedly from comparable material in the rest of Egypt (Pl. 11b; WILLEMS 1988: 102).

Several seated calcite statuettes representing a peculiar style give clear evidence for a local workshop of sculptors (VANDIER 1958: 161; TEFNIN 1988: 25-27; TEETER 1990: 104-106). Two of these statues come from the tombs of Mesehti and Nakhti, respectively, and point to the existence of this local workshop during the early Middle Kingdom. Altogether nine statues of this local style are known: Brussels E. 5596; Cairo CG 235 (JE 30971); Cairo JE 44986; Boston MFA 1971.20; Hannover, Kestner-Museum 1935.200.40; Moscow, Pushkin Museum 4760; Paris, private collection; San

Jose, Rosicrucian Museum 1763; Seattle Art Museum 44.34.

Other Middle Kingdom statues show peculiarities that can be interpreted as being specific Asyuti features, for example disproportionately long hands (Figs. 42, 77).

Thus we may conclude that Asyut was witness to an excellent school of scribes, theologians, architects, and sculptors during the First Intermediate Period and the Middle Kingdom. They were able to produce high quality texts and art works, while at the same time paying regard to local types and style. Presumably they worked at the nomarchs' court or the temples and were in touch with artists and scholars from the Residence.

This high cultural standard was resumed during the New Kingdom (cf. Pl. 12). Statues and reliefs of the early Ramesside Period are linked with the style of the late Eighteenth Dynasty and point once again to an accomplished atelier of sculptors (HAYES 1959: 347-349; KARIG 1968: 34). Statues of the overseer of the double granary of Upper and Lower Egypt Si-Ese III (Pl. 13), and of the king's scribe Iuny, as well as reliefs from the Tomb of Amen-hotep (Fig. 82) are especially worth mentioning.

More than 140 graffiti in Tomb N13.1 give evidence of school teaching and school excursions during the New Kingdom, particularly during the

Fig. 111: Statue of a dog, Paris, Louvre E 11657 (© Musée du Louvre/Maurice et Pierre Chuzeville).

Eighteenth Dynasty (KAHL 2006). Since some of these graffiti quote literary texts, this find attests to a classical education for—presumably Asyuti—scribes. Drawings are also among the graffiti, some of them bearing comparison with graffiti from Deir el-Medineh (Pl. 14a). A limestone ostracon found in the debris of Tomb III can also be

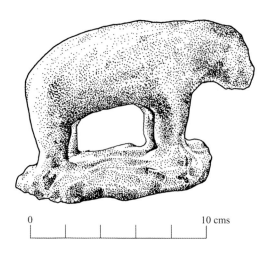

Fig. 112: Figure of a hippopotamus (Tomb N13.1; S06/022; drawing: Ammar Abu Bakr).

connected with scribal or artistic exercises (Pl. 14b).

Despite meagre evidence of Late statuary from Asyut, the statue of a dog (Fig. 111) attributed to the Graeco-Roman Period foreshadows the continuity of good quality workshops in the town.

From the Roman Period there is also inscriptional evidence for a group statue made of gold and iron ore representing the contending gods Horus and Seth (OSING 1998b: 143-150). The fact that this statue is explicitly mentioned points to its extraordinary importance in respect of religion but presumably also in regard to its workmanship.

Today almost completely destroyed Coptic wall paintings still reveal good artistic quality (JOHANN GEORG 1914: 45).

Beside these high quality works of art there are many artifacts that give evidence of "popular art," for example ceramic statuettes of hippopotamoi (Fig. 112; cf. also TONY-RÉVILLON 1950: 59-61) or some of the votives found in the Salakhana Tomb (cf. Chapter Seven and DUQUESNE 2007).

At present our knowledge about potters' workshops, faience production, and glass studios in Asyut is still too limited to make a clear statement about local features. Examinations of pottery (cf. Pl. 15; Figs. 38-39), faience (Pl. 16a, b), and glass (Pl. 16c) found in Asyut have only just started. For example, one cannot definitely answer the question whether there was a glass studio at Asyut during the Amarna Period. The discovery of a thin fragment of translucent turquoise-blue glass, having a slender flame or feather pattern in yellow, white, and dark blue, is said to come from el-Amarna, because there is no evidence for a glass studio at Asyut (COONEY 1976: 49). The present state of Asyut's archaeological exploration, however, does not permit a final decision on this matter; the entire city has not been explored yet. It would be rash to conclude that there had not been a glass studio simply because we do not have any positive evidence at the moment. We still have to solve the question of workshops, not only for the Amarna Period, but for later periods as well.

The study of regional workmanship in Ancient Egypt is still at the beginning. A case study concerning Asyut will contribute essentially to the much too long neglected topic.

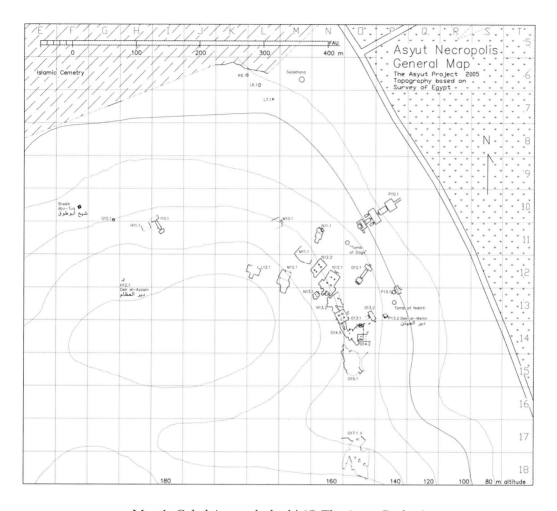

Map 1: Gebel Asyut al-gharbi (© The Asyut Project)

Chronology of Ancient Egypt

Early Dynastic Period (c. 3040-2731 BC)
    Dynasty 1 (c. 3040-2870 BC)
    Dynasty 2 (2870-2731 BC)

Old Kingdom (c. 2731-2205 BC)
    Dynasty 3 (2731-2658 BC)
    Dynasty 4 (2658-2539 BC)
    Dynasty 5 (2539-2390 BC)
    Dynasty 6 (2390- 2226 BC)
    Dynasties 7/8 (2226-2205 BC)

First Intermediate Period (c. 2205-2020 BC)
    Dynasties 9/10 (Herakleopolitan) (2205-2020 BC)
    Early Dynasty 11 (Theban) (2125-c. 2020 BC)

Middle Kingdom (c. 2020-1630 BC)
    Late Dynasty 11 (c. 2020-1985 BC)
    Dynasty 12 (1985-1773 BC)
    Dynasty 13 (1773-c. 1630 BC)

Second Intermediate Period (c. 1630-1540 BC)
    Dynasty 14
    Dynasty 15 (Hyksos) (-c. 1530 BC)
    Dynasty 16
    Dynasty 17 (Theban) (c. 1580-1540 BC)

New Kingdom (c. 1539-c. 1077 BC)
    Dynasty 18 (c. 1539-1292 BC)
    Dynasty 19 (Ramesside) (1292-1191 BC)
    Dynasty 20 (Ramesside) (1190-c. 1077 BC)

Third Intermediate Period (c. 1076-664 BC)
    Dynasty 21 (Tanite) (c. 1076-944 BC)
    Dynasty 22 (Bubastite) (943-c. 746 BC)
    Dynasty 23 (c. 845-c. 730 BC)
    Dynasty 24 (Saite) (736-723 BC)
    Dynasty 25 (722-655 BC)

Late Period (664-332 BC)
- Dynasty 26 (Saite) (664-525 BC)
- Dynasty 27 (First Persian Period) (525-404 BC)
- Dynasty 28 (404-399 BC)
- Dynasty 29 (Mendes) (399-380 BC)
- Dynasty 30 (Sebennytos) (380-343 BC)
- Second Persian Period (343-332 BC)

Graeco-Roman Period (332 BC-AD 642)
- Macedonian Dynasty (332-305 BC)
- Ptolemaic Dynasty (305-30 BC)
- Roman, later Byzantine, Empire (30 BC-AD 642)
- Coptic Period (Late second century AD-AD 642)
- Third Persian Period (AD 618/619-AD 629)

Arab Conquest (AD 642)

Bibliography

ALBERTZ 1978: Rainer Albertz, *Persönliche Frömmigkeit und offizielle Religion* (Stuttgart 1978).

ANDREU 2002: Guillemette Andreu, *Les artistes de Pharaon. Deir el-Médineh et la Vallée des Rois* (Paris 2002).

ANTONINI 1940: Luciana Antonini, Le chiese cristiane nell'Egitto dal IV al IX secolo secondo i documenti dei papiri greci, in: *Aegyptus. Rivista italiana di egittologia e di papirologia* 20, 1940, 160-208.

ASSMANN 1992: Jan Assmann, *Das kulturelle Gedächtnis: Schrift, Erinnerung und politische Identität in frühen Hochkulturen* (München 1992).

ASSMANN 1999: Jan Assmann, *Ägyptische Hymnen und Gebete* (Fribourg ²1999).

BAEDEKER 1929: *Baedeker's Egypt* ⁸1929 (reprint Norwich 1974).

BAGNALL 1998: Roger S. Bagnall, "Cults and Names of Ptolemais in Upper Egypt", in: Willy Clarysse/Antoon Schoors/Harco Willems (eds.), *Egyptian Religion. The Last Thousand Years. Studies Dedicated to the Memory of Jan Quaegebeur* (*Orientalia Lovanensia Analecta* 85; Leuven 1998) II, 1093-1101.

BAGNALL/FRIER 1994: Roger S. Bagnall/Bruce W. Frier, *The demography of Roman Egypt* (*Cambridge Studies in Population, Economy and Society in Past Time* 23; Cambridge 1994).

BAGNALL/FRIER/RUTHERFORD 1997: Roger S. Bagnall/Bruce W. Frier/Ian C. Rutherford (eds.), *The Census Register P.Oxy. 984: The Reverse of Pindar's Paeans* (*Papyrologica Bruxellensia* 29; Bruxelles 1997).

BAILLET 1926: Jules Baillet, *Inscriptions Grecques et Latines des Tombeaux des Rois ou Syringes* (*Mémoires publiés par les membres de l'Institut Français d'Archéologie Orientale du Caire* 42; Le Caire 1926).

BAINES 1987: John Baines, "Practical Religion and Piety", in: *Journal of Egyptian Archaeology* 73, 1987, 79-98.

BAINES 1991: John Baines, *Society, Morality and Religious Practice*, in: Byron E. Shafer (ed.), *Religion in Ancient Egypt. Gods, Myths, and Personal Practice* (London 1991) 123-200.

BAYLE 1852: Bayle St. John, *Village Life in Egypt*, vol. II (London 1852).

BECKER 2004: Meike Becker, *Varietäten inoffizieller Religion am Beispiel von Assiut: definitorische Überlegungen anhand ausgewählter Belege* (unpublished M.A. thesis; Münster 2004).

BECKER 2006: Meike Becker, Djefaihapi – ein Name mit langer Tradition, in: *Göttinger Miszellen. Beiträge zur ägyptologischen Diskussion* 210, 2006, 7-11.

BEINLICH 1975: Horst Beinlich, Assiut, in: *Lexikon der Ägyptologie*. I (Wiesbaden 1975) 489-495.

BEINLICH 1976: Horst Beinlich, *Studien zu den „Geographischen Inschriften" (10.-14. o.äg.Gau)* (*Tübinger Ägyptologische Beiträge* 2; Bonn 1976).

BEINLICH 2000: Horst Beinlich, *Das Buch vom Ba* (*Studien zum Altägyptischen Totenbuch* 4; Wiesbaden 2000).

BERMAN 1999: Lawrence M. Berman, *The Cleveland Museum of Art. Catalogue of Egyptian Art* (New York 1999).

BIERBRIER 1993: Morris L. Bierbrier, *Hieroglyphic Texts from Egyptian Stelae etc.*, Part 12 (London 1993).

BIETAK 1985: Manfred Bietak, Zu den nubischen Bogenschützen aus Assiut: ein Beitrag zur Geschichte der Ersten Zwischenzeit, in: Paule Posener-Kriéger (ed.), *Mélanges Gamal Eddin Mokhtar* (*Bibliothèque d'Étude* 97/1; Le Caire 1985) 87-97.

BIETAK 1994: Manfred Bietak (ed.), *Pharaonen und Fremde. Dynastien im Dunkel* (Wien 1994).

BILABEL 1950: Friedrich Bilabel, *Sammelbuch Griechischer Urkunden aus Ägypten* 5/3 (Wiesbaden 1950).

BLUMENTHAL 1998: Elke Blumenthal, Sinuhes persönliche Frömmigkeit, in: Irene Shirun-Grumach (ed.) *Jerusalem Studies in Egyptology* (Ägypten und das Alte Testament 40; Wiesbaden 1998) 213-231.

BOCK 1901: W. de Bock, *Matériaux pour servir à l'archéologie de l'Égypte chrétienne* (St. Pétersbourg 1901).

BOGDANOVIĆ 1993: Bogdan Bogdanović, *Die Stadt und der Tod* (Klagenfurt – Salzburg 1993).

BOGDANOVIĆ 1994: Bogdan Bogdanović, *Architektur der Erinnerung* (Klagenfurt – Salzburg 1994).

BOHLEKE 1993: Briant Bohleke, *The Overseers of Double Granaries of Upper and Lower Egypt in the Egyptian New Kingdom, 1570-1085 B.C.* (New Haven 1993).

BORCHARDT 1911: Ludwig Borchardt, *Statuen und Statuetten von Königen und Privatleuten im Museum von Kairo, CG 1-380* (*Catalogue Général des Antiquités Égyptiennes du Musée du Caire*; Berlin 1911).

BORCHARDT/RICKE 1929: L. Borchardt/H. Ricke, *L'Égypte. Architecture, paysages, scènes populaires* (Paris 1929).

BOURRIAU 1988: Janine Bourriau, *Pharaohs and Mortals. Egyptian Art in the Middle Kingdom. Exhibition organised by the Fitzwilliam Museum Cambridge 19 April to 26 June, Liverpool 18 July to 4 September 1988* (Cambridge 1988).

BOWMAN/ROGAN 1999: Alan K. Bowman/Eugene Rogan, Agriculture in Egypt from Pharaonic to Modern Times, in: Alan K. Bowman/Eugene Rogan (eds.), *Agriculture in Egypt. From Pharaonic to Modern Times* (*Proceedings of the British Academy* 96; Oxford 1999) 1-32.

BOWRING 1998: (Sir) John Bowring, *Report on Egypt 1823-1838 under the reign of Mohamed Ali* (London 1998).

BOYAVAL 1965: B. Boyaval, Les ostraca d'Edfa, in: *Bulletin de l'Institut Français d'Archéologie Orientale du Caire* 63, 1965, 37-72.

BOYLAN 1922: Patrick Boylan, *Thoth, the Hermes of Egypt: A Study of Some Aspects of Theological Thought in Ancient Egypt* (London 1922).

BREASTED 1906: James Henry Breasted, *Ancient Records of Egypt. Historical Documents from the Earliest Times to the Persian Conquest. Volume 1: The First to the Seventeenth Dynasties* (New York 1906).

BRUNNER 1937: Hellmut Brunner, *Die Texte aus den Gräbern der Herakleopolitenzeit von Siut mit Übersetzungen und Erläuterungen* (*Ägyptologische Forschungen* 5; Glückstadt 1937).

BRUNNER 1958: Hellmut Brunner, Eine Dankstele an Upuaut, in: *Mitteilungen des Deutschen Archäologischen Instituts Abteilung Kairo* 16, 1958, 5-19.

BRUNNER-TRAUT 1974: Emma Brunner-Traut, *Die Alten Ägypter: Verborgenes Leben unter Pharaonen* (Stuttgart 1974).

BRUNNER-TRAUT/BRUNNER 1981: Emma Brunner-Traut/Hellmut Brunner, *Die ägyptische Sammlung der Universität Tübingen* (Mainz 1981).

BRUNNER-TRAUT/HELL 1962: Emma Brunner-Traut/Vera Hell, *Aegypten. Studienreiseführer mit Landeskunde* (Stuttgart 1962).

BRUYÈRE 1948: Bernard Bruyère, *Rapport sur les Fouilles de Deir el-Médineh 1935-40* (*Fouilles de l'Institut Français de l'Archéologie Orientale* 20; Le Caire 1948).

BUCHBERGER 1993: Hannes Buchberger, *Transformation und Transformat. Sargtextstudien I* (*Ägyptologische Abhandlungen* 52; Wiesbaden 1993).

DE BUCK 1947: Adriaan de Buck, *The Egyptian Coffin Texts. III. Texts of Spells 164-267* (*The University of Chicago Oriental Publications* 64; Chicago 1947).

DE BUCK 1961: Adriaan de Buck, *The Egyptian Coffin Texts. VII. Texts of Spells 787-1185* (*The University of Chicago Oriental Publications* 87; Chicago 1961).

BUDGE 1911: E.A. Wallis Budge, *Cook's Handbook for Egypt and the Egyptian Sûdân* (London ³1911).

BUDGE 1921: E.A. Wallis Budge, *Cook's Handbook for Egypt and theEgyptian Sûdân* (London ⁴1921).

BUHL 1959: Marie-Louise Buhl, *The Late Egyptian Anthropoid Stone Sarcophagi* (*Nationalmuseets Skrifter. Arkæologisk-Historisk Række* VI; København 1959).

BUTLER 1898: Cuthbert Butler, *The Lausiac History of Palladius: a critical discussion together with notes on early Egyptian monachism* (Cambridge 1898).

CALDERINI 1922: Aristide Calderini, Nella Patria di Plotino, in: *Aegyptus. Rivista italiana di egittologia e di papirologia* 3, 1922, 255-274.

CALDERINI 1980: Aristide Calderini, *Dizionario dei nomi geografici e topografici dell'Egitto greco-romano a cura di Sergio Daris* 3,3 (Milano 1980).

CAPART 1936: Jean Capart (ed.), *Travels in Egypt [December 1880 to May 1891]. Letters of Charles Edwin Wilbour* (Brooklyn N.Y. 1936).

CAPEL/MARKOE 1996: Anne K. Capel/Glenn E. Markoe (eds.), *Mistress of the House, Mistress of Heaven. Women in Ancient Egypt* (New York 1996).

CAUVILLE 1997: Sylvie Cauville, *Le Temple de Dendara. Les chapelles osiriennes.* (*Dendara* X/1; Le Caire 1997).

ČERNÝ 1927: Jaroslav Černý, Le culte d'Amenophis Ier chez les ouvriers de la Nécropole thébaine, in: *Bulletin de l'Institut Français de l'Archéologie Orientale* 27, 1927, 159-203.

ČERNÝ 1954: Jaroslav Černý, Consanguineous Marriages in Pharaonic Egypt, in: *Journal of Egyptian Archaeology* 40, 1954, 23-29.

CHADEFAUD 1982: Catherine Chadefaud, *Les statues porte-enseignes de l'Égypte ancienne (1580 – 1085 avant J.C.). Signification et insertion dans le culte du Ka royal* (Paris 1982).

CHARRON 1990: Alain Charron, Massacres d'animaux à la Basse Epoque, in: *Révue d'Égyptologie* 41, 1990, 209-213.

CHARRON 2002: Alain Charron, *La mort n'est pas une fin. Pratiques funéraires en Égypte d'Alexandre à Cléopâtre* (Arles 2002).

CHASSINAT 1912: Émile Chassinat, La déesse Djéritef, in: *Bulletin de l'Institut Français d'Archéologie Orientale* 10, 1912, 159-160.

CHASSINAT/PALANQUE 1911: È. Chassinat/Ch. Palanque, *Une campagne des fouilles dans la nécropole d'Assiout* (*Mémoires publiés par les membres de l'Institut Français d'Archéologie Orientale du Caire* 24; Le Caire 1911).

CHÉHAB 1969: Maurice Chéhab, Noms de personnalités égyptiennes découverts au Liban, in: *Bulletin du Musée de Beyrouth* 22, 1969, 1-47.

CLARYSSE 1979: Willy Clarysse, Ptolemaic Papyri from Lycopolis, in: Jean Bingen/Georges Nachtergael (eds.), *Actes du XVe Congrès International de Papyrologie. Quatrième partie: Papyrologie documentaire* (*Papyrologica Bruxellensia* 19; Bruxelles 1979) 101-106.

CLÉDAT 1908: Jean Clédat, Notes d'archéologie copte, in: *Annales du Service des Antiquités de l'Égypte* 9, 1908, 213-230.

CLÉRE 1969: J.J. Clére, A propos du nom du XIIIe nome de Haute Égypte, in: *Mitteilungen des Deutschen Archäologischen Instituts Abteilung Kairo* 24, 1969, 93-95.

COONEY 1976: John D. Cooney, *Catalogue of Egyptian Antiquities in the British Museum. IV. Glass* (London 1976).

COQUIN 1975: René-Georges Coquin, Le catalogue de la bibliothèque du couvent de Saint Elie « du rocher » (ostracon IFAO 13315), in: *Bulletin de l'Institut Français d'Archéologie Orientale* 75, 1975, 207-239.

COQUIN 1991: René-Georges Coquin, Constantine: History, in: Aziz S. Atiya (ed.), The *Coptic Encyclopedia* 2 (New York 1991) 590-592.

COQUIN/MARTIN 1991a: René-Georges Coquin/Maurice Martin, Dayr al-Izam, in: Aziz S. Atiya (ed.), *The Coptic Encyclopedia* 3 (New York 1991) 809.

COQUIN/MARTIN 1991b: René-Georges Coquin/Maurice Martin, Dayr al-Muttin, in: Aziz S. Atiya (ed.), *The Coptic Encyclopedia* 3 (New York 1991) 842-843.

CRUM 1902: W.E. Crum, Coptic Monuments (*Catalogue général des Antiquités Égyptiennes du Musée du Caire*, Le Caire 1902).

CRUM 1927: W.E. Crum, Some Further Meletian Documents, in: *Journal of Egyptian Archaeology* 13, 1927, 19-26.

CURTO 1973-1975: Silvio Curto, I contributi all'egittologia di Pietro Barocelli, Giovanni Marro, Michele Pizzio, Virginio Rosa, in: *Bollettino della Società Piemontese di Archeologia e Belle Arti, Nuova Serie* 27-29, 1973-1975, 5-25.

CURTO 1976: Silvio Curto, *Storia del Museo Egizio di Torino* (Torino 1976).

DARESSY 1917a: G. Daressy, Sarcophage ptolémaïque d'Assiout, in: *Annales du Service des Antiquités de l'Égypte* 17, 1917, 95-96.

DARESSY 1917b: G. Daressy, L'art tanite, in: *Annales du Service des Antiquités de l'Égypte* 17, 1917, 164-176.

DARIS 1958: Sergio Daris, Dai papiri inediti della raccolta milanese, in: *Aegyptus. Rivista italiana di egittologia e di papirologia* 38, 1958, 28-68.

DARIS 1963: Sergio Daris, Su un nuovo Archivio Licopolitano, in: *Studia Papyrologica. Revista Española de Papirologia* 2, 1963, 77-84.

DAVIES 1953: Norman De Garis Davies, *The Temple of Hibis in El Khargeh Oasis. Part III. The Decoration*, edited by Ludlow Bull and Lindsley F. Hall (*Publications of The Metropolitan Museum of Art Egyptian Expedition* 17; New York 1953).

DAVIES 1995: W.Vivian Davies, Ancient Egyptian Timber Imports: An Analysis of Wooden Coffins in the British Museum, in: W. Vivian Davies/Louise Schofield (eds.), *Egypt, the Aegean and the Levant. Interconnections in the Second Millennium BC* (London 1995) 146-156.

DAVIES 2003a: Vivian Davies, Sobeknakht of Elkab and the coming of Kush, in: *Egyptian Archaeology. The Bulletin of the Egypt Exploration Society* 23, 2003, 3-6.

DAVIES 2003b: Vivian Davies, Kurgus 2002: the inscriptions and rock-drawings, in: *Sudan & Nubia. The Sudan Archaeological Research Society Bulletin* 7, 2003, 55-57.

DAWSON/GRAY 1968: Warren R. Dawson/P.H.K. Gray, *Mummies and Human Remains* (*Catalogue of Egyptian Antiquities in the British Museum* 1; London 1968).

DELANGE 1987: Elisabeth Delange, *Catalogue des statues égyptiennes du Moyen Empire. 2060-1560 avant J.-C.* (Paris 1987).

DELEHAYE 1922: Hippolytus Delehaye, Les Martyrs d'Egypte, in: *Analecta Bollandiana* 40, 1922, 7-154.

DEMARÉE 1983: Robert J. Demarée, *The $ȝḥ-iḳr-n-R^c.w$ stelae. On ancestor worship in Ancient Egypt* (*Egyptologische Uitgaven* 3; Leiden 1983).

DENNISON 1918: W. Dennison, *A Gold Treasure of the Late Roman Period* (Studies in East Christian and Roman Art 2; New York 1918).

DESROCHES NOBLECOURT/VERCOUTTER 1981: Christiane Desroches Noblecourt/Jean Vercoutter (eds.), *Un siècle de fouilles françaises en Égypte 1880-1980* (Paris 1981).

DESROSIERS 2002: Sophie Desrosiers, Techniques des textiles médiévaux égyptiens d'époque islamique, in: Maximilien Durand/Florence Saragoza (eds.), *Égypte, la trame de l'Histoire. Textiles pharaoniques, coptes et islamiques* (Paris 2002) 163-166.

DEVOS 1969a: Paul Devos, La « servante de Dieu » Poemenia d'après Pallade, la tradition Copte et Jean Rufus, in: *Analecta Bollandiana* 87, 1969, 189-212.

DEVOS 1969b: Paul Devos, Fragments Coptes de l' »Historia Monachorum » (Vie de S. Jean de Lycopolis BHO. 515), in: *Analecta Bollandiana* 87, 1969, 417-440.

DEVOS 1969c: Paul Devos, S. Jean de Lyco et la tentatrice, in: *Analecta Bollandiana* 87, 1969, 441.

DEVOS 1970: Paul Devos, Feuillets Coptes nouveaux et anciens concernant S. Jean de Siout, in: *Analecta Bollandiana* 88, 1970, 153-187.

DEVOS 1976: Paul Devos, « Saint Jean de Lycopolis et l'empereur Marcien. À propos de Chalcédoine », in: *Analecta Bollandiana* 94, 1976, 303-316.

DEVOS 1978: Paul Devos, De Jean Chrysostome à Jean de Lycopolis. Chrysostome et Chalcèdôn, in: *Analecta Bollandiana* 96, 1978, 389-403.

DEVOS 1988: Paul Devos, Jean de Lycopolis revisité. Nouveaux feuillets du « Codex B », in: *Analecta Bollandiana* 106, 1988, 183-200.

DEVOS 1991: Paul Devos, John of Lycopolis, Saint, in: Aziz S. Atiya (ed.), *The Coptic Encyclopedia* 5 (New York 1991) 1363-1366.

DEVOS 1994: Paul Devos, De Saint Jean de Lycopolis aux règlements de vie chrétienne, in: *Christianisme d'Égypte. Hommages à René-Georges Coquin* (*Cahiers de la Bibliothèque Copte* 9; Paris – Louvain 1994) 76-86.

VAN DIJK 2000: Jacobus v. Dijk, The Amarna Period and the Later New Kingdom (c. 1352-1069 BC), in: Ian Shaw (ed.), *The Oxford History of Ancient Egypt* (Oxford 2000) 272-313.

DOXEY 1998: Denise M. Doxey, *Egyptian Non-Royal Epithets in the Middle Kingdom: A Social and Historical Analysis* (*Probleme der Ägyptologie* 12; Leiden – Boston - Köln 1998).

DOXEY 2001a: Denise M. Doxey, Anubis, in: Donald B. Redford (ed.), *The Oxford Encyclopedia of Ancient Egypt*, vol. 1 (Oxford 2001) 97-98.

DOXEY 2001b: Denise M. Doxey, Thoth, in: Donald B. Redford (ed.), *The Oxford Encyclopedia of Ancient Egypt*, vol. 3 (Oxford 2001) 398-400.

DREYER 1986: Günter Dreyer, *Elephantine VIII. Der Tempel der Satet. Die Funde der Frühzeit und des Alten Reiches* (*Archäologische Veröffentlichungen* 39; Mainz 1986).

DUNHAM 1937-1938: Dows Dunham, An Egyptian Statuette of the Middle Kingdom, in: *Worcester Art Museum Annual* 3, 1937-1938, 9-16.

DUNHAM 1982: Dows Dunham, *Excavations at Kerma. Part VI* (Boston 1982).

DUQUESNE 2000: Terence DuQuesne, Votive Stelae for Upwawet from the Salakhana trove, in: *Discussions in Egyptology* 48, 2000, 5-47.

DUQUESNE 2002a: Terence DuQuesne, Documents on the Cult of the Jackal Deities at Asyut: Seven more ramesside stelae from the Salakhana trove, in: *Discussions in Egyptology* 53, 2002, 9-30.

DUQUESNE 2002b: Terence DuQuesne, Hathor of Medjed, in: *Discussions in Egyptology* 54, 2002, 39-60.

DUQUESNE 2003: Terence DuQuesne, Exalting the god. Processions of Upwawet at Asyut in the New Kingdom, in: *Discussions in Egyptology* 57, 2003, 21-45.

DUQUESNE 2004: Terence DuQuesne, Empowering the Divine Standard: an unusual motif on the Salakhana stelae, in: *Discussions in Egyptology* 58, 2004, 29-56.

DUQUESNE 2005: Terence DuQuesne, *The Jackal Divinities of Egypt. I. From the Archaic Period to Dynasty X* (Oxfordshire Communications in Egyptology VI; London 2005).

DUQUESNE 2007: Terence DuQuesne, *Anubis, Upwawet, and other Deities, Personal Worship and Official Religion in Ancient Egypt. Catalogue of the Exhibition at the Egyptian Museum, Cairo. March 2007* (Cairo 2007).

DURISCH 1993: Nicole Durisch, Culte des canidés à Assiout: Trois nouvelles stèles dédiées à Oupouaout, in: *Bulletin de l'Institut Français d'Archéologie Orientale* 93, 1993, 205-221.

DUYRAT 2005: Frédérique Duyrat, Le trésor de Damanhour (*IGCH* 1664) et l'évolution de la circulation monétaire en Égypte hellénistique, in: Frédérique Duyrat/Olivier Picard (eds.), *L'exception égyptienne? Production et échanges monétaires en Égypte hellénistique et romaine. Actes du colloque d'Alexandrie, 13-15 avril 2002* (*Études alexandrines* 10; Le Caire 2005) 10-51.

EBERS 1880: Georg Ebers, *Aegypten in Bild und Wort dargestellt von unseren ersten Künstlern beschrieben von Georg Ebers. Zweiter Band* (Stuttgart - Leipzig 1880).

EBERS 1886: Georg Ebers, *Cicerone durch das alte und neue Ägypten. Ein Lese- und Handbuch für Freunde des Nillandes II* (Stuttgart - Leipzig 1886).

EDEL 1955: Elmar Edel, Inschriften des Alten Reiches. V. Die Reiseberichte des ḥrw-ḫwjf (Her-chuf), in: O. Firchow (ed.), *Ägyptologische Studien* (Berlin 1955) 51-75.

EDEL 1970: Elmar Edel, *Die Inschriften am Eingang des Grabes des „Tef-ib" (Siut Grab III) nach der Description de l'Egypte. Ein Wiederherstellungsversuch* (*Abhandlungen für die Kunde des Morgenlandes* 39.1; Wiesbaden 1970).

EDEL 1984: Elmar Edel, *Die Inschriften der Grabfronten der Siut-Gräber in Mittelägypten aus der Herakleopolitenzeit. Eine Wiederherstellung nach den Zeichnungen der Description de l'Égypte* (*Abhandlungen der Rheinisch-Westfälischen Akademie der Wissenschaften* 71; Opladen 1984).

EGBERTS 1987: Arno Egberts, A divine epithet in P. dem. Cairo CG 50058 and 50059, in: *Enchoria. Zeitschrift für Demotistik und Koptologie* 15, 1987, 25-31.

EISSA 1991: Ahmed Eissa, Zum Lepidotos-Fisch als eine Erscheinungsform des Osiris, in: *Göttinger Miszellen. Beiträge zur ägyptologischen Diskussion* 124, 1991, 43-49.

EISSA 1994: Ahmed Eissa, Zwei Votivstelen eines Beamten namens Parênacht aus Siût, in: *Studien zur Altägyptischen Kultur* 21, 1994, 59-64.

EISSA 1995: Ahmed Eissa, Zur Etymologie des modernen Namens vom großen Amuntempel in Theben: "Karnak", in: *Göttinger Miszellen. Beiträge zur ägyptologischen Diskussion* 144, 1995, 31-41.

EISSA 1996: Ahmed Eissa, Zwei königliche Stelen der 18. Dynastie aus Siût, in: *Mitteilungen des Deutschen Archäologischen Instituts Abteilung Kairo* 52, 1996, 83-85.

EL-KHADRAGY 2006a: Mahmoud El-Khadragy, The Northern Soldiers-Tomb at Asyut, in: *Studien zur Altägyptischen Kultur* 35, 2006, 147-165.

EL-KHADRAGY 2006b: Mahmoud El-Khadragy, New Discoveries in the Tomb of Khety II at Asyut, in: *The Bulletin of the Australian Centre for Egyptology* 17, 2006, 79-95.

EL-KHADRAGY 2007: Mahmoud El-Khadragy, The Shrine of the Rock-cut Chapel of Djefaihapi I at Asyut, in: *Göttinger Miszellen. Beiträge zur ägyptologischen Diskussion* 212, 2007, 41-62.

EL-KHADRAGY/KAHL 2004: Mahmoud El-Khadragy/Jochem Kahl, The First Intermediate Period Tombs at Asyut Revisited, in: *Studien zur Altägyptischen Kultur* 32, 2004, 233-243.

EL SABBAN 2005: Sherif El Sabban, Coffin of *p3 di n 3st* in Cairo Museum, in: *Discussions in Egyptology* 61, 2005, 25-30.

EMMEL 1998: Stephen Emmel, The Historical Circumstances of Shenute's Sermon God Is blessed, in: Martin Krause/Sofia Schaten (eds.), ΘΕΜΕΛΙΑ. *Spätantike und koptologische Studien. Peter Grossmann zum 65. Geburtstag* (Sprachen und Kulturen des Christlichen Orients 3; Wiesbaden 1998) 81-96.

ENGEL/KAHL forthcoming: Eva-Maria Engel/Jochem Kahl, Die Grabanlage Djefaihapis I. in Assiut, in: Joanna Popielska-Grzybowska/Olga Białostocka (eds.), *Proceedings of the Third Central European Conference of Young Egyptologists. Egypt 2004: Perspectives of Research. Warsaw 12-14 May 2004*.

ERMAN 1929: Adolf Erman, *Mein Werden und mein Wirken. Erinnerungen eines alten Berliner Gelehrten* (Leipzig 1929).

ERMAN/GRAPOW 1926-1931: Adolf Erman/Hermann Grapow (eds.), *Wörterbuch der Ägyptischen Sprache* (Leipzig 1926-1931).

EVETTS/BUTLER 1895: T.A. Evetts/Alfred J. Butler, *The Churches & Monasteries of Egypt and Some Neighbouring Countries Attributed to Abû Sâlih, The Armenian* (Oxford 1895).

FAUERBACH 2005: Ulrike Fauerbach, in: Jochem Kahl/Mahmoud El-Khadragy/Ursula Verhoeven in collaboration with Eva-Maria Engel/Ulrike Fauerbach/Yasser Mahmoud/Omar Nour el-Din/Monika Zöller, The Asyut Project: fieldwork season 2004, in: *Studien zur Altägyptischen Kultur* 33, 2005, 166-167.

FESTUGIÈRE 1971: André-Jean Festugière (ed.), *Historia Monachorum in Aegypto. Édition critique du texte grec et traduction annotée* (Subsidia Hagiographica 53; Bruxelles 1971).

FILER 1999: Joyce Filer, Both Mummies as *Bakshish*, in: W.V. Davies (ed.), *Studies in Egyptian Antiquities. A Tribute to T.G.H. James* (British Museum Occasional Paper 123; London 1999) 23-27.

FINNESTAD 1988: Ragnhild Bjerre Finnestad, Religion as a Cultural Phenomenon, in: G. Englund (ed.), *The religion of the ancient Egyptians. Cognitive structures and popular expressions* (*BOREAS* 20; Uppsala 1988) 73-76.

FORBES 1996: D.C. Forbes, Giants of Egyptology, 8th of a Series: Ernesto Schiaparelli (1856-1928), in: *KMT. A Modern Journal of Ancient Egypt* 7.2, 1996, 82-84.

FORBES 2005: D.C. Forbes, Giants of Egyptology. 22nd of a Series: Ahmed Kamal (Pasha) (1851-1923), in: *KMT. A Modern Journal of Ancient Egypt* 16.1, 2005, 82-84.

FRANK 1998: Georgia Frank, Miracles, Monks and Monuments: The *Historia Monachorum in Aegypto* as pilgrims' tales, in: David Frankfurter (ed.), *Pilgrimage and Holy Space in Late Antique Egypt* (*Religions in the Graeco-Roman World* 134; Leiden – Boston - Köln 1998) 483-505.

FRANKE 1987: Detlef Franke, Zwischen Herakleopolis und Theben: Neues zu den Gräbern von Assiut, in: *Studien zur Altägyptischen Kultur* 14, 1987, 49-60.

FRANKE 1994: Detlef Franke, *Das Heiligtum des Heqaib auf Elephantine. Geschichte eines Provinzheiligtums im Mittleren Reich* (*Studien zur Archäologie und Geschichte Altägyptens* 9; Heidelberg 1994).

GABRA 1931: Sami Gabra, Un temple d'Aménophis IV à Assiout, in: *Chronique d'Égypte* 6, 1931, 237-243.

GABRA 2001: Gawdat Gabra (ed.), *Be Thou There. The Holy Family's Journey in Egypt* (Cairo – New York 2001).

GAILLARD 1927: Claude Gaillard, Les animaux consacrés à la divinité de l'ancienne Lycopolis, in : *Annales du Service des Antiquités de l'Égypte* 27, 1927, 33-42.

GARDINER 1947: Alan H. Gardiner, *Ancient Egyptian Onomastica. Text, Volume II* (Oxford 1947).

GARDINER 1957: Alan Gardiner, *Egyptian Grammar Being an Introduction to the Study of Hieroglyphs* (Oxford ³1957).

GARITTE 1950: Gérard Garitte, Constantin, évêque d'Assiout, in: *Coptic Studies in Honor of Walter Ewing Crum* (Boston 1950) 187-304.

GAUTHIER/LEFEBVRE 1923: H. Gauthier/G. Lefebvre, Sarcophages du Moyen Empire provenant de la nécropole d'Assiout, in: *Annales du Service des Antiquités de l'Égypte* 23, 1923, 1-33.

GEISSEN/WEBER 2004: Angelo Geissen/Manfred Weber; Untersuchungen zu den ägyptischen Nomenprägungen. III, in: *Zeitschrift für Papyrologie und Epigraphik* 149, 2004, 283-306.

GOLDAMMER 1960: Kurt Goldammer, *Die Formenwelt des Religiösen. Grundriß der systematischen Religionswissenschaft* (Stuttgart 1960).

GOMAÀ 1986: Farouk Gomaà, *Die Besiedlung Ägyptens während des Mittleren Reiches. I. Oberägypten und das Fayyum* (*Beihefte zum Tübinger Atlas des Vorderen Orients. Reihe B (Geisteswissenschaften)* 66/1; Wiesbaden 1986).

GOYON 1967: Jean Claude Goyon, Le cérémonial de glorification d'Osiris du Papyrus du Louvre I. 3079 (colonnes 110 à 112), in: *Bulletin de l'Institut Français d'Archéologie Orientale* 65, 1967, 89-156.

GRAEFE 1986: Erhart Graefe, Upuaut, in: Wolfgang Helck/Wolfhart Westendorf (eds.), *Lexikon der Ägyptologie*. VI (Wiesbaden 1986) 862-864.

GRAHAM 2005: Angus Graham, Plying the Nile: Not all plain sailing, in: Kathryn Piquette/Serena Love (eds.), *Current Research in Egyptology 2003. Proceedings of the Fourth Annual Symposium which took place at the Institute of Archaeology, University College London 18-19 January 2003* (Oxford 2005) 41-56.

GRANDET 1994: Pierre Grandet, *Le Papyrus Harris I (BM 9999)* (*Bibliothèque d'Étude* 109.1-2; Le Caire 1994).

GRÉBAUT 1890-1900: E. Grébaut, *Le Musée Égyptien. Recueil de monuments et de notices sur les fouilles d'Égypte. Tome premier* (Le Caire 1890-1900).

GRIFFITH 1889a: Francis Llewellyn Griffith, The Inscriptions of Siût and Dêr Rîfeh, in: *The Babylonian and Oriental Record* 3, 1888-1889, 121-129, 164-168, 174-184, 244-252.

GRIFFITH 1889b: F.L. Griffith, *The Inscriptions of Siût and Dêr Rîfeh* (London 1889).

GRIFFITHS 2001: J. Gwyn Griffiths, Osiris, in: Donald B. Redford (ed.), *The Oxford Encyclopedia of Ancient Egypt*, vol. 2 (Oxford 2001) 615-619.

GROSSMANN 1991: Peter Grossmann, Dayr al-Izam, in: Aziz S. Atiya (ed.), *The Coptic Encyclopedia* 3 (New York 1991) 809-810.

GROSSMANN 2002: Peter Grossmann, *Christliche Architektur in Ägypten* (*Handbook of Oriental Studies* 62; Leiden – Boston - Köln 2002).

GUERMEUR 2005: Ivan Guermeur, *Les cultes d'Amon hors du Thèbes. Recherches de géographie religieuse* (*Bibliothèque de l'École des Hautes Études Sciences Religieuses* 123; Turnhout 2005).

GUNN 1926: Battiscombe Gunn, The Coffins of Heny, in: *Annales du Service des Antiquités de l'Égypte* 26, 1926, 166-171.

HABACHI 1977: Labib Habachi, *Tavole d'Offerta Are e Bacili da Libagione n. 22001 – 22067* (*Catalogo del Museo Egizio di Torino. Serie Seconda – Collezioni* 2; Torino 1977).

HALFWASSEN 2004: Jens Halfwassen, *Plotin und der Neuplatonismus* (München 2004).

HARDY 1952: Edward Rochie Hardy, *Christian Egypt: Church and People. Christianity and Nationalism in the Patriarchate of Alexandria* (New York 1952).

HARVEY 1990: Julia Harvey, Some Notes on the Wooden Statues from the Tomb of Nakht at Assiut, in: *Göttinger Miszellen. Beiträge zur ägyptologischen Diskussion* 116, 1990, 45-50.

HASSAN 1976: Ali Hassan, *Stöcke und Stäbe im Pharaonischen Ägypten bis zum Ende des Neuen Reiches* (*Münchner Ägyptologische Studien* 33; München/Berlin 1976).

HASSAN 2001: Fekri Hassan, Cities, in: Donald B. Redford, *The Oxford Encyclopedia of Ancient Egypt*, vol. 1 (Oxford 2001) 268-273.

HAYES 1937: William C. Hayes, *The Texts in the Mastabeh of Se'n Wosret-'Ankh at Lisht* (*Publication of the Metropolitan Museum of Art* 12; New York 1937).

HAYES 1959: William C. Hayes, *The Scepter of Egypt. A Background for the Study of the Egyptian Antiquities in The Metropolitan Museum of Art. Part II: The Hyksos Period and the New Kingdom (1675-1080 B.C.)* (New York 1959).

HELCK 1956: Wolfgang Helck, *Urkunden der 18. Dynastie. Heft 18. Biographische Inschriften von Zeitgenossen Thutmosis' III. und Amenophis' II.* (Berlin 1956).

HELCK 1958: Wolfgang Helck, *Zur Verwaltung des Mittleren und Neuen Reiches* (*Probleme der Ägyptologie* 3; Leiden – Köln 1958).

HELCK 1961: Wolfgang Helck, *Urkunden der 18. Dynastie. Übersetzung zu den Heften 17-22* (Berlin 1961).

HELCK 1976: Wolfgang Helck, Ägyptische Statuen im Ausland – ein chronologisches Problem, in: *Ugarit Forschungen* 8, 1976, 101-115.

Hodjash/Berlev 1982: Svetlana Hodjash/Oleg Berlev, *The Egyptian Reliefs and Stelae in the Pushkin Museum of Fine Arts, Moscow* (Leningrad 1982).

Hofmann 2004: Eva Hofmann, *Bilder im Wandel. Die Kunst der ramessidischen Privatgräber* (Theben 17; Mainz 2004).

Hogarth 1910: D.G. Hogarth, *Accidents of an Antiquary's Life* (London 1910).

Hombert/Préaux 1947: Marcel Hombert/Claire Préaux, Les papyrus de la Fondation Égyptologique Reine Élisabeth. XII, in: *Chronique d'Égypte* 22, 1947, 123-132.

Hombert 1964: Marcel Hombert, (Review) Sergio Daris, Su un nuovo Archivio Licopolitano. Studia Papyrologica 2 (1963) pp. 77-84, in: *Chronique d'Égypte* 39, 1964, 204.

Hoogendijk 1997: Franciska Hoogendijk, Ein Unicum beim ägyptischen Zensus-Vorgang: Die zusätzliche Eingabe SPP II, S. 31, in: *Tyche. Beiträge zur Alten Geschichte, Papyrologie und Epigraphik* 12, 1997, 125-129.

Houser-Wegner 2001: Jennifer Houser-Wegner, Wepwawet, in: Donald B. Redford (ed.), *The Oxford Encyclopedia of Ancient Egypt*, vol. 3 (Oxford 2001) 497.

Ikram 2002: Salima Ikram, The Animal Mummy Project at the Egyptian Museum, Cairo, in: Mamdouh Eldamaty/Mai Trad (eds.) *Egyptian Museum Collections around the world. Studies for the centennial of the Egyptian Museum* (Cairo 2002) 235-39.

Ikram 2005: Salima Ikram, *Divine Creatures. Animal Mummies in Ancient Egypt* (Cairo 2005).

Janssen 1995: Jac. J. Janssen, Papyrus Baldwin Rediscovered, in: *Göttinger Miszellen. Beiträge zur ägyptologischen Diskussion* 147, 1995, 53-60.

Janssen 2004: Jac. J. Janssen, *Grain Transport in the Ramesside Period. Papyrus Baldwin (BM EA 10061) and Papyrus Amiens* (Hieratic Papyri in the British Museum 8; London 2004).

Jaroš-Deckert 1987: Brigitte Jaroš-Deckert, *Statuen des Mittleren Reichs und der 18. Dynastie* (Corpus Antiquitatum Aegyptiacarum Kunsthistorisches Museum Wien, Lieferung 1; Mainz 1987).

Jarry 1964: J. Jarry, Histoire d'une sédition à Siout à la fin du IVe siècle, in: *Bulletin de l'Institut Français d'Archéologie Orientale* 62, 1964, 129-145.

Johann Georg 1913: Johann Georg, Herzog von Sachsen, Fresken bei Assiut, in: *Römische Quartalschrift für christliche Altertumskunde und für Kirchengeschichte* 27, 1913, 76-78.

Johann Georg 1914: Johann Georg, Herzog zu Sachsen, *Streifzüge durch die Kirchen und Klöster Ägyptens* (Leipzig – Berlin 1914).

Johnson 1994: Janet H. Johnson, "Annuity Contracts" and Marriage, in: David P. Silverman (ed.), *For his Ka. Essays Offered in Memory of Klaus Baer* (Studies in Ancient Oriental Civilization 55; Chicago 1994) 113-132.

Jollois/Devilliers 1821: (René Édouard) Devilliers (du Terrage)/(Jean Baptiste Prosper) Jollois, Description de Syout, et des Antiquités qui paraissent avoir appartenu a l'ancienne ville de Lycopolis, in: *Description de l'Égypte ou recueil des observations et des recherches qui ont été faites en Égypte pendant l'Expédition de l'armée française*, Seconde édition, publiée par C.L.F. Panckoucke, Tome quatrième, Antiquités-desriptions (Paris 1821) 125-157.

Kahl 1993: Jochem Kahl, Textkritische Bemerkungen zu den Diagonalsternuhren des Mittleren Reiches, in: *Studien zur Altägyptischen Kultur* 20, 1993, 95-107.

Kahl 1994: S1S 380-418: Eine Textidentifizierung, in: *Göttinger Miszellen. Beiträge zur ägyptologischen Diskussion* 139, 1994, 41-42.

Kahl 1999: Jochem Kahl, *Siut-Theben: zur Wertschätzung von Traditionen im alten Ägypten* (Probleme der Ägyptologie 13; Leiden – Boston – Köln 1999).

Kahl 2006: Jochem Kahl, „Ein Zeugnis altägyptischer Schulausflüge", in: *Göttinger Miszellen. Beiträge zur ägyptologischen Diskussion* 211, 2006, 25-29.

KAHL/EL-KHADRAGY/VERHOEVEN 2005a: Jochem Kahl/Mahmoud El-Khadragy/Ursula Verhoeven in collaboration with Eva-Maria Engel/Ulrike Fauerbach/Yasser Mahmoud/Omar Nour el-Din/Monika Zöller, The Asyut Project: fieldwork season 2004, in: *Studien zur Altägyptischen Kultur* 33, 2005, 159-167.

KAHL/EL-KHADRAGY/VERHOEVEN 2005b: Jochem Kahl/Mahmoud El-Khadragy/Ursula Verhoeven, „Dornröschen" Assiut: Erste Ergebnisse einer Deutsch-Ägyptischen Grabungskooperation, in: *Sokar* 11, 2005, 43-47.

KAHL/EL-KHADRAGY/VERHOEVEN 2006: Jochem Kahl/Mahmoud El-Khadragy/Ursula Verhoeven, The Asyut Project: Third season of fieldwork, in: *Studien zur Altägyptischen Kultur* 34, 2006, 241-249.

KAHL/VERHOEVEN 2006: Jochem Kahl/Ursula Verhoeven, Die „Wächter-Stadt": Assiut – eine Stadt und ihre Nekropole in Mittelägypten gewähren wieder Einblicke, in: *ANTIKE WELT* 4, 2006, 65-72.

KAMAL 1910: Ahmed Bey Kamal, Rapport sur les fouilles faites dans la montagne de Sheîkh Saîd, in: *Annales du Service des Antiquités de l'Égypte* 10, 1910, 145-154.

KAMAL 1916: Ahmed Bey Kamal, Fouilles à Deir Dronka et à Assiout (1913-1914), in: *Annales du Service des Antiquités de l'Égypte* 16, 1916, 65-114.

KAMAL 1934a: Moharram Kamal, Trois sarcophages du Moyen Empire provenant de la nécropole d'Assiout, in: *Annales du Service des Antiquités de l'Égypte* 34, 1934, 49-53.

KAMAL 1934b: Moharram Kamal, Un nouveau sarcophage du Moyen Empire provenant de la nécropole d'Assiout, in: *Annales du Service des Antiquités de l'Égypte* 34, 1934, 125-126.

KAPLONY-HECKEL 1986: Ursula Kaplony-Heckel, *Ägyptische Handschriften. Teil 3*. Herausgegeben von Erich Lüddeckens (Stuttgart 1986).

KARIG 1968: Joachim Selim Karig, Die Kultkammer des Amenhotep aus Deir Durunka, in: *Zeitschrift für Ägyptische Sprache und Altertumskunde* 95, 1968, 27-34.

KASSER 1991: Rodolphe Kasser, Geography, Dialectal, in: Aziz S. Atiya (ed.), *The Coptic Encyclopedia* 8 (New York 1991) 133-141.

KEES 1956: Hermann Kees, *Der Götterglaube im Alten Ägypten* (Berlin ²1956).

KENDALL 1997: Timothy Kendall, *Kerma and the Kingdom of Kush, 2500-1500 B.C.: the archaeological discovery of an ancient Nubian empire* (Washington 1997).

KESSLER 1989: Dieter Kessler, *Die heiligen Tiere und der König* (Ägypten und das Alte Testament 16; Wiesbaden 1989).

KESSLER 2001: Dieter Kessler, „Kultische Bindung der Ba-Konzeption II", in: *Studien zur Altägyptischen Kultur* 29, 2001, 139-186.

KINSLEY 1986: David Kinsley, in: Mircea Eliade (ed.), *Encyclopedia of Religion* (New York 1986) 321-326, s.v. devotion.

KITCHEN 1975: K.A. Kitchen, *Ramesside Inscriptions. Historical and Biographical. I* (Oxford 1975).

KITCHEN 1976: K.A. Kitchen, Encore la famille de Iouny (RdE 26, 123-4), in: *Revue d'Égyptologie* 28, 1976, 156-158.

KITCHEN 1979: K.A. Kitchen, *Ramesside Inscriptions. Historical and Biographical, II* (Oxford 1979).

KITCHEN 1980: K.A. Kitchen, *Ramesside Inscriptions. Historical and Biographical, III* (Oxford 1980).

KITCHEN 1986: K.A. Kitchen, *The Third Intermediate Period in Egypt (1100-650 B.C.)* (Warminster ²1986).

KITCHEN 1993a: K.A. Kitchen, *Ramesside Inscriptions. Translated and Annotated: Translations. I* (Oxford 1993).

KITCHEN 1993b: K.A. Kitchen, *Ramesside Inscriptions. Translated and Annotated: Notes and Comments. I* (Oxford 1993).

KITCHEN 2000: K.A. Kitchen, *Ramesside Inscriptions. Translated an Annotated. Translations, III* (Oxford 2000).

KLEMM/KLEMM 1993: Rosemarie Klemm/Dietrich D. Klemm, *Steine und Steinbrüche im Alten Ägypten* (Berlin – Heidelberg 1993).

KLEMM/KLEMM 2006: Rosemarie Klemm/Dietrich D. Klemm, *Geological Report (on occasion of a visit at Gebel Asyut in 2005)* (January 2006; unpublished).

KOEMOTH 2001: Pierre P. Koemoth, À propos de la stèle d'Apollônios (Louvre N 328): Ophoïs, Osiris et Sérapis en Abydos, in: *Studien zur Altägyptischen Kultur* 29, 2001, 217-233.

LACAU 1922: Pierre Lacau, Rapport sur les travaux du Service des Antiquités de l'Égypte en 1921-1922, in: *Académie des Inscriptions & Belles-Lettres. Comptes rendus des séances de l'année 1922* (Paris 1922) 372-380.

LACAU/ CHEVRIER 1956-1969: Pierre Lacau/Henri Chevrier, *Une chapelle de Sésostris Ier à Karnak.* 2 vols. (Le Caire 1956-1969).

LANCZKOWSKI 1971: Günter Lanczkowski, *Begegnung und Wandel der Religionen* (Düsseldorf – Köln) 1971.

LANCZKOWSKI 1980: Günter Lanczkowski, *Einführung in die Religionswissenschaft* (Darmstadt 1980).

LANGE/SCHÄFER 1902: H.O. Lange/H. Schäfer, *Grab- und Denksteine des Mittleren Reiches im Museum von Kairo. No. 20001-20780. Theil 1* (*Catalogue Général des Antiquités Égyptiennes du Musée du Caire*; Berlin 1902).

LEAHY 1999: Anthony Leahy, More fragments of the Book of the Dead of Padinemty, in: *Journal of Egyptian Archaeology* 85, 1999, 230-232.

LEFEBVRE 1909: Gustave Lefebvre, Égypte chrétienne, in: *Annales du Service des Antiquités de l'Égypte* 10, 1909, 50-65.

LEFEBVRE 1914: G. Lefebvre, A travers la Moyenne-Égypte. Documents et notes, § IX-X, in: *Annales du Service des Antiquités de l'Égypte* 13, 1914, 5-18.

LEIPOLDT 1902/03: Johannes Leipoldt, Berichte Schenutes über Einfälle der Nubier in Ägypten, in: *Zeitschrift für Ägyptische Sprache und Altertumskunde* 40, 1902/3, 126-140.

LEITZ 1995: Christian Leitz, *Altägyptische Sternuhren* (*Orientalia Lovaniensia Analecta* 62; Leuven 1995).

LEITZ 2002: Christian Leitz (ed.), *Lexikon der ägyptischen Götter und Götterbezeichnungen. VII* (*Orientalia Lovanensia Analecta* 116; Leuven – Paris – Dudley 2002).

LEOSPO 1988: Enrichetta Leospo, Gebelein e Asiut tra Primo Periodo Intermedio e Medio Regno, in: Anna Maria Donadoni Roveri (ed.), *Civiltà degli Egizi. Le credenze religiose* (Milano 1988).82-103.

LEOSPO 1989: Enrichetta Leospo et alii, Asiut, in: Anna Maria Donadoni Roveri (ed.), *Passato e futuro del Museo Egizio di Torino* (Torino 1989) 188-194.

LEOSPO 1990: Enrichetta Leospo, Assiut, in: Gay Robins (ed.), *Beyond the Pyramids. Egyptian Regional Art from the Museo Egizio, Turin* (Atlanta 1990) 34-38, 75-83.

LEOSPO/FOZZATI 1992: Enrichetta Leospo/Luigi Fozzati, I modelli navali del Museo Egizio di Torino. Prospettive per un'indagine storico-antropologica, in: *Sesto Congresso Internazionale di Egittologia. Atti. I* (Torino 1992) 391-396.

LESKO 1979: Leonard H. Lesko, *Index of the Spells on Egyptian Middle Kingdom Coffins and Related Documents* (Berkeley 1979).

L'HÔTE 1840: Nestor L'Hôte, *Lettres écrites d'Égypte en 1838 et 1839 contenant de observations sur divers monuments égyptiens nouvellement explorés et dessinés* (Paris 1840).

LICHTHEIM 1973: Miriam Lichtheim, *Ancient Egyptian Literature. A Book of Readings. Volume I: The Old and Middle Kingdoms* (Berkeley – Los Angeles – London 1973).

LOCHER 1983: Kurt Locher, A Further Coffin-lid with a Diagonal Star-clock from the Egyptian Middle Kingdom, in: *Journal for the History of Astronomy* 14, 1983, 141-144.

LOCHER 1992: Kurt Locher, Two Further Coffin Lids with Diagonal Star Clocks from the Egyptian Middle Kingdom, in: *Journal for the History of Astronomy* 23, 1992, 201-207.

LORTET/GAILLARD 1903-1909: Louis Lortet/Claude Gaillard, *La faune momifiée de l'Ancien Ègypte. I-V* (Lyon 1903-1909).

LUCAS 1719: *Troisieme Voyage du Sieur Paul Lucas fait en M. DCCXIV, &C. par ordre de Louis XIV. Dans la Turquie, l'asie, la Sourie, la Palestine, la Haute et la Basse Egypte, &C. Tome Second* (Rouen 1719).

LUISIER 2004: Philippe Luisier, Jean de Lycopolis. Derniers fragments Parisiens réunis par le Père Devos, in: Ugo Zanetti/Enzo Lucchesi (eds.), *Aegyptus Christiana. Mélanges d'hagiographie égyptienne et orientale dédiés à la mémoire du P. Paul Devos Bollandiste* (*Cahiers d'Orientalisme* 25; Genève 2004) 175-193.

MAGEE 1988: Diana Magee, *Asyût to the End of the Middle Kingdom: a historical and cultural study* (unpublished Ph.D. thesis; Oxford 1988).

MAGEE 1998: Diana Magee, A Small Tomb at Asyut Based on the Mss of P.E. Newberry, in: C.J. Eyre (ed.), *Proceedings of the Seventh International Congress of Egyptologists. Cambridge, 3-9 September 1995* (*Orientalia Lovaniensia Analecta* 82; Leuven 1998) 717-729.

MANLEY/ABDEL-HAKIM 2004: Deborah Manley/Sahar Abdel-Hakim (eds.), *Travelling through Egypt. From 450 B.C. to the Twentieth Century* (Cairo 2004).

MARRO 1913: Giovanni Marro, Osservazioni morfologiche ed osteometriche sopra lo scheletro degli Egiziani antichi (Necropoli di Assiut, 2500-3000 anni av. Cr.), in: *Rivista di Antropologia. Atti della Società Romana di Antropologia* 18, 1913, 63-109.

MASALI/CHIARELLI 1972: M. Masali/B. Chiarelli, Demographic Data on the Remains of Ancient Egyptians, in: *Journal of Human Evolution* 1, 1972, 161-169.

MASPERO 1900: G. Maspero, Les fouilles de Deir el Aizam (Septembre 1897), in: *Annales du Service des Antiquités de l'Égypte* 1, 1900, 109-119.

MAXWELL-HYSLOP 1971: K. R. Maxwell-Hyslop, *Western Asiatic Jewellery c. 3000-612 B.C.* (London 1971).

MCGING 1997: Brian C. McGing, Revolt Egyptian Style. Internal Opposition to Ptolemaic Rule, in: *Archiv für Papyrusforschung und verwandte Gebiete* 43, 1997, 273-314.

MEINARDUS 1965: Otto F.A. Meinardus, *Christian Egypt, Ancient and Modern* (Cairo 1965).

MELLY 1852: Andrè Melly, *Souvenir d'André Melly. Lettres d'Egypte et de Nubie. Septembre 1850 à June 1851* (Londres 1852).

MONTET 1928: Pierre Montet, Les tombeaux de Siout et de Deir Rifeh, in: *Kêmi. Revue de philologie et d'archéologie égyptiennes et coptes* 1, 1928, 53-68.

MONTET 1930-35: Pierre Montet, Les tombeaux de Siout et de Deir Rifeh (suite), in: *Kêmi. Revue de philologie et d'archéologie égyptiennes et coptes* 3, 1930-35, 45-111.

MONTET 1936: Pierre Montet, Les tombeaux de Siout et de Deir Rifeh (troisième article), in: *Kêmi. Revue de philologie et d'archéologie égyptiennes et coptes* 6, 1936, 131-163.

MONTEVECCHI 1998: Orsolina Montevecchi, La provenienza di P.Oxy. 984, in: *Aegyptus. Rivista italiana di egittologia e di papirologia* 78, 1998, 49-76.

MONTEVECCHI 2000a: Orsolina Montevecchi, Ritorniamo a Licopoli e a Plotino, in: *Aegyptus. Rivista italiana di egittologia e di papirologia* 80, 2000, 139-143.

MONTEVECCHI 2000b: Orsolina Montevecchi, Ancora su Lycopolis, in: *Aegyptus. Rivista italiana di egittologia e di papirologia* 80, 2000, 145-146.

Moss 1933: Rosalind Moss, An Unpublished Rock-Tomb at Asyût, in: *Journal of Egyptian Archaeology* 19, 1933, 33.

Münster 1968: Maria Münster, *Untersuchungen zur Göttin Isis vom Alten Reich bis zum Ende des Neuen Reiches* (*Münchner Ägyptologische Studien* 11; Berlin 1968).

Munro 1963: Peter Munro, Einige Votivstelen an *Wp w3wt*, in: *Zeitschrift für Ägyptische Sprache und Altertumskunde* 88, 1963, 48-58.

Nagel 1991: Peter Nagel, Lycopolitan (or Lyco-Diospolitan or Subakhmimic), in: Aziz S. Atiya (ed.), *The Coptic Encyclopedia* 8 (New York 1991) 151-159.

Najmabadi/Weber 1993: Seyfeddin Najmabadi/Siegfried Weber (eds.), *Naser e-Khosrou, Safarname. Ein Reisebericht aus dem Orient des 11. Jahrhunderts* (München 1993).

Neugebauer/Parker 1960: O. Neugebauer/Richard A. Parker, *Egyptian Astronomical Texts. I. The Early Decans* (London 1960).

Neugebauer/Parker 1969: O. Neugebauer/Richard A. Parker, *Egyptian Astronomical Texts. III. Decans, Planets, Constellations and Zodiacs* (London 1969).

Norden 1784: *Sammlung der besten Reisebeschreibungen. Dritter Band. Friedrich Ludwig Nordens Reisen durch Aegypten und Nubien.* (Troppau 1784).

Norden 1795-1798: Frédéric-Louis Norden, *Voyage d'Égypte et du Nubie. Nouvelle édition* (Paris 1795-1798)

Nunn 1996: John F. Nunn, *Ancient Egyptian Medicine* (London 1996).

Obsomer 1995: Claude Obsomer, *Sésostris Ier. Etude chronologique et historique du règne* (*Connaissance de l'Egypte Ancienne* 5; Bruxelles 1995).

Onasch 1994: Hans-Ulrich Onasch, *Die assyrischen Eroberungen Ägyptens. Teil 1: Kommentare und Anmerkungen* (*Ägypten und Altes Testament. Studien zu Geschichte, Kultur und Religion Ägyptens und des Alten Testaments* 27/1; Wiesbaden 1994).

Osing 1976: Jürgen Osing, *Die Nominalbildung des Ägyptischen* (Mainz 1976).

Osing 1998a: Jürgen Osing, PSI inv. I 3 + pCarlsberg 305 + pTebt. Tait Add. 2 e PSI inv. I 4 + pCarlsberg 306 + pTebt. Tait Add. 3. Copie delle iscrizioni nelle tombe di Assiut, in: Jürgen Osing/Gloria Rosati (eds.), *Papiri geroglifici e ieratici da Tebtynis* (Firenze 1998) 55-100.

Osing 1998b: Jürgen Osing, PSI inv. I 72: Manuale mitologico per i nòmi VII – XVI dell' Alto Egitto, in: Jürgen Osing/Gloria Rosati (eds.), *Papiri geroglifici e ieratici da Tebtynis* (Firenze 1998) 129-188.

Palanque 1903: Charles Palanque, Notes de fouilles dans la nécropole d'Assiout, in: *Bulletin de l'Institut Français d'Archéologie Orientale* 3, 1903, 119-128.

Panckoucke 1822: C.L.F. Panckoucke, *Description de l'Égypte ou recueil des observations et des recherches qui ont été faites en Égypte pendant l'Expédition de l'armée française*, Seconde édition (Paris 1822).

Peet/Woolley 1923: T. Eric Peet/C. Leonard Woolley, *City of Akhenaten. Excavations of 1921 and 1922 at El-'Amarneh* (*Memoirs of the Egypt Exploration Society* 38; London 1923).

Perry 1743: Charles Perry, *A View of the Levant, particularly of Constantinople, Syria, Egypt and Greece* (London 1743).

Pestman 1995: P.W. Pestman, Haronnophris and Chaonnophris. Two Indigenous Pharaohs in Ptolemaic Egypt (205-186 B.C.), in: S.P. Vleeming (ed.), *Hundred-Gated Thebes. Acts of a Colloquium on Thebes and the Theban Area in the Graeco-Roman Period* (*Papyrologica Lugduno-Batava* 27; Leiden – New York – Köln 1995) 101-137.

Petrie 1888: W.M. Flinders Petrie, *Tanis. Part II. Nebesheh (AM) and Defenneh (Tahpanhes)* (*Memoirs of the Egypt Exploration Fund* 4; London 1888).

Petrie 1891: William Matthew Flinders Petrie, *Illahun, Kahun and Gurob* (London 1891).

PINCH 1993: Geraldine Pinch, *New Kingdom Votive Offerings* (Oxford 1993).

PLATZ-HORSTER 2004: Gertrud Platz-Horster, Schmuck und Private Frömmigkeit: Der Goldschmuck von Assiût, Ägypten, in: Ludwig Wamser (ed.), *Die Welt von Byzanz – Europas östliches Erbe. Glanz, Krisen und Fortleben einer tausendjährigen Kultur* (München 2004) 286-304.

PODVIN 2000: Jean-Louis Podvin, Position du mobilier funéraire dans les tombes égyptiennes privées du Moyen Empire, in: *Mitteilungen des Deutschen Archäologischen Instituts Abteilung Kairo* 56, 2000, 277-334.

PORTER/MOSS 1934: Bertha Porter/Rosalind L.B. Moss, *Topographical Bibliography of Ancient Egyptian Hieroglyphic Texts, Reliefs, and Paintings. IV. Lower and Middle Egypt* (Oxford 1934).

POSENER 1971: George Posener, Amon juge du pauvre, in: G. Haeny (ed.), *Aufsätze zum 70. Geburtstag von Herbert Ricke* (Beiträge zur Bauforschung 12; Wiesbaden 1971) 59-63.

POSENER 1975: George Posener, La piété personelle avant l'âge amarnien, in: *Révue d'Égyptologie* 27, 1975, 195-206.

PRICE/WAGGONER 1975: Martin Price/Nancy Waggoner, *Archaic Greek Coinage. The Asyut Hoard* (London 1975).

QUACK 1992: Joachim Friedrich Quack, *Studien zur Lehre für Merikare* (Göttinger Orientforschungen. IV. Reihe: Ägypten 23, Wiesbaden 1992).

RADWAN 1983: Ali Radwan, *Die Kupfer- und Bronzegefäße Ägyptens (Von den Anfängen bis zum Beginn der Spätzeit)* (Prähistorische Bronzefunde, Abteilung II, 2; München 1983).

REISNER 1918: George A. Reisner, The Tomb of Hepzefa, Nomarch of Siût, in: *Journal of Egyptian Archaeology* 5, 1918, 79-98.

REISNER 1923a: George A. Reisner, *Excavations at Kerma. Parts I-III* (Harvard African Studies V; Cambridge, Mass. 1923).

REISNER 1923b: George A. Reisner, *Excavations at Kerma. Parts IV-V* (Harvard African Studies VI; Cambridge, Mass. 1923).

REISNER 1931: G. A. Reisner, Inscribed Monuments from Gebel Barkal, in: *Zeitschrift für Ägyptische Sprache und Altertumskunde* 66, 1931, 76-100.

REVEZ 2002: Jean Revez, Photos inédites de la statue du Moyen Empire d'Hapidjefa, découverte à Kerma (BMFA 14.724), in: *Revue d'Égyptologie* 53, 2002, 245-249.

RICHTER 2003: Siegfried G. Richter, Beobachtungen zur dritten persischen Eroberung und Besetzung Ägyptens in den Jahren 618/19 bis 629 n. Chr., in: Anke Ilona Blöbaum/Jochem Kahl/Simon D. Schweitzer (eds.), *Ägypten – Münster. Kulturwissenschaftliche Studien zu Ägypten, dem Vorderen Orient und verwandten Gebieten donum natalicium viro doctissimo Erharto Graefe sexagenario ab amicis collegis discipulis ex aedibus Schlaunstraße 2/Rosenstraße 9 oblatum* (Wiesbaden 2003) 221-232.

RIDLEY: Ronald T. Ridley, *Napoleon's Proconsul in Egypt. The life and times of Bernardino Drovetti* (London; n.d.).

RIGGS/STADLER 2003: A Roman Shroud and its Demotic Inscriptions in the Museum of Fine Arts, Boston, in: *Journal of the American Research Center in Egypt* 40, 2003, 69-87.

ROCCATI 1974: A. Roccati, Una tomba dimenticata di Asiut, in: *Oriens Antiquus. Rivista del Centro per le Antichità e la Storia dell'Arte del Vicino Oriente* 13, 1974, 41-52.

ROEDER 1929: Günther Roeder, Ein namenloser Frauensarg des Mittleren Reiches um 2000 v.Chr. aus Siut (Oberägypten) im Städtischen Museum zu Bremen, in: *Niederdeutsche Zeitschrift für Volkskunde* 6, 1929, 191-243.

RUSSELL 1981: Norman Russell, *The Lives of the Desert Fathers. The Historia Monachorum in Aegypto* (Cistercian Studies 34; Kalamazoo 1981).

RUSSELL 2001: Terence M. Russell, *The Napoleonic Survey of Egypt Description de L'Égypte. The monuments and customs of Egypt: selected engravings and texts, II* (Aldershot 2001).

RYAN 1988: Donald Paul Ryan, *The Archaeological Excavations of David George Hogarth at Asyut, Egypt* (Cincinnati 1988).

RYAN 1996: Donald P. Ryan, David George Hogarth. A Somewhat Reluctant Egyptologist, in: *KMT. A Modern Journal of Ancient Egypt* 7.2, 1996, 77-81.

SADEK 1988: Ashraf Iskander Sadek, *Popular Religion in Egypt during the New Kingdom* (*Hildesheimer Ägyptologische Beiträge* 27; Hildesheim 1988).

SÄVE-SÖDERBERGH 1941: Torgny Säve-Söderbergh, *Ägypten und Nubien. Ein Beitrag zur Geschichte altägyptischer Aussenpolitik* (Lund 1941).

SAMIR 1991: Khalil Samir, Constantine: Constantine's Writings, in: Aziz S. Atiya (ed.), *The Coptic Encyclopedia* 2 (New York 1991) 592-593.

SATZINGER 1978: Helmut Satzinger, Der Leiter des Speicherwesens Si-Êse Sohn des Qeni und seine Wiener Statue, in: *Jahrbuch der Kunsthistorischen Sammlungen in Wien* 74, Wien 1978, 7-28.

SATZINGER 1989: Helmut Satzinger, Die Zeugnisse persönlicher Frömmigkeit im pharaonischen Ägypten, in: Hubert Christian Ehalt (ed.), *Volksfrömmigkeit. Von der Antike bis zum 18. Jahrhundert* (*Kulturstudien* 10; Wien 1989) 13-27.

SAUNERON 1952: Serge Sauneron, *Rituel de l'Embaumement: Pap. Boulaq III, Pap. Louvre 5.158* (Le Caire 1952).

SAUNERON 1967: S. Sauneron, Villes et légendes d'Égypte, § XII-XIV, in: *Bulletin de l'Institut Français d'Archéologie Orientale* 65, 1967, 157-168.

SAUNERON 1983: Serge Sauneron, *Villes et légendes d'Égypte* (*Bibliothèque d'Étude* 90; Le Caire ²1983).

SCHAFF/WACE 1995: Philip Schaff/Henry Wace (eds.), *Nicene and Post-Nicene Fathers. Vol. 11. Sulpitius Severus, Vincent of Lerins, John Cassian.* Second Series (reprint; Peabody ²1995).

SCHEIDEL 2001: Walter Scheidel, (Review) Bagnall/Frier/Rutherford, The Census Register P.Oxy. 984: The Reverse of Pindar's Paeans (Brussels 1997), in: *Bulletin of the American Society of Papyrologists* 38, 2001, 147-151.

SCHENKEL 1962: Wolfgang Schenkel, *Frühmittelägyptische Studien* (*Bonner Orientalistische Studien, Neue Serie* 13; Bonn 1962).

SCHENKEL 1965: Wolfgang Schenkel, *Memphis – Herakleopolis – Theben. Die epigraphischen Zeugnisse der 7.-11. Dynastie Ägyptens* (*Ägyptologische Abhandlungen* 12; Wiesbaden 1965).

SCHENKEL 1978: Wolfgang Schenkel, *Die Bewässerungsrevolution im Alten Ägypten* (Mainz 1978).

SCHENKEL 1996: Wolfgang Schenkel, Eine Konkordanz zu den Sargtexten und die Graphien der 1. Person Singular, in: Harco Willems (ed.), *The World of the Coffin Texts. Proceedings of the Symposium Held on the Occasion of the 100ᵗʰ Birthday of Adriaan De Buck, Leiden, December 17-19, 1992* (*Egyptologische Uitgaven* 9; Leiden 1996) 115-127.

SCHMELZ 2003: Georg Schmelz, Konstantin, Bischof von Assiut, in: Friedrich-Wilhelm Bautz/Traugott Bautz (eds.), *Biographisch-Bibliographisches Kirchenlexikon* 22 (Nordhausen 2003) 732-734.

SCHNEIDER/SUSSER 2003: Jane Schneider/Ida Susser (eds.), *Wounded Cities. Destruction and Reconstruction in a Globalized World* (Oxford – New York 2003).

SCHRAMM 1981: Matthias Schramm, Astronomische Interpretation der Diagonalsternuhr, in: Emma Brunner-Traut/Hellmut Brunner, *Die ägyptische Sammlung der Universität Tübingen* (Mainz 1981) 219-227.

SCOTT 1986: Gerry D. Scott III, *Ancient Egyptian Art at Yale* (New Haven 1986).

SEIDLMAYER 1990: Stephan Johannes Seidlmayer, *Gräberfelder aus dem Übergang vom Alten zum Mittleren Reich. Studien zur Archäologie der Ersten Zwischenzeit* (*Studien zur Archäologie und Geschichte Altägyptens* 1; Heidelberg 1990).

SEIDLMAYER 1997: Stephan Johannes Seidlmayer, Zwei Anmerkungen zur Dynastie der Herakleopoliten, in: *Göttinger Miszellen. Beiträge zur ägyptologischen Diskussion* 157, 1997, 81-90.

SEIDLMAYER 2000: Stephan Seidlmayer, The First Intermediate Period (c.2160-2055 BC), in: Ian Shaw (ed.), *The Oxford History of Ancient Egypt* (Oxford 2000) 118-147.

SETTGAST 1972: Jürgen Settgast, Ein anthropoider Sarkophagdeckel der 19. Dynastie, in: *Jahrbuch Preussischer Kulturbesitz* 10, 1972, 245-249.

SHAW 1929: W.B.K. Shaw, Darb el Arba'in. The Forty Days' Road, in: *Sudan Notes & Records* 12, 1929, 63-71.

SHORE 1988: A.F. Shore, Swapping Property at Asyut in the Persian Period, in: John Baines/T.G.H. James/Anthony Leahy/A.F. Shore (eds.), *Pyramid Studies and other Essays Presented to I.E.S. Edwards* (*The Egypt Exploration Society Occasional Publications* 7; London 1988) 200-206.

SHORE/SMITH 1959: A.F. Shore/H.S. Smith, Two Unpublished Demotic Documents from the Asyut Archive, in: *Journal of Egyptian Archaeology* 45, 1959, 52-60.

SHORE/SMITH 1960: A.F. Shore/H.S. Smith, A Demotic Embalmers' Agreement (Pap. Dem. B.M. 10561), in: *Acta Orientalia* 25, 1960, 277-294.

SIMPSON 1969: William Kelly Simpson, *Papyrus Reisner III. Transcription and Commentary* (Boston 1969).

SMITH 1957: William Stevenson Smith, A Painting in the Assiut Tomb of Hepzefa, in: *Mitteilungen des Deutschen Archäologischen Institutes Abteilung Kairo* 15, 1957, 221-224.

SOTTAS 1923: Henri Sottas, Sur quelques papyrus dèmotiques provenant d'Assiout, in: *Annales du Service des Antiquités de l'Égypte* 23, 1923, 34-46.

SPANEL 1989: Donald B. Spanel, The Herakleopolitan Tombs of Kheti I, *Jt(.j)jb(.j)*, and Kheti II at Asyut, in: *Orientalia* 58, 1989, 301-314.

SPANEL 2001: Donald B. Spanel, Asyut, in: Donald B. Redford (ed.), *The Oxford Encyclopedia of Ancient Egypt*, vol. 1 (Oxford 2001) 154-156.

SPELEERS 1923: Louis Speleers, *Recueil des inscriptions egyptiennes des Musées Royaux du Cinquantenaire à Bruxelles* (Bruxelles 1923).

SPIEGELBERG 1932: Wilhelm Spiegelberg, *Die demotischen Denkmäler. III. Demotische Inschriften und Papyri (CG 50023-50165)* (*Catalogue Général des Antiquités Égyptiennes du Musée du Caire;* Berlin 1932).

STEINDORFF 1946: George Steindorff, *Catalogue of the Egyptian Sculpture in the Walters Art Gallery* (Baltimore 1946).

STEWART 1991: Randall Stewart, Asyut, in: Aziz S. Atiya (ed.), *The Coptic Encyclopedia* 1 (New York 1991) 296-297.

STUART 1879: Villiers Stuart, *Nile Gleanings concerning the Ethnology. History and Art of Ancient Egypt as revealed by Egyptian Paintings and Bas-Reliefs. With descriptions of Nubia and its Great Rock Temples to the Second Cataract* (London 1879).

SUSSER/SCHNEIDER 2003: Ida Susser/Jane Schneider, Wounded Cities: Deconstruction and Reconstruction in a Globalized World, in: Jane Schneider/Ida Susser (eds.), *Wounded Cities. Destruction and Reconstruction in a Globalized World* (Oxford – New York 2003) 1-23.

TEETER 1990: Emily Teeter, How Many Statues of Nakhti?, in: *Göttinger Miszellen. Beiträge zur ägyptologischen Diskussion* 114, 1990, 101-106.

TEETER 2001: Emily Teeter, Maat,in: Donald B. Redford (ed.), *The Oxford Encyclopedia of Ancient Egypt*, vol. 2 (Oxford 2001) 319-321.

TEFNIN 1988: Roland Tefnin, *Statues et Statuettes de l'ancienne Égypte* (Bruxelles 1988).

THÉODORIDÈS 1971: Aristide Théodoridès, Les contrats d'Hâpidjefa, in: *Revue Internationale des Droits de l'Antiquité* (3ᵉ série) 18, 1971, 109-251.

THÉODORIDÈS 1973: Aristide Théodoridès, À propos du sixième contrat du gouverneur Hâpidjefa, in: *Annuaire de l'Institut de Philologie et d'Histoire Orientales et Slaves* 30 (1968-1972), 1973, 439-466.

THOMPSON 1934: Herbert Thompson, *A Family Archive from Siut from Papyri in the British Museum* (Oxford 1934).

TILL 1935: Walter Till, *Koptische Heiligen- und Martyrerlegenden. Erster Teil* (*Orientalia Christiana Analecta* 102; Roma 1935).

TILL 1936: Walter Till, *Koptische Heiligen- und Martyrerlegenden. Zweiter Teil* (*Orientalia Christiana Analecta* 108; Roma 1936).

TIMBIE 1991a: Janet Timbie, Melitian Schism, in: Aziz S. Atiya (ed.), *The Coptic Encyclopedia* 5 (New York 1991) 1584-1585.

TIMBIE 1991b: Janet Timbie, Melitius, in: Aziz S. Atiya (ed.), *The Coptic Encyclopedia* 5 (New York 1991) 1585.

TIMM 1984: Stefan Timm, *Das christlich-koptische Ägypten in arabischer Zeit. Teil 1 (A-C)* (*Beihefte zum Tübinger Atlas des Vorderen Orients, Reihe B (Geisteswissenschaften)* 41/1; Wiesbaden 1984).

TONY-RÉVILLON 1950: Adrienne Tony-Révillon, À propos d'une statuette d'hippopotame récemment entrée au Musée de Boston, in: *Annales du Service des Antiquités de l'Égypte* 50, 1950, 47-63.

TOOLEY 1989: Angela Mary Johanne Tooley, *Middle Kingdom Burial Customs. A Study of Wooden Models and Related Material* (Liverpool 1989).

ULLMANN 2002: Martina Ullmann, *König für die Ewigkeit – Die Häuser der Millionen von Jahren. Eine Untersuchung zu Königskult und Tempeltypologie in Ägypten* (*Ägypten und Altes Testament* 51; Wiesbaden 2002).

VALBELLE 1998: Dominique Valbelle, The Cultural Significance of Iconographic and Epigraphic Data Found in the Kingdom of Kerma, in: Timothy Kendall (ed.), *Nubian Studies 1998. Proceedings of the Ninth Conference of the International Society of Nubian Studies, August 21-26, 1998, Boston, Massachusetts* (Boston 2004) 176-183.

VANDIER 1958: J. Vandier, *Manuel d'Archéologie égyptienne. Tome III. Les grandes époques. La Statuaire* (Paris 1958).

VANDONI 1976: Mariangela Vandoni, Le prebende sacerdotali nei documenti greco-egizi, in: *Aegyptus. Rivista italiana di egittologia e di papirologia* 56, 1976, 104-108.

VATIN 1989: *Vivant Denon, Voyage dans la Basse et la Haute Égypte.* Présentation de Jean-Claude Vatin (Le Caire 1989).

VEÏSSE 2004: Anne-Emmanuelle Veïsse, *Les « révoltes égyptiennes ». Recherches sur les troubles intérieurs en Égypte du règne de Ptolémée III à la conquète romaine* (*Studia Hellenistica* 41; Leuven – Paris – Dudley, MA 2004).

VERHOEVEN-VAN ELSBERGEN 2004: Ursula Verhoeven-van Elsbergen, Zwischen Memphis und Theben: Die Gräber politischer Drahtzieher in Assiut/Mittelägypten, in: *Natur und Geist. Das Forschungsmagazin der Johannes Gutenberg-Universität Mainz*, 2004, 14-17.

VERNUS 1996: Pascal Vernus, Langue litteraire et diglossie, in: Antonio Loprieno (ed.), *Ancient Egyptian Literature: history and forms* (*Probleme der Ägyptologie* 10; Leiden – New York – Köln 1996) 555-564.

VIVIAN 2000: Cassandra Vivian, *The Western Desert of Egypt. An Explorer's Handbook* (Cairo 2000).

VLEEMING 1989: S.P. Vleeming, Strijd om het erfdeel van Tefhapi, in: P.W. Pestman (ed.), *Familiearchieven uit het land van Pharao* (Zutphen 1989) 31-45.

VOLKOFF 1979: Oleg V. Volkoff, Siout au temps des caravans, in: Jean Vercoutter (ed.), *Hommages à Serge Sauneron. II. Égypte post-pharaonique* (*Bibliothèque d'Étude* 88; Le Caire 1979).

VON BECKERATH 1977: Jürgen von Beckerath, in: Wolfgang Helck/Wolfhart Westendorf (eds.), *Lexikon der Ägyptologie* II (Wiesbaden 1977) 566-568, s.v. Geschichtsschreibung.

VON KÄNEL 1984: Frédérique von Känel, *Les prêtres-ouâb de Sekhmet et les conjurateurs de Serket* (*Bibliothèque de l'École des Hautes Études. Section des sciences religieuses* 87; Paris 1984).

WAINWRIGHT 1926: G.A. Wainwright, A Subsidiary Burial in Hap-Zefi's Tomb at Assiut, in: *Annales du Service des Antiquités de l'Égypte* 26, 1926, 160-166.

WAINWRIGHT 1928: G.A. Wainwright, The Aniconic Form of Amon in the New Kingdom, in: *Annales du Service des Antiquités de l'Égypte* 28, 1928, 175-189.

WALZ 1978: Terence Walz, Asyut in the 1260's (1844-53), in: *Journal of the American Research Center in Egypt* 15, 1978, 113-126.

WEILL 1950: Raymond Weill, Un nouveau pharaon de l'époque tardive en Moyenne Égypte et l'Horus de Deir el-Gebrâwi (XIIe nome), in: *Bulletin de l'Institut Français d'Archéologie Orientale* 49, 1950, 57-65.

WILD 1971: Henri Wild, Note concernant des antiquités trouvées, non à Deir Dronka, mais dans la nécropole d'Assiout, in: *Bulletin de l'Institut Français d'Archéologie Orientale* 69, 1971, 307-309.

WILKINSON 1837: John Gardner Wilkinson, *Manners and customs of the ancient Egyptians. Including their private life, government, laws, arts, manufactures, religion, and early history. III* (London 1837).

WILKINSON 1843: Gardner Wilkinson, *Modern Egypt and Thebes: being a description of Egypt; including the information required for travellers in that country. II* (London 1843).

WILLEMS 1983-1984: H.O. Willems, The Nomarchs of the Hare Nome and Early Middle Kingdom History, in: *Jaarbericht van het Vooraziatisch-Egyptisch Genootschap Ex Oriente Lux* 28, 1983-1984, 80-102.

WILLEMS 1988: Harco Willems, *Chests of Life. A Study of the Typology and Conceptual Development of Middle Kingdom Standard Class Coffins* (*Mededelingen en Verhandelingen van het Vooraziatisch-Egyptisch Genootschap "Ex Oriente Lux"* 25; Leiden 1988).

WILLIAMS 1924: Caroline Ransom Williams, *Gold and Silver Jewelry and Related Objects* (New York 1924).

WÜSTENFELD 1845: Ferdinand Wüstenfeld, *Macrizi's Geschichte der Copten. Aus den Handschriften zu Gotha und Wien mit Übersetzung und Anmerkungen* (Göttingen 1845).

ZECCHI 1996: Marco Zecchi, In Search of Merymutef, "Lord of Khayet", in: *Aegyptus. Rivista italiana di egittologia e di papirologia* 76, 1996, 7-14.

ZÖLLER 2007: Monika Zöller, *Holzmodelle aus dem Grab des Gaufürsten Jtj-Jbj (Siut III) in Assiut/Mittelägypten*. 2 vols. (unpublished M.A. thesis; Mainz 2007).

Indices

Index of deities

Akhenitief	38	Maat (cf. Temple of Maat)	54, 99
Amenhotep I	142	Merymutef	38
Amun	38, 55, 133, 135, 146	Min-Amun	55
Amun-Ra (cf. Temple of Amun-Ra)	38, 55, 58, 133	Mut (cf. Temple of Mut)	58
Amun-Ra-Kamutef	38	Neith	56
Amun-Ra-Ope	55-56	Nemti	136
Anubis (cf. Temple of Anubis)	3, 9, 49-50, 59, 84, 110, 128, 131-132, 146, 148-149	Nephthys	19, 35, 50
		Onuris	58
Apollo	58	Osiris (cf. Temple of Osiris)	3, 19, 35, 38, 50-51, 56, 59, 107, 110, 117, 124, 134-135, 144, 149
Ares	58		
Aten (cf. Temple of Aten)	55	Ptah	38, 41
Atum	40, 134	Ra	44, 99
Baal	117	Ra-Atum and his hand	38
Djefai-Hapi (cf. Temple of Djefai-Hapi)	57, 132	Ra-Horakhti	38
		Ramesses Meryamun, the god in Asyut	57
Harsaphes	38	Reshef	117
Hathor (cf. Temple of Hathor)	3, 38, 51-52, 58, 78, 99, 110, 124, 133, 144, 149, Pl. 5b	Sahet	38
		Sakhmet	56, 98, 132
		Serapis	48, 50-51
Herakles	128	Seth	3, 35, 154
Hereret	38	Sobek	38
Heritepsenuef	38	Tatenen	38
Hermes (cf. Temple of Hermes)	53, 117	Tatenenet	38
		Taweret	38
Horus	3, 35, 58, 76, 131, 154	Thoth (cf. Temple of Thoth)	3, 38, 41, 53-54
Horus, son of Isis	39	Wepwawet (cf. Temple of Wepwawet)	3, 9, 15, 35, 37-51, 54, 56, 58, 84, 89, 93, 99, 107, 124, 126-129, 131-135, 142, 144, 147-149, Pl. 2a
Horus, son of Isis and son of Osiris	56		
Isis	19, 35, 39, 49-50, 56		
Isis-Hathor	35, 56, 76, 135		
Khnum	57	Wepwawet-Ra	38, 146-147
Khonsu	56	Wennofer	50

Index of kings

Akhenaten	44	Amenemhat II	17, 92
Alexander Severus	50, 121	Amenemhat III	52
Amasis	47-49, 51-52, 56, 123-124	Amenhotep I	142
		Amenhotep II	43
Amenemhat I	9	Amenhotep III	42, Pl. 5a

Ankhwennefer	12, 114	Nubkheperra Antef VI	10
Assarhaddon	11, 136	Pa-di-Nemti	136
Assurbanipal	11-12, 136	Pepy I (cf. Ka-House of Pepy I)	57
Bonaparte	22-23		
Cambyses	44-45, 48, 51-52, 56, 123-124	Piye	136
Chaonnophris: cf. Ankhwennefer		Psametik I	17
		Ptolemy V Epiphanes	114, 125
Christian VI	21	Ptolemy VI Philometor	69, 117, 125-126
Darius I	38		
Diocletian	114, 122	Ramesses II	11, 42, 44, 46-47, 52, 55-57, 133-134
Eugenius	139		
Gallenius	137	Ramesses III	42-43, 47
Hadrian	39	Senwosret I	9, 16-17, 40, 45-46, 48-51, 54, 86, 88-89, 130, Pl. 7a
Hatshepsut	16-17		
Horemhab	43, 133-134		
Louis XIV	21	Senwosret III	52
Maximus	139	Sety I	46, 133-134
Mentuhotep II	8	Taharqa	136
Merenptah	42, 134	Theodosius I	20, 120, 138-139
Merikara	7, 17, 41, 46, 49, 52, 77-78, 129	Thutmose III	43
		Thutmose IV	134
Mohamed Ali	26	Tutankhamun	40-41

Index of private names (for Asyuti people, the elements of compounded names are indicated by a stroke)

Abu Salih	58, 111, 123	Ankhefenkhons	17
Abu-Tug (Sheikh)	68, 71-72	Ankh-en-mer	41
Agatharchides of Knidos	13	Anu (cf. Tomb of Anu)	8-9, 17, 46, 49-50, 84-85, 112
Agathokles	117	Apalos	122
Agylos	117	Aphous	122
Ah-mose	36-37	Apollonios	121
Aiglos	125	Apollonios (bishop)	122
Akakios	122	Apollos	122
Akoris	122	A(p ?)y-nofret	54
Aleet	122	Areion	122
Amenaphis	121	Arianus	122
Amen-hotep (cf. Tomb of Amen-hotep)	55-56, 97-99, 132-133, 153	Aristion	117
		Arsenophis	122
		Arundale, F.	27
Amen-hotep (first prophet of Wepwawet)	46, 67	Aset-resh	124
		Athanasia	122
		Athanasius I	137, 140
Ammenius	137	Baket-Djehuti	54
Ammonius Saccas	137	Ber	126
Andromachos	127	Bogdanoviæ, B.	5
Aniketos the younger	111	Bohleke, B.	134
Ankh-ef	32	Browne, W.G.	116

Brunner, H.	28	Grébaut, E.	28, 68
Cailliaud, F.	14, 27	Griffith, F.Ll.	27-28, 72, 97
Cassian	138	Halfawee, M.	28, 68
Champollion, J.F.	22	Har-im-hotep	127
Chassinat, É.G.	28, 30-32, 64, 82, 93, 103	Harwa	17
		Hassan, A.	29
Claudius the Martyr	122, 138, 140	Hathor	133
Clédat, J.	106	Heny	91-92
Constantine (bishop of Asyut)	122, 138, 140	Heraklides	117, 126
		Her-khuf	15
Damian	140	Hetepi	112
Danielios	122	Hetep-nebi	57
Denon, D.V.	25	Hierax	121
Desaix	24	Hogarth, D.G.	29-30, 32-33, 61, 82, 148
Devilliers du Terrage, R.É.	23-24	Hor	125, 127
Dionysios (bishop)	139	Hor I	47, 123-124
Dionysos	117, 125, 127	Hor II	124
Djed-Djehuti-iu-ef-ankh	48, 50-51, 53, 55-56	Horeau, H.	23
		Hori	46, 147
Djed-Hor: cf. Sikhâ	136-137	Hotep	48
Djed-Wepwawet-iu-ef-ankh	40	Huy	133
		Iay	47
Djefai-Hapi I	8-11, 16-18, 39, 41-43, 45-46, 48-51, 54, 57, 60, 69, 85-86, 88-89, 91-92, 103, 111, 116, 118, 130-132, 151, Pl. 7	Ibn Said	21
		Idu	52
		Idy	Pl. 11
		Idy, the elder (f.)	131
		Idy (f.)	131
		I-kau	47
Djefai-Hapi II	8, 17, 46, 50-51, 54, 85, 132	Ikher-nofret	50
		Ioannes	122
Djefai-Hapi III	17, 61, 68, 92-93, 132, 143-144, 148-149	Iobinos	122
		Ipuemra	17
		Iserikh	134
Djefai-Hapi	51, 57, 131, 152	Isidor	139
Djefai[…]	37	Isidorus of Antioch	140
Djehuti-em-hab	53, 58	Iti-ibi	6-8, 17-18, 46, 49-50, 74, 76, 78, 82, 129, 148, 151
Djehuti-heri	53		
Djehuti-iir-di-es	53		
Djehuti-setem	53	Iti-ibi (f.)	52, 78
DuQuesne, T.	93	Iti-ibi(-iqer)	8, 17, 46, 49-50, 79, 129
Ebers, G.	148		
Edel, E.	14, 28, 74	Iuny	56, 98, 120, 132-133, 153
Elias	140		
Erman, A.	32	Iw	32
Farag	28, 82	Iy(?)	47
Farag Ismail	28	Iyt-nofret	57
Forbin, A.	27	John of Heraclea	140
Gardiner, A.H.	18	John of Lycopolis	19-21, 99-100, 120-121, 138-139
George	140		
Georgios	122	Jollois, J.B.P.	23-24

Kait Idenit	52	Miusis	126
Kamal, A.	29, 62, 98, 132	Moje, J.	135
Kamal, M.	29	Montet, P.	28
Keky	112	Nakht	52
Khaa	134	Nakhti (cf. Tomb of Nakhti)	31, 64, 93, 95, 152
El-Khadragy, M.	8, 89		
Kha-em-waset	133	Naser-e Khosru	21
Kha-nub	55	Nau-kau-mer Pa-si-en-metek(?)	47, 124
Khashaba, S.	29, 98		
Khay	133	Nebet-em-qis	52
Khety I	8, 17-18, 46, 49, 51, 60, 74, 82, 120, 122, 129, 151	Neferabu	147
		Nefret-Aset	46
		Nes-Hor	124
Khety II	7-8, 17-18, 31, 42, 46, 49, 60, 77-78, 120, 129, 142, 144, 151	Nes-pa-met-shepes 1	48, 51-52, 124
		Nes-pa-met-shepes 2	56, 124
		Nes-pa-met-shepes 3	48, 51-52, 124
Khety (Newberry Tomb 1 or Tomb 8)	120	Nes-ta-henut	124
		Newberry, P.E.	28, 120
Khonsardais	17	Nofret-Ptah	134
Khonsu	57	Norden, F.L.	21-22
Khrati-ankh	125, 127	Onnaphris	121
Khuit	52	On-nophris	69
Klemm, D.	59-60	Osman, M.	62
Klemm, R.	59-60	Ouertes	117
Konon	122	Pa-di-Imen	Pl. 4
Kyriakos	122	Pa-di-Wepuy	40
Kyros	122	Pa-di-Wepuy-iu	40
Lanczkowski, G.	141	Pa-heb	53
Leo Africanus	58	Pakoris	122
L'Hôte, N.	27	Palanque, Ch.	28, 31-32, 64, 82, 93, 103
Lucas, P.	21-22, 88		
Luke, the physician	105	Palladius	138
Lysimachos	117	Pa-nehesi	134
Magee, D.	29, 84	Pa-Ra-hotep	135
al-Maqrizi	12, 58, 100, 103	Parresia	122
Maria	122	Pa-sher-Djehuti	53
Martha	122	Pa-ta-weret	145-147
Matrai	125	Pay-ef-tjau-em-awy-Wepwawet	40
Mehyt-khayt	47		
Melitius	137-138, 140	Pekusis	125
Menas	122	Perry, Ch.	88
Menekh-ib-Ra	48	Pet-Amen-ophis	69, 126
Menkheperraseneb	17	Petamenophis	17
Meri-mose	42, Pl. 12	Peter I	137
Meryt	133	Pe-te-tum	54, 69, 124-127
Mesehti (cf. Tomb of Mesehti)	8-9, 17, 28, 46, 82-83, 105, 152	Pe-te-Wepwawet	125, 127
		Petophois	40
Metiay	133	Petros	122
Metri, Hany Sadek	111	Phoibammon	122
Min-mose	43, 113	Pliny the Elder	13
Min-nefer	49-50, 109, 112	Plotinus	137

Plousammon	122
Poemen	139
Poimenia	139
Poncet, Ch.	21, 99, 110
Porphyry	137
Psois	122
Pybes	125
Qeny	134-135
Ra	133
Ra-mose	133
Rekhmira	17
Renenut I	46, 55, 98, 133
Renenut II	46, 52, 55, 98, 120, 133
Renenut	47
Rosa, V.	32
Ryan, D.P.	29
Sakhmet	47, 134
Sat-Aset	47
Schenkel, W.	28
Schiaparelli, E.	28, 32, 84, 148
Schneider, J.	5
Senebet	52
Senebtisi	52
Senenmut	17
Sen-Ese	125-126
Senet-user	52
Sennwy	10-11, 116, 119, 130-131
Senwosretankh	112
Sheb-Hor	124
Shemes (cf. Tomb of Shemes)	84
Shenute	12, 140
Shep-Min (cf. Spemminis)	53, 126
Si-Ese I	134
Si-Ese II	134-135
Si-Ese III	42, 56, 64, 134-135, 153, Pl. 13
Sikhâ (cf. Djed-Hor)	137
Sois	122
Spanel, D.B.	29
Spemminis (cf. Shep-Min)	115, 126
Stephens, J. Ll.	107
Stuart, H.W.V.	26
Susser, I.	5
Tadros, Y.	28
Ta-Ese	125
Ta-iay	47
Ta-ket	46
Ta-na-hibu	53
Ta-py	124
Ta-sheret-Hor-udja	50
Ta-sheret-Khonsu	55
Ta-wa	124-125, 127
Ta-weneshet	47
Ta-weret	134
Tay-sen-nefret	47
Tay-wahet(?)	47
Tef-Hape	53, 69, 117, 124-127
Te-nai-nefer	64
Tenit-en-Hor 1	124
Tenit-en-Hor 2	124
Tep-shena-iir-di-es	124
Te-te-Ese	125
Te-te-imhotep	124-125
Thekla	122
Theomnestos	127
Thortaios	53
Thothortaios	53
Tipay	133
Tothoes	53
Tourbon	111
T-shen-tuot	124-125
Tuot	54, 117, 124-127
Ty	55
Valentinos	122
Viktor	122
Viktorine	122
Wainwright, G.A.	29, 93, 123, 143
Wepa	40
Wepai	40
Wepay	40, 131
Wepi-mose	40
Wepuy-iu	40
Wepwawet-em-hat	32, 40-41
Wepwawet-iir-di-es	40
Wepwawet-iu	40, 125
Wepwawet-mose I	134
Wepwawet-mose II	134
Wepwawet-mose	40, 47, 134
Wepwawet-nakht	40
Wepwawet-hotep I	124
Wepwawet-hotep II	48, 51-52, 123-124
Wepwawet-hotep III	124
Wepwawet-hotep	40, 123-124
Wenep	46
Wen-nefer	134
Wia	134
Wilbour, Ch. E.	68
Wild, H.	29

Wilkinson, J.G.	27, 72, 109, 148	Yia	133

Index of buildings in Asyut

Alwet el-Nasara	58	Magee Tomb 13: cf. Northern Soldiers-Tomb	
Amphitheatre	21, 110		
Bab el-Arman: cf. Gate of the Armenians		Mausolea, Roman	21, 99
		Mausoleum of Sheikh Abu-Tug	68, 71-72
Bank building	110		
Bath	110	Monastery of Seven Mountains	12, 100
Chassinat/Palanque Tombeau no. 7: cf. Tomb of Nakhti		Newberry Tomb 1	52, 120
		Newberry Tomb 8	52, 120
Chassinat/Palanque Tombeau no. 13	109	N12.1: cf. Tomb III	
		N12.2: cf. Tomb IV	
Christian chapel	104-105	N13.1 (tomb)	8, 17, 42, 46, 49-52, 58, 63, 65, 79-82, 112, 149, 153-154, Pl. 5, Pl. 14a
Deir el-Azzam	12, 28, 71, 99-102, 114, 139		
Deir el-Mazall: cf. Deir el-Meitin			
		N13.2 (quarry)	86
Deir el-Meitin	12, 71, 93, 102-103	Northern Soldiers-Tomb	8, 17, 83
Deir el-Muttin: cf. Deir el-Meitin			
		O13.1: cf. Tomb II	
Gate of the Armenians	111	O13.2 (tomb)	71
		O15.1 (quarry)	63, 71
G10.1 (Christian chapel)	105-106	O17.1 (quarry)	61-62
		Obelisk	3, 35
H11.1: cf. Northern Soldiers-Tomb		Old Kingdom Tomb	69, 72
		P10.1: cf. Tomb I	
Hall of the Sistrum	35	Salakhana Tomb	17, 28-29, 38, 61, 66, 68, 85, 92, 121, 123, 132, 142-144, 148-149, 151, 154
al-Hanadah, monastery	140		
Hippodrome	110		
		Siut I: cf. Tomb I	
Hogarth Tomb III: cf. Tomb of Mesehti		Siut II: cf. Tomb II	
		Siut III: cf. Tomb III	
House of Eight Trees	3, 35	Siut IV: cf. Tomb IV	
House of Wennofer (cf. Temple of Osiris)	50	Siut V: cf. Tomb V	
		Temple of Amun-Ra	55
I10.1 (tomb)	30, 62, 96-98, 105	Temple of Anubis	49, 50-56, 69, 89, 126, 131-132
Ka-House of Djefai-Hapi I	57		
		Temple of Aten	55
Ka-House of Pepy I	57, 109	Temple of Djefai-Hapi	57, 132, 149
L6.2 (tomb)	62		
M10.1 (tomb)	95, 105	Temple of Hathor	51-52
M11.1: cf. Tomb V		Temple of Hermes (cf. Temple of Thoth)	53
Magazine for a group statue	3		
		Temple of Maat	54

Temple of Mut	58	Tomb V	8, 17-18, 26-30, 60, 70, 74, 85, 122, 129
Temple of Osiris	50-51		
Temple of Thoth	53	Tomb VI	28, 93
Temple of Wepwawet	3, 9, 35-36, 39, 41-45, 48-49, 55-56, 58, 89, 93, 109, 129, 131-132, 135	Tomb VII: cf. Salakhana Tomb	
		Tomb VIII	93
		Tomb of Amen-hotep	97-99, 132
Tomb I	11, 17-18, 21-22, 27, 29-30, 39, 45, 60, 68, 85-93, 130, 151, Pls. 6-8	Tomb of Anu	84-85, 112
		Tomb of Mesehti	8, 17, 28, 82, 105, 152
		Tomb of Nakhti	31, 64, 93-95, 102, 152
Tomb II	16-17, 27, 30, 50, 61, 68, 71, 77, 85-86, 132, 139	Tomb of Shemes	84
		Tomb of the Dogs	68
Tomb III	8, 17-18, 26-33, 50, 60, 62, 66, 68, 71-77, 79, 85-86, 129, 135, 139, 148, 151, 153, Pl. 2a, Pl. 2c, Pls. 3-4, Pl. 9, Pl. 14b	Tomb of the Old Kingdom: cf. Old Kingdom Tomb	
		Tomb with Coptic paintings: cf. Christian chapel	
Tomb IV	8, 17-18, 26-32, 60-62, 71-72, 74, 77-78, 84-85, 129, 139, 144		

Index of buildings outside Asyut

Deir Rifeh, Tomb VII	112	P (pyramid of Pepy I)	112
KV 62 (Tomb of Tutankhamun)	41	Serapeum, Saqqara	39
		T (pyramid of Teti)	112
M (pyramid of Merenra)	112	Temple of Amun, Luxor	55, 113
Mastaba of Senwosretankh, al-Lisht	112	Temple of Dendara	113
		Temple of Hibis	38, 113
Monastery of Apa Elias	140	Tomb of Khonsardais, Naga el-Hasaya	17
Monastery of the Holy Virgin, Deir Drunka	121	White Monastery, Sohag	12
N (pyramid of Pepy II)	112		

Index of objects

Berlin Ägyptisches Museum 2/63	46	Berlin Ägyptisches Museum 10481	152
Berlin Ägyptisches Museum 10480	152	Berlin Ägyptisches Museum 10482	152

Berlin Ägyptisches Museum 31010/1	98	Dublin Trinity College Pap. Gr. 274	12
Berlin Antikensammlung, Inv. 30219,505	Pl. 10a	Hannover Kestner-Museum 1935.200.40	152
Berlin Antikensammlung, Inv. 30219,506	Pl. 10b-c	Leiden RMO AMT 106	49, 109, 112
Boston MFA 14.720	119, 152	Leiden RMO AP 8	134
Boston MFA 14.724	118	Liverpool Museum 1966.178	41
Boston MFA 54.993	48, 51, 53	London BM EA 891	146-147
Boston MFA 1971.20	152	London BM EA 1430	37
Brussels MRAH E. 3036	112	London BM EA 1632	145
Brussels MRAH E. 5596	152	London BM EA 1725	37
Cairo CG 235	152	London BM EA 10561	45, 69
Cairo CG 257	83, 116	London BM EA 10575	53, 125
Cairo CG 258	83	London BM EA 10589	125
Cairo CG 20266	112	London BM EA 10591	53, 125, 127
Cairo CG 28118	46, 83, 112	London BM EA 10592	53, 125
Cairo CG 28119	46, 83	London BM EA 10593	53, 125
Cairo CG 50058	37, 48-49, 51-53, 56, 123	London BM EA 10594	53, 125
Cairo CG 50059	37, 44, 47-48, 51-52, 56, 123	London BM EA 10595	125
Cairo CG 50060	53, 123	London BM EA 10596	125
Cairo CG 50061	53, 123	London BM EA 10597	53, 126
Cairo CG 50062	123	London BM EA 10598	53, 126
Cairo JE 30971	152	London BM EA 10599	53, 126
Cairo JE 39014	112	London BM EA 10600	126
Cairo JE 44019	52	London BM EA 10601	126
Cairo JE 44986	152	London BM EA 10676: cf. Papyrus Gardiner II	
Cairo JE 47383	47		
Cairo JE 47384	48		
Cairo JE 47969	55		
Cairo JE 48862: cf. Victory Stela of Piye			
Cairo JE 68570	47		
Cairo JE 68576	47		
Cairo JE 68582	47		
Cairo Masp. 67032: cf. Papyrus Cairo Masp. 67032			
Cincinnati Art Museum 1966.266	37	London BM EA 10792	47-48, 51-52, 123
Cleveland Museum of Art 63.100	98	London BM EA 24388	55
Cologne 3410	39		

London BM EA 46629	57	S04/008	144
London BM EA 46634	52	S04/020	144
		S04/171	48, Pl. 2a
London BM EA 46637	52	S04/231	135
		S04/st307	119, Pl. 9b
London BM EA 47521	154	S04/st313	31
		S04/st418	Pl. 14b
London BM EA 47615	148	S04/st517.5	Pl. 16c
		S05/016	37
London BM EA 47622	148	S05/017	37
		S05/019	36, 37
London BM EA 47623	148	S05/022	53, 54
		S05/029	46, 65
Mediolanum inv. 47 (papyrus)	53	S05/046	Pl. 2c
		S05/065	68
		S05/071	Pl. 4
Moscow, Pushkin Museum I.1.a 5636	46-47	S05/072	Pl. 16a
		S05/073	117, Pl. 9a
Moscow, Pushkin Museum 4760	152	S05/112	66
		S05/st066	32, 33
New York Brooklyn Museum 47.120.2	42, 135	S06/015	Pl. 16b
		S06/022	154
New York MMA 15.2.1	52, 133	S06/024	65
		S06/025	65
New York MMA 17.2.5	135	S06/st930	63
		S1C: cf. Cairo CG 28118	
New York MMA 33.2.1	46, 52	San Jose, Rosicrucian Museum 1763	153
Ostracon Golenischeff	113	Seattle Art Museum 44.34	153
Oxford Ashmolean Museum 1883.14	133	Sq3C: cf. Cairo JE 39014	
Papyrus Amiens	121	Toledo (Ohio), Museum of Art 62/64	98
Papyrus Baldwin	121		
Papyrus Cairo Masp. 67032	120		
		Tübingen, Ägyptische Sammlung der Universität 6	Pl. 11
Papyrus Gardiner II	112		
Papyrus Harris I	43		
Papyrus of Pa-di-Nemti	136		
Papyrus Oxrhynchos 984	45, 58, 121, 128, 137	Turin Museo Egizio Sup. 14378	52
		Turin Museo Egizio Sup. 14439	41
Paris Louvre A 73	113		
Paris Louvre C 89	133	Victory Stela of Piye	136
Paris Louvre E 11657	153	Vienna, Kunsthistorisches Museum ÄS 34	42, Pl. 13
Paris Louvre E 11937	95		
Paris Louvre E 11977	114		
Paris Louvre E 12003	66		
Paris Louvre E 26915	130, 151	Vienna, Kunsthistorisches Museum ÄS 36	42, Pl. 12
Paris mss. Arabe 4893	140		

Vienna, Kunsthistorisches Museum ÄS 126	134	Homily "On the Fallen Soul and Its Exit from This World"	140
Worcester Art Museum 1938.9	51	Institutiones coenobiticae 4.23 (John Cassian)	138
Yale Art Gallery 1947.81	47, 53, 58	Lettre à Monsieur Dacier	22
Zürich, Kunsthaus 1963/36	98	London BM EA 891	147
Index of texts and text passages		London BM EA 1632	146
Book of the Dead 18-24	136	Loyalistic Teaching	79
Book of the Dead 125	99	Mortuary Liturgy no. 7	91, 151
Book of the Dead 142	136	Natural History V, 61 (Pliny the Elder)	13
Book of the Dead 145	136		
Book of the Dead 146	136	New York Brooklyn Museum 47.120.2	135
Buch vom Ba	113	New York MMA 17.2.5	135
Canon of Athanasius (25)	137	Notitia Dignitatum	15
CT III, 190b	112	Notitia Dignitatum Orient., no. XXXI: 17	116
CT VII, 227i	112		
CT VII, 245c	112		
Dialogue of a Man with his Soul	18	Notitia Dignitatum Orient., no. XXXI: 23	116
Herodotus, History, II, 37	141	Panegyric on John of Heraclea	140
Historia Lausiaca	138	Panegyric on Saint Athanasius of Alexandria	140
Historia Lausiaca XXXV	139		
Historia Monachorum in Aegypto	21, 138-139	Panegyric on Saint Claudius the Martyr	140
Historia Monachorum in Aegypto I, 4	139	Panegyric on Saint George	140
Historia Monachorum in Aegypto I, 6	139	Panegyric on Saint Isidorus of Antioch	140
Historia Monachorum in Aegypto I, 11	138	Panegyric on Shenute	140
		Papyri della Società Italiana inv. I, 72	35
Historia Monachorum in Aegypto I, 16	139	Papyri della Società Italiana inv. I, 72, x+3,1-3	113
Historia Monachorum in Aegypto I, 17	139	Papyri della Società Italiana inv. I, 72, x+3,12	35
Historia Monachorum in Aegypto I, 65	140	Papyri della Società Italiana inv. I, 72, x+3,15	113

Papyri della Società Italiana inv. I, 72, x+3,17-18	113
Papyrus Boulaq III, 4.23-5.1	35, 113
Papyrus Harris I, 58,12-59,3	44
Papyrus Harris I, 59,2	42
Papyrus Insinger 28,4	143
Papyrus London BM EA 10575,6	48, 53
Papyrus London BM EA 10589,14	45
Papyrus London BM EA 10591 rto. I.2	45
Papyrus London BM EA 10591 rto. I.7	45
Papyrus London BM EA 10591 rto. I.24	117
Papyrus London BM EA 10591 rto. II.14	45
Papyrus London BM EA 10591 rto. III.8	117
Papyrus London BM EA 10591 rto. V.1-2	127
Papyrus London BM EA 10591 rto. V.26-VI.2	127
Papyrus London BM EA 10591 rto. VI.4	36
Papyrus London BM EA 10591 rto. VI.11	117
Papyrus London BM EA 10591 rto. VI.22	54
Papyrus London BM EA 10591 rto. VII.13	36, 41
Papyrus London BM EA 10591 rto. VIII.3	53
Papyrus London BM EA 10591 rto. VIII.7	49, 56
Papyrus London BM EA 10591 rto. VIII.19	36
Papyrus London BM EA 10591 rto. VIII.24	54
Papyrus London BM EA 10591 rto. IX.12	45
Papyrus London BM EA 10591 rto. X.13-15	127
Papyrus London BM EA 10591 rto. X.16	45
Papyrus London BM EA 10591 vso. IV.18	45
Papyrus London BM EA 10591 vso. VI.4	53
Papyrus London BM EA 10591 vso. VI.11	117
Papyrus London BM EA 10597,16	45
Papyrus Louvre I.3079, col. 111, 76	113
Papyrus Mediolanum inv. 47, I 31	53
Papyrus Reisner III suppl. verso 10	112
Papyrus Reisner III suppl. verso 20	112
Papyrus Reisner III suppl. verso 22-24	112
Papyrus Trinity College Dublin Gr. 274, 39-48	115
Papyrus Vindob. G 19769, 10-11	50
P.O. III 488,3	53
Prism A	11, 136
PT 366	19
Pyr § 630 a-c	19, 35, 50
Pyr § 630 b	112
Pyr § 1634 a	112
Pyr § 1634 a-c	35, 50
Rituel de l'embaumement	35, 113
SB VI 9310 A5	50
SB VI 9310 B6	50
Shipwrecked Sailor	18
Siut I, 2	112
Siut I, 4	131
Siut I, 80-81	46
Siut I, 81	112
Siut I, 132	88, 151
Siut I, 150	46
Siut I, 152	131
Siut I, 155	46, 112
Siut I, 157	46

Siut I, 173	131	Siut II, 13	54
Siut I, 180	46	Siut II, 21	50
Siut I, 183	131	Siut III, 1	112
Siut I, 212	131	Siut III, 2	46
Siut I, 214	131	Siut III, 12	112
Siut I, 217	46	Siut III, 18	111
Siut I, 218	46	Siut III, 28	112
Siut I, 221	131	Siut III, 33	38
Siut I, 222	131	Siut III, 57	46
Siut I, 223	112	Siut III, 61	49
Siut I, 230-231	8	Siut III, 67	49
Siut I, 231	51	Siut IV, 10-18	7
Siut I, 232	46	Siut IV, 15	111
Siut I, 232-233	40	Siut IV, 17-18	120
Siut I, 234	49	Siut IV, 19-20	42, 142
Siut I, 234-236	9, 43	Siut IV, 21	41, 112
Siut I, 235-236	42	Siut IV, 21-22	41
Siut I, 238	131	Siut IV, 24	41
Siut I, 240	46	Siut IV, 30	48
Siut I, 241	131	Siut IV, 32	112
Siut I, 245	131	Siut IV, 38	52
Siut I, 260	46	Siut IV, 45	46
Siut I, 268	46	Siut IV, 53	49
Siut I, 269-272	90	Siut IV, 54	38
Siut I, 273	45	Siut IV, 61	46, 112
Siut I, 273-274	49	Siut V, 1	46, 112
Siut I, 273-276	132	Siut V, 9	122
Siut I, 278-279	35	Siut V, 14	41
Siut I, 281-282	45	Siut V, 18	111
Siut I, 283-284	41, 45	Siut V, 20-22	120
Siut I, 290	41	Siut V, 23	112
Siut I, 299	45	Siut V, 33	112
Siut I, 305	50	Siut V, 41	46
Siut I, 307	50	Siut V, 42	49
Siut I, 312	50	Siut V, 43	51
Siut I, 312-326	69	Siut V, 45	46
Siut I, 330	46	Siut VIII, 1	112
Siut I, 335	46	Synaxarion, Copto-Arabic	12
Siut I, 337	46		
Siut I, 338	131	Tale of Sinuhe	9
Siut I, 345	46	Teaching of Amenemhat to his Son	9
Siut I, 358	54		
Siut I, 380-417	91		
Siut II, 3	46, 112	Teaching of Duaf's Son Khety	81-82
Siut II, 11	51		

PLATES

Pl. 1

Pl. 1a: View of Asyut in 1839 (water-colour drawing by Hector Horeau).

Pl. 1b: Gebel Asyut al-gharbi in 2005 (© Verhoeven).

Pl. 2

Pl. 2a: Cartonnage-fragment mentioning the title "scribe of the house of Wepwawet" (Tomb III; S04/171; © Kahl).

Pl. 2b: Gebel Asyut al-gharbi (MELLY 1852: opposite p. 37).

Pl. 2c: Magical text inscribed on a camel(?) bone, Coptic Period (Tomb III; S05/046; © Kahl).

Pl. 3

Pl. 3a: Modern graffiti in Tomb III (© Kahl).

Pl. 3b: Tomb III, northern wall, autobiographical inscription, detail (© Kahl).

Pl. 4

Pl. 4a: Mummy cartonnage of Pa-di-Imen, Late Period (Tomb III; S05/071; © Kahl).

Pl. 4b: Mummy cartonnage of Pa-di-Imen, Late Period, detail (Tomb III; S05/071; © Kahl).

Pl. 5a: Tomb N13.1, northern wall, graffito mentioning the names of King Amenhotep III (© Kahl).

Pl. 5b: Tomb N13.1, northern wall, graffito mentioning the temple of Hathor, lady of Medjeden, early New Kingdom, detail (© Kahl).

Pl. 6

Pl. 6a: Tomb I (© Barthel).

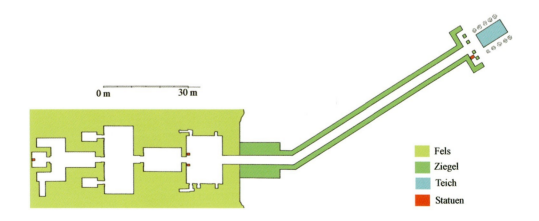

Pl. 6b: Tomb I, reconstruction (© Engel/Kahl).

Pl. 7a: Tomb I, great transverse hall, eastern wall, southern part, Djefai-Hapi I in front of the names of King Senwosret I (© Barthel).

Pl. 7b: Tomb I, great transverse hall, eastern wall, northern part, the ten contracts (© Barthel).

Pl. 8

Pl. 8a: Tomb I, great transverse hall, ceiling (© Barthel).

Pl. 8b: Tomb I, first corridor (© Verhoeven).

Pl. 9

Pl. 9a: Golden earring, Late Period (Tomb III; S05/073; © Kahl).

Pl. 9b: Amphora stamp from Rhodes, Ptolemaic Period (Tomb III; S04/st307; © Kahl).

Pl. 10a: Golden necklace with pendants and jewels, Early Byzantine Period, Berlin, Antikensammlung, Inv. 30219,505, Geschenk F.L. von Gans (© Bildarchiv Preußischer Kulturbesitz, Berlin, 2007).

Pl. 10b: Golden pectoral with large medallion (*enkolpion*), obverse, Early Byzantine Period, Berlin, Antikensammlung Inv. 30219,506, Geschenk F.L. von Gans (© Bildarchiv Preußischer Kulturbesitz, Berlin, 2007).

Pl. 10c: Golden pectoral with large medallion (*enkolpion*), reverse, Early Byzantine Period, Berlin, Antikensammlung Inv. 30219,506a, Geschenk F.L. von Gans (© Bildarchiv Preußischer Kulturbesitz, Berlin, 2007).

Pl. 11

Pl. 11a: Diagonal star clock, coffin of Idy, lid, Twelfth Dynasty (Tübingen, Ägyptische Sammlung der Universität 6).

Pl. 11b: Coffin of Idy, chest, Twelfth Dynasty (Tübingen, Ägyptische Sammlung der Universität 6).

Pl. 12: Statue of Meri-mose, Eighteenth Dynasty (Vienna, Kunsthistorisches Museum ÄS 36).

Pl. 13: Statue of Si-Ese III, Nineteenth Dynasty (Vienna, Kunsthistorisches Museum ÄS 34).

Pl. 14

Pl. 14a: Graffito showing a dog, New Kingdom (Tomb N13.1, western wall; © Kahl).

Pl. 14b: Limestone ostracon representing a nursing woman (Tomb III; S04/st418; © Kahl).

Pl. 15

Pl. 15: Pottery, Christian Era (© Kahl).

Pl. 16

Pl. 16a: Erotic figurine, faience (S05/072; © Kahl).

Pl. 16b: Udjat-eye, faience, Third Intermediate Period (S06/015; © Kahl).

Pl. 16c: Fragment of a glass beaker with a horizontal band of blobs, fourth century AD (S04/st517.5; © Kahl).